*Michel de L'Hôpital*

*Habent sua fata libelli*

Volume XXXVI
of
Sixteenth Century Essays & Studies

Charles G. Nauert, Jr., and Raymond A. Mentzer
General Editors

Composed at Truman State University, Kirksville, Missouri 63501 USA. Cover art and title page by Teresa Wheeler, Truman State University designer. Manufactured by Edwards Brothers, Ann Arbor, Michigan. Text is set in Palatino 10/12

# Michel de L'Hôpital

The *Vision* of a
Reformist
Chancellor
*during the French
Religious Wars*

## Seong-Hak Kim

SIXTEENTH CENTURY ESSAYS & STUDIES
VOLUME XXXVI

Copyright © 1997
Sixteenth Century Journal Publishers, Inc.
Kirksville, Missouri 63501-4221 USA
*escj@truman.edu*

This book has been brought to publication
with the generous support
of Truman State University, Kirksville, Missouri

**Library of Congress Cataloging-in-Publication Data**

Kim, Seong-Hak, 1958—
    Michel de L'Hôpital : the vision of a reformist chancellor during the
French religious wars / Seong-Hak Kim.
        p.     cm. — (Sixteenth century essays and studies ; v. 36)
    Includes bibliographical references and index.
    ISBN 0-940474-38-7 (alk. paper)
    1. L'Hospital, Michel de, 1507–1573—Political and social views. 2.
Statesmen—France—Biography. 3. Toleration—France—History—16th
century. 4. France—History—Wars of the Huguenots, 1562–1598. 5.
France—Politics and government—16th century—Religious aspects. I.
Title. II. Series
DC112.L6K55   1997                                97–2252
944'.028'092—dc21                                    CIP

*To the memory of my father,*
*The Honorable Yoon-Haeng Kim (†1990)*
*and to my mother,*
*Eung-Kyu Chung*

Michel de L'Hôpital

# Contents

# Foreword

SEONG-HAK KIM DEPLORES the fact that the myths about Michel de L'Hôpital should mask the realities of both his achievements and his failures. In this scholarly biography she sets the record straight. The chancellor was not the philosophic advocate of religious toleration: He was a pragmatic statesman who defended royal authority amid religious conflict and noble faction in the early phases of the sixteenth-century civil wars.At first he sought to find religious concord through compromise; when this could not be attained, he tried to recognize the coexistence of two religions within the state. The separation of politics from religion proved an impossible task in the climate of opinion that prevailed at the time.

If there was a streak of idealism in the chancellor (and Dr. Kim shows that he was not free from inconsistencies), it was evident in his attempts to reform the judicial system. While he himself used patronage and venality to rise through the Parlement and the Chamber of Accounts to the highest judicial office, L'Hôpital strove to break the system that gave the judges propertied rights in their offices, and to deny their constitutional claims to restrain the crown. For their part, the magistrates resisted his reforming ordinances and delayed his edicts of pacification. In the course of this struggle the chancellor seems to have held a doctrine of the legislative sovereignty of the king similar to that which Jean Bodin was to set forth in his *Six Livres de la République* a few years later. Dr. Kim argues that L'Hôpital's brief regime formed a bridge between the authoritarian trend in the French monarchy in the first half of the sixteenth century and the absolutism of the first Bourbon kings.

Before he became chancellor, L'Hôpital, despite his humanist dislike of war, supported the policy of his patrons in the family of Guise to continue the conflict with the Habsburgs. His inherent pacifism was modified by his patriotic acceptance of military action in the interests of the state, which did not include French ambitions in Italy. This, like his readiness to tolerate heresy as the only alternative to civil anarchy, earned him a reputation for dissimulation, if not hypocrisy. Indeed, his attempt to procure recognition of the French Calvinist reformed churches provoked accusations of Nicodemism. Dr. Kim admits vacillations in his behavior born of necessity, but insists upon the coherence of his statesmanship and the sincerity of his humanist Catholic beliefs.

She also examines his role in the development of royal Gallicanism, asserting the crown's administrative control of the French Catholic church against the claims of the papacy. Here he shared the views of one of the most fervent polemicists against Rome, Charles Du Moulin, who was also accused of Protestant leanings. It was L'Hôpital who drew up instructions for the French delegation to the Council of Trent, and who resisted the demands of his powerful patron, the Guisard cardinal of Lorraine, to receive the Tridentine decrees in France. It was also the chancellor, on this occasion with support from the Parlement, who persuaded the French clergy to contribute to the national finances.

L'Hôpital was early exposed to new humanist learning when he was studying law at Padua and Bologna and visiting the court of the French princess, Renée of Ferrara. His later appointment as personal chancellor to another humanistically inclined member of the royal family, the duchess of Berry, enabled him to dispense her patronage to poets of the Pléiade and to the University of Bourges. He secured the appointment of leading legal humanists such as Jacques Cujas and François Hotman, and emulated his friends among the poets with his own verses. Dr. Kim has used both his poetry and the juristic writings with which he was associated to provide new insights into the chancellor's personal system of values.

One of the most puzzling issues concerning L'Hôpital is his relationship to the ultra-Catholic Guises. This book provides definitive answers to this vexed question, showing that the cardinal of Lorraine was neither so inflexible nor his relatives so monolithic in their family attitudes as has commonly been assumed. This explains how the chancellor, despite differences of opinion with the cardinal, could remain on reasonably good terms with him until near the end of L'Hôpital's exercise of his office. In fact, it was not until the notorious quarrel within the royal council in September 1568, when the two threatened to pull each other's beards, that the definitive break occurred. It was at this point that the queen mother, Catherine de Médicis, who for the most part had followed L'Hôpital's guidance, withdrew her support and used him as a scapegoat. Nevertheless, the crown retained respect for the disgraced chancellor through the remaining five years of his life, when he retired to his estates to write verses and letters to his friends, hoping in vain to be recalled. The massacre of St. Bartholomew's Day, a few months before his death, signaled the abject failure of his policy. This book shows the firmness and integrity that underlay the seeming inconsistencies in his endeavor. Dr. Kim has made a most valuable contribution to our understanding of L'Hôpital and his era.

J. H. M. Salmon
Bryn Mawr College

# Acknowledgments

THIS STUDY is a revised version of a doctoral dissertation completed for the University of Minnesota in 1991. I am grateful to Professors James D. Tracy and Paul W. Bamford of the University of Minnesota, who kindly agreed to serve as my dissertation supervisors and who gave me valuable comments and guidance throughout this study. Professor John H. M. Salmon of Bryn Mawr College, to whom I owe a special thanks, gave the manuscript a careful and judicious reading and has been most gracious in his continuing encouragement of my work. I am especially grateful to two scholars in France, Father Guillaume de Bertier de Sauvigny, SJ, and Professor Bernard Barbiche of L'École des Chartes, who facilitated a foreign graduate student's stay in Paris, and who have since offered personal friendship and unwavering support of my scholarly efforts. To my husband, Joel Alan Shoemaker, I owe my greatest thanks.

# Introduction

T HIS IS THE FIRST CRITICAL POLITICAL BIOGRAPHY in over a hundred years of Michel de L'Hôpital. L'Hôpital served as chancellor of France between 1560 and 1568 during the Wars of Religion under the reigns of Francis II and Charles IX and the regency of Catherine de Médicis. L'Hôpital's principal claim to prominence in history is that he alone, or at least with more consistency than anyone else, pursued a policy of coexistence of Catholics and Protestants during the religious wars. The French Religious Wars, which lasted from 1562 to 1598, had been touched off by religious dissent but were soon complicated by political struggle. When many of his contemporaries were swept away by overwhelming religious passion and factional enmity, L'Hôpital played the role of mediator between antagonistic factions at the royal court. L'Hôpital tried to resolve the crisis of civil wars by refusing to view the current situation from a religious angle, insisting on dealing with the troubles only in political terms. His main goal was to separate politics and religion by drawing a line between political sedition and religious misbelief: Those Huguenots who resorted to violence should be punished, but the rest should be left in peace. Judging that the urgent task of the government was to preserve the unity of the kingdom, L'Hôpital advocated granting limited toleration to Protestants as the only alternative to civil war. But this matter-of-fact approach proved ill-fated in the face of engulfing religious zeal, and L'Hôpital's disgrace in 1568 seemed to mark the end of any lingering hopes of resolving through peaceful means the unprecedented crisis of civil strife.

L'Hôpital espoused the cause of toleration, less because of moral or philosophical convictions than by a recognition of the fundamental need for national unity and stability. But this pragmatic attitude accounts for only part of L'Hôpital's political outlook and perspectives. In fact, L'Hôpital's attempt to separate politics from religion was decidedly unrealistic, given the assumptions of the age and France's peculiar Catholic identity. L'Hôpital resolutely pursued his religious policy even when all the evidence suggested that religious coexistence could not work in France in the 1560s. L'Hôpital's misfortune was that his defense of religious moderation clashed with the religious idealism of the time. His vision of divorcing politics from religion was too far ahead of his time.

L'Hôpital is one of those pivotal figures in history whose policy seems familiar but who remain largely unknown and frequently misunderstood. L'Hôpital has been a victim of his own legend. Historians have hailed L'Hôpital as a lonely apostle of toleration, driven off the stage of history by religious fanaticism. The overpowering legacy of toleration has confounded the history of the chancellor, whose veritable tenet has almost vanished in the midst of timeless celebrations of his cause. Many studies of L'Hôpital tend to depict him as an aloof idealist, and his toleration policy has been treated as an abstract philosophy. Yet L'Hôpital had more tangible and limited objectives than converting his contemporaries to a doctrine of toleration. His idea of religious toleration was not so much the outcome of philosophical reflection as the result of his keen understanding of the desperate financial situation of the kingdom and his strong wish for peace and order. A sound assessment of the life and political career of L'Hôpital is long overdue, especially one free of both hagiographic treatment characteristic of his panegyrists and the collection of disjointed anecdotes crowding available biographies. This study provides a more dispassionate appraisal of L'Hôpital's career by examining what he thought and what he actually did, and presents a portrait of L'Hôpital that is closer to historical reality.

L'Hôpital's legendary reputation is a by-product of the eighteenth-century Enlightenment, when the name of L'Hôpital was conjured up in a campaign for religious tolerance. It was no mere accident that L'Hôpital was the subject of an essay contest sponsored by the Académie Française in 1777.[1] The exalting portrait of L'Hôpital was completed by nineteenth-century liberal historians who anachronistically acclaimed the "liberal" chancellor as a harbinger of freedom of conscience. This portrayal of L'Hôpital as a champion of freedom of conscience has been uncritically accepted by many authors, and their encomiums have continued to form our view of the chancellor. Several books exploiting manuscript sources were published in the late nineteenth century. Most notable was Emile

[1]Successful contestants included Abbé Remy, who received the first prize, and the Marquis de Condorcet, the renowned philosophe; see Abbé Remy, *Eloge de Michel de L'Hôpital, chancelier de France, discours présenté à l'Académie Française* (Paris, 1777); Condorcet (Jean-Antoine-Nicolas de Caritat, marquis de), *Eloge de Michel de L'Hôpital, chancelier de France* (Paris, 1777). The result of the contest was not without scandal. Many contemporaries, including Voltaire, claimed that the first prize should have gone to Condorcet instead of Remy; see *Voltaire's Correspondence*, ed. Theodore Besterman, vol. 96 (Geneva: Institut et Musée Voltaire, 1964), 67 (Amélie Suard to Voltaire, September 1, 1777), 76 (Jean de Vaines to Voltaire, September 6, 1777, and Voltaire to Jean le Rond d'Alembert, September 22, 1777).

Dupré Lasale's two-volume study based on extensive archival research. Unfortunately, it only covered L'Hôpital's pre-chancellor years.[2] L'Hôpital's chancellorship was earlier dealt with by A. H. Taillandier, who proposed to present L'Hôpital's history, and not his saga, but it was still overly generous.[3] Taillandier's work was supplemented by a study by P. D. L. [Paul de La Faye de L'Hôpital], a descendant of Chancellor L'Hôpital, who relied mainly on his family papers to write a polemical defense of the chancellor.[4] All three books are now outdated.[5] The twentieth century has seen, apart from those which warrant no serious consideration as history, biographies by Jean Héritier and by Albert Buisson.[6] Both are intended for a general readership. Buisson's, published in 1950, remains the most recent book on L'Hôpital. No book on the chancellor has appeared in English since 1905.[7]

Mario Turchetti has recently provided a significant insight for our understanding of the French religious wars by convincingly arguing that toleration edicts issued by the government in the second half of the sixteenth century were only temporary steps towards "concord," or a kind of forced religious compromise between Catholics and Protestants.[8] Accord-

[2]Emile Dupré Lasale, *Michel de L'Hospital avant son élévation au poste de chancelier de France* (Paris: Ernest Thorin, 1875, 1890), 2 vols., remains the best treatment of L'Hôpital, for little has been added to our knowledge during the past hundred years.

[3]A. H. Taillandier, *Nouvelles recherches historiques sur la vie et les ouvrages du chancelier de L'Hospital* (Paris: Firmin Didot Frères et Fils, 1861).

[4]P. D. L. [Paul de La Faye de L'Hôpital], *Quelques éclaircissements historiques et généalogiques sur Michel de L'hôpital et sa famille* (Clermont-Ferrand: Imprimerie de Ferdinand Thibaud, 1863).

[5]Jean Marie, *Essai sur la vie & les ouvrages du Chancelier Michel de L'Hospital* ( Rennes: Oberthus & Fils, 1868), and Henri Amphoux, *Michel de l'Hôpital et la liberté de conscience au XVIe siècle* (Paris, 1900; Geneva: Slatkine Reprints, 1969), are often anachronistic and suffer from the problem of a preconceived view portraying L'Hôpital as a saintly figure.

[6]Jean Héritier, *Michel de L'Hospital* (Paris: Flammarion, 1943); Albert Buisson, *Michel de L'Hospital* (Paris: Hachette, 1950). Buisson provides a very thorough bibliography.

[7]To my knowledge, only two books have ever been published in English on L'Hôpital: C. T. Atkinson, *Michel de L'Hospital* (London: Longmans, Green, 1900), and A. E. Shaw, *Michel de L'Hospital and His Policy* (London: Henry Frowde, 1905). Richard A. Hunt, "Religion and Law: The Chancellorship of Michel de L'Hospital, 1560-1562" (Ph.D. dissertation, University of Pennsylvania, 1973), remains the most recent study of considerable length, but it only deals with the first two years of L'Hôpital's chancellorship.

[8]Mario Turchetti, *Concordia o tolleranza? François Bauduin (1520-1573) e i "Moyenneurs"* (Geneva: Droz, 1984); idem, "Concorde ou tolérance? Les Moyenneurs à la veille des guerres de religion en France," *Revue de théologie et de philosophie* 118 (1986): 255–67; idem, "Religious Concord and Political Tolerance in Sixteenth- and Seventeenth-Century France," *Sixteenth Century Journal* 22 (1991): 15–25; idem, "Une question mal posée: La qualification de 'perpétuel et irrévocable' appliquée à l'Edit de Nantes (1598)," *Bulletin de la société de l'histoire du protestantisme français* 139 (1993): 41-78.

ing to him, Catherine de Médicis, Chancellor L'Hôpital, the Cardinal of Lorraine, and others at the royal court pursued religious toleration with a clear goal of attaining the ultimate restoration of religious unity in France. Turchetti's view is an important corrective to the traditional interpretation of L'Hôpital as a sixteenth-century advocate of the freedom of conscience. It also sheds light on the political opinion and the religious policy of L'Hôpital. L'Hôpital was one of the few members of the royal council who, while sincerely wishing for religious uniformity, realized that toleration of Protestants was the only alternative to civil war. He was aware that in the current situation religious uniformity under Catholicism could not be achieved without endangering the state. The fiasco of the Colloquy of Poissy in 1561 convinced L'Hôpital that limited toleration of Protestants was the only way of escape from prolonged anarchic confusions and crisis. When efforts to achieve unity of faith caused violence and disorder, they were no longer promoting stability of the state.

L'Hôpital did not deny the unquestioned value of religious agreement. He believed, as did other members of the royal council, that religious uniformity was important for maintaining the unity of the kingdom. But L'Hôpital was also convinced, perhaps more so than has been acknowledged by Turchetti, that a measure of toleration had a better chance to spare the kingdom from civil conflict. L'Hôpital was not an advocate of a full-blown theory of toleration, yet his ideals were not dictated by the goal of concord. Indeed, L'Hôpital does not seem to fit into the dichotomy of concord and toleration in the sixteenth century. The key to understanding L'Hôpital's religious policy instead seems to lie in his steadfast focus on finding a mean between persecution and toleration by distinguishing seditious Huguenots from Huguenots of conscience. He struggled to preserve peace, and to achieve that end, he was prepared, although reluctantly, to tolerate Protestantism. L'Hôpital's position eventually caused his estrangement from his former patron, the cardinal of Lorraine, who did not contemplate the possibility of legalizing the Huguenot religious services.

L'Hôpital's uphill battle for religious moderation during his chancellorship represented his fundamentally idealistic belief that religious coexistence could work in France. An indelible trace of idealism in his thought was more dramatically revealed in his advocacy of unchallenged royal authority and his reform programs. During the troubled age of the religious conflicts, L'Hôpital believed that only strong royal authority would spare France from further calamities of civil war. He believed that contemporary society, on the verge of fragmentation, needed a powerful prince with absolute sovereignty to hold it together. One major interpretive proposition of this study is that L'Hôpital represents a rare force of continuity in a long evolutionary trend towards royal absolutism in France. The French religious wars have been viewed as an interlude in this movement toward greater authority of the crown. France had experienced national consolidation under Francis I and Henry II, and after more than thirty years of civil war, emerged with renewed centralization under Henry IV. Defending and reasserting royal authority during this unprecedented civil conflict, L'Hôpital occupied an important position in the development of the French monarchy, linking the powerful rule of Francis I and Henry II to that of the early Bourbon kings. Apart from his constitutional ideas that emphasized royal power—which were the natural outgrowth of his strong national feeling—it is possible to find in L'Hôpital's policies many anticipations of later absolutist policies. Most notable were the sweeping ordinances he drafted and intended to apply across the whole kingdom. Furthermore, his head-on confrontations with the powerful interest groups such as the clergy and the Parlement of Paris clearly foreshadowed a more absolute form of monarchy. These efforts amply attest to his serious intentions of reasserting royal authority, and L'Hôpital can thus legitimately be viewed as a prototype of the seventeenth-century absolutist ministers.

L'Hôpital articulated his apology for unchallenged royal authority in his responses to systematic opposition from the Parlement of Paris. The alienation of L'Hôpital from the Parlement of Paris serves as an important point of reference in this study. During the religious wars, repeated resistance by the Parlement of Paris to the registration of the edicts of toleration convinced the chancellor that the intransigence of parlements constituted the main obstacle to royal efforts to bring the civil conflicts to a close. It has been argued that L'Hôpital's policy of religious toleration was unsuccessful because it was incompatible with the orthodox mentality of the Parlement of Paris. The remarkable lack of collaboration between the royal government which L'Hôpital headed and the magistrates requires, however, an examination of the full ramifications of the Parlement's opposition, not just from the religious angle but also from the perspective of conflicting constitutional pretensions as well as separate interests. L'Hôpital's reassertion of royal authority, in particular his efforts to limit the Parlement's right of remonstrance, clashed with the *parlementaires'* claim of their venerable historical role in the legislative process. This constitutional tension was, in turn, exacerbated by the religious issue, because the Parlement was vehemently opposed to the chancellor's toleration policy.

L'Hôpital was convinced that disorder in society was prompted by the disarrayed legal system and judicial breakdown. He thus sought for a strong centralized government that could carry out judicial reforms and provide impartial administration of justice. L'Hôpital's reform plans represented an unequivocal political vision that perceived the restoration of the integrity of royal justice as an essential solution to the crisis. L'Hôpital's resolute efforts to create a reformed judicial structure were illustrative of his distinct idealism. As an outspoken critic of venality and heredity of office, L'Hôpital made massive efforts to suppress the practice of selling judicial offices and consistently challenged the principle of irremovability of royal officials. In fact, L'Hôpital was one of the first statesmen in the sixteenth century who warned that the growing recalcitrance of the officeholders to the crown, while they remained entrenched in their offices as a result of venality, was the main predicament of the monarchy. The chancellor's attempts to limit the privileges of magistrates were perceived by the parlementaires as intrusive innovations that must be resisted to preserve their own self-interest as well as the corporate values of the institution. To the magistrates, the unyielding efforts of L'Hôpital for judicial reforms appeared excessively hostile. Humiliated, and threatened, the parlementaires resented L'Hôpital's authoritarian attitude and felt betrayed by their former colleague. They were among the bitterest opponents of L'Hôpital's chancellorship, not only thwarting the execution of his judicial reforms but obstructing the implementation of his religious policies. L'Hôpital did not like the Parlement, and he was not liked by the Parlement. This strained relationship between the chancellor and the Parlement of Paris eventually proved most damaging to L'Hôpital's political career.

L'Hôpital was a man of great intellectual diversity, and the tendency of his philosophical and political thought was conspicuously eclectic. Efforts to explain him and his politics in categorical terms tend to bring more confusion than clarity to the understanding of his place in history. L'Hôpital shared with the Christian humanists their pacifism. His denunciation of violence and embrace of pacifism did not, however, deter him from idealizing military glory and patriotism. L'Hôpital consciously attempted to benefit from patriotic enthusiasm, which he hoped would generate an overriding sense of national unity cutting across the polarization within the kingdom, whether religious or political. Endowed with a skeptical perspective, apparently a result of his humanist erudition, L'Hôpital believed that all things, including religious schism, were in the providence of God. His was too pragmatic a mind to rank among Erasmian humanists, however, because he considered the matter of religious differences mainly in the context of the state's interests. He opposed the notion that false religion must not be tolerated—an idea that was ingrained deeply during the sixteenth century—yet his toleration policies were based less on a conviction than on circumstance. The profound Christian spirit in L'Hôpital combined with his keen understanding of the dynamics of power and practical political considerations to engender a rare intellectual outlook, one that can probably be termed "Christian rationalism." L'Hôpital was a striking representative of Gallican royalists, who asserted that the crown, not the pope, held control over the organization and discipline of the clergy in France. For all his fundamental Gallican stance, however, L'Hôpital was unable to share the confessional rigidity of Gallican royalists. His persistent efforts for reconciliation of Catholics and Protestants even aroused the suspicions of his contemporaries as to his personal stance in religion. Numerous and unceasing charges by L'Hôpital's opponents that he was a Protestant sympathizer haunted him throughout his chancellorship, despite his repeated refutation of such allegations.

If L'Hôpital had an ideology, it could be found in his attempt to strike an equilibrium between Christian liberty on the one hand and law and order on the other. L'Hôpital believed that law could change the kingdom. There was an inherent limit to L'Hôpital's pursuit of such goals, however, because he relied entirely on uncertain royal favor for the power he wielded. The fundamental cause for the ultimate failure of L'Hôpital's policy thus appears to lie in the fact that he derived his power exclusively from the king. As long as Catherine de Médicis was inclined to support L'Hôpital, he was able to push his program forward. But she became increasingly impatient and disillusioned with the policy of conciliation, and when criticisms were heaped on the chancellor who stubbornly asserted that pacification hinged upon concessions to Protestants, she was ready to hold him responsible for the ill-fated policy of toleration. When L'Hôpital found himself abandoned by the king whose interest he was serving, he admitted his defeat and submitted the royal seals in 1568. During St. Bartholomew's Day in 1572, a few months before his death, L'Hôpital saw all his efforts to prevent civil wars prove to have been in vain. Chancellor L'Hôpital's religious policy was not successful. Yet his eloquent advocacy of toleration and the subordination of religion to civil policy inspired moderate Catholics. L'Hôpital was a spiritual precursor of the *Politique* party of the late sixteenth century.

L'Hôpital did not leave behind any vast volume of writings. His public speeches at the Estates General and the parlements, a few memoranda, Latin poems, several letters, and a testament complete the list.[9] The

---

[9]*Oeuvres complètes de Michel de L'Hospital,* ed. Pierre Joseph Spiridion, 3 vols. (Paris: Boulland, 1824; Geneva: Slatkine Rep[rints, 1968); *Michel de L'Hospital: Discours pour la majorité de Charles IX et trois autres discours,* ed. Robert Descimon (Paris, 1993) includes "Remonstrance de Monsieur le chancelier faite en l'assemblée tenue à Moulins" (January 1566), BN 8° Lf 25 40, an important discourse that is not printed in Duféy's collection. The present study relies on both Duféy's collection, hereafter *Oeuvres complètes,* and Descimon's edition, hereafter *Discours pour l'majorité de Charles IX.* When the two editions conflict, I de-

authenticity of the *Traité de la réformation de la justice*, the only treatise of considerable length, has recently been effectively disputed.[10] A few unpublished manuscripts, scattered in the Bibliothèque Nationale in Paris, are often either fragmentary or unimportant. When contrasting the meagerness of L'Hôpital's extant correspondence to the enormous collection of letters written by Catherine de Médicis, historian Jean H. Mariéjol once commented that it almost looked as if the queen mother had been L'Hôpital's chancellor.[11] This study mainly relies on printed material, but also utilizes extant archival sources which have not been printed. Most manuscript research was conducted in the Bibliothèque Nationale and Archives Nationales in Paris, and Bibliothèque Municipale et Interuniversitaire de la Ville de Clermont-Ferrand.[12] The problem of limited sources has dissuaded historians from writing a history of L'Hôpital, while many writers who tried succeeded only in perpetuating his saintly portrait. But the demand for a new study of L'Hôpital cannot be exaggerated, especially when he faces the threat of degenerating into a myth. This study proposes to elucidate L'Hôpital's aspirations, frustrations, and contradictions, and to clear the ground of old legends and polemics abounding in the history of the French religious wars.

---

pend on Descimon and note the corresponding page nos. in Duféy. L'Hôpital's Latin poems, constituting vol. 3 of Duféy's edition, were originally published by Guy du Faur, Jacques-Auguste de Thou, and Scévole de Sainte-Marthe, *Michaelis Hospitalii, Epistolarum* (Paris, 1585). The second edition appeared in 1592 in Geneva; a third edition is *Michaelis Hospitalii, Carmina: Editio a prioribus diversa et auctior*, ed. P. Vlaming (Amsterdam: B. Lakeman, 1732). There are two French editions: *Essai de traduction de quelques épitres et autre poésies latines de Michel de l'Hôpital*, tr. J. M. L. Coupé (Paris, 1778), and *Poésies complètes du chancelier Michel de L'Hospital*, tr. Louis Bandy de Nalèche (Paris: Hachette, 1857) (hereafter *Poésies complètes*).

[10]Duféy published the two-volume *Oeuvres inédites de Michel de L'Hospital* in 1825, which included the *Traité de la réformation de la justice*. Since then, the *Traité* has been used, mistakenly, as the only political treatise of any significant length for gleaning L'Hôpital's political ideas. The moderate political views expressed in the *Traité*, along with his policy of religious toleration, were mainly responsible for the formation of the anachronistic reputation of L'Hôpital as a "liberal chancellor." Yet many historians have questioned L'Hôpital's authorship of this work; Sylvia Neely, "Michel de L'Hospital and the *Traité de la Réformation de la Justice*: A Case of Misattribution," *French Historical Studies* 14 (1986): 339-66, cogently argues that Duféy incorrectly attributed the *Traité* to L'Hôpital. The main basis for Neely's assertion is that some phrases found in the *Traité* could not have been written during L'Hôpital's lifetime. Refutation of L'Hôpital's authorship of the *Traité*, a work which has been the major source in interpreting L'Hôpital's political thought, calls for an overall reappraisal of his political ideas. Hunt, "Religion and Law," with its heavy reliance on the *Traité*, requires the caution of a reader. In this study, I do not rely on the *Traité*.

[11]J.-H. Mariéjol, *Catherine de Médicis* (Paris: Tallandier, 1979), 214.

[12]Clermont-Ferrand is approximately twenty miles from Aigueperse, which is believed to be L'Hôpital's birthplace. Bibliothèque Municipale et Interuniversitaire de la Ville de Clermont-Ferrand preserves manuscrit no. 740, which concerns L'Hôpital.

# CHAPTER 1

# Exile's Son

IN MARCH 1642, the Conseil d'Etat examined an appeal by Gilbert de L'Hôpital, seigneur of La Roche and Montbardon and grandnephew of Chancellor Michel de L'Hôpital. A royal intendant in the *généralité* of Moulins had assessed the *tailles* for Gilbert in the amount of four hundred livres, although Gilbert claimed exemption on the grounds that his family had been known as seigneur of La Roche for "more than four hundred years." As evidence of his noble lineage, Gilbert submitted to the conseil a 1547 document which passed the land and lordship of La Roche from his granduncle Michel, then *conseiller* at the Parlement of Paris and future chancellor of France, to his grandfather Pierre, *gentilhomme ordinaire* in the house of the duc de Lorraine. The royal council accepted Gilbert's appeal and issued an *arrêt* on March 14, 1643, which upheld his tax privileges.[1] This incident exemplifies the difficulties of tracing the lineage of the L'Hôpitals. Although the descendants of Chancellor L'Hôpital managed to have their noble pedigree confirmed, their legal proof of nobility was less than a hundred years' standing. In fact they could not provide any records that furnished ancestry more remote than the chancellor's father, Jean.[2] The lack of such documentary evidence has led historians to either vilify or ennoble Michel de L'Hôpital's ancestors. Some allege that Michel's grandfather was a Jew from Avignon, a claim that is no more

---

[1]Arrêt du Conseil d'Etat du 14 mars 1643, printed in P. D. L. [Paul La Faye de L'Hôpital], *Quelques éclaircissements historiques et généalogiques sur M. de L'Hospital et sa famille* (Clermont-Ferrand, 1862), 135–40.

[2]The nobility of the family was again disputed in 1700, in the wake of Louis XIV's pursuit of false nobles who were unable to prove their noble lineage prior to 1560. But the family's legal proof of noble title dating to 1547 satisfied the requirement, and an edict issued on August 9, 1700, confirmed the family's nobility; see Emil Dupré Lasale, *Michel de L'Hospital avant son élévation au poste de chancelier de France*, 2 vols. (Paris, 1875–1899), 1:280.

9

credible than his descendants' claim that their nobility dated back to the thirteenth century.[3]

Not much is known about Michel de L'Hôpital's family. The few extant sources are often inaccurate or contradictory. Michel was the eldest child, with two brothers and at least one sister—possibly two.[4] His father, Jean, was a personal physician and at the same time a trusted councillor of Charles de Bourbon, comte de Montpensier and the constable of France. In 1515, Jean was appointed *bailli* of Montpensier; seven years later he received the post of *auditeur des comptes* at Moulins.[5] Virtually nothing is known about Michel's mother; although Michel made frequent references to his father in his writings, he remained silent about his mother.[6] His parents failed to tell Michel his own birth date. L'Hôpital's testament, drawn up on March 12, 1573, and signed by him the following day, two hours before his death, is the most reliable source for his biographical details.[7] In his testament, L'Hôpital stated that he was "always uncertain of age," and at best surmised that he had been born either "before the war against the Genoese" (who rebelled against the French in June 1506) or

[3]François Duchesne, *Histoire des chanceliers et gardes des sceaux de France* (Paris, 1680), 643; *Biographie universelle ancienne et moderne*, 2d ed. Joseph François Michaud (Paris: Desplaces, 1854–1865),24:451. On the other hand, some claimed that Jean's father, Charles, was from Murat, fief of Pierre de Bourbon, future father-in-law of the constable of Bourbon. Pierre Merle; e.g. "Jean de L'Hospital, père du chancelier et médecin du connétable de Bourbon," *L'Auvergne littéraire, artistique et historique* 37 (1960): 3. The strongest, albeit emotional, rebuttal of L'Hôpital's Jewish ancestry thesis can be found in P.D.L., *Eclaircissements,* 1–5. The author did not disclose his full name, but sources reveal that P.D.L., Paul de La Faye de L'Hôpital, was the grandson of Jean-François de L'Hôpital, descendant of Chancellor L'Hôpital's brother, Pierre; see "Lhospital ou L'Hôpital," *Chercheurs et Curieux* (1957): 65; Jean Baptiste Bouillet, *Nobiliaire d'Auvergne* (Clermont-Ferrand: Peron, 1846–1853), 3:271–73. The manuscripts preserved at the Bibliothèque Municipale et Interuniversitaire de la Ville de Clermont-Ferrand (hereafter BCF), apparently collected by P.D.L., contain various sources related to descendants of Chancellor L'Hôpital; see BCF, MS 740.

[4]Dupré Lasale, *L'Hospital,* 1:14, quoting a manuscript in the Bibliothèque Nationale, asserted that Michel had two brothers, Pierre and Jean, and two sisters, Françoise and Madeleine. Père Anselme de Sainte-Marie, Histoire généalogique et chronologique de la maison royale de France (Paris, 1726–1733), 6:489, omits Madeleine. P.D.L., *Eclaircissements,* 7–8, indicates that Jean de L'Hôpital had at least five children.

[5] Anselme, *Histoire généalogique,* 6:489.

[6]We do not know even her correct name. Some historians propose Marie de la Guiole, others Marguerite de Ladiot; see Dupré Lasale, *L'Hospital,* 1:13.

[7]Testament, BN, *Collection Dupuy* 491, fols. 38–41. There are several copies of this original testament scattered in the Collection Dupuy and Manuscrits français. The text of the testament is printed in *Oeuvres complètes de Michel de L'Hospital,* ed. P. J. S. Duféy, 3 vols. (Paris, 1824–182), 2:501–31 (hereafter *Oeuvres complètes*).

"during their subjugation to Louis XII" (which occurred in April 1507).[8] Michel was probably born and raised at the Château de La Roche, in the commune of Chaptuzat in Aigueperse, some twenty miles northeast of Clermont-Ferrand. The register of 1516 of the municipality of Aigueperse styled his father seigneur de La Roche, although he held the right of simple possession of the domain, "sans justice," subject to feudal dues to the comte de Montpensier.[9] A true feudal manor with its walls and towers dating from the eleventh or twelfth century, the Château de La Roche stands to this day on the top of a rugged hill, overlooking the vast surrounding fields of the Puys.[10] Among the few memories of his childhood, Michel recalled that his father, concerned about Michel's infatuation with literature, especially poetry, had warned him of the dismal poverty that doomed the majority of poets.[11] Perhaps that warning had some effect on young Michel's decision to study law at the University of Toulouse to pursue a legal career.[12]

In September 1523, Michel's education was interrupted suddenly by the constable of Bourbon's rebellion against Francis I. Jean de L'Hôpital faithfully joined his master in the abortive scheme, and was among the few who successfully fled the country with the constable to serve Emperor Charles V.[13] On August 13, 1524, Jean was sentenced in absentia to death

---

[8]L'Hôpital wrote that he was eighteen years old in September 1523, which would put his birth date at 1505; see *Oeuvres complètes*, 2:503. Duchesne, *Histoire des chanceliers*, 643, puts the date as early as 1504; Dupré Lasale, *L'Hospital*, 1:10, contends that Jean accompanied his master to the Genoese expedition.

[9]BCF, MS 740, fol. 45. The text is printed in Dupré Lasale, *L'Hospital*, 1:11–12. It was not until 1525 that Jean was granted the lordship of La Roche; see n. 19 below.

[10]The castle was owned by the L'Hôpital family until the eighteenth century. It has since remained uninhabited, but receives curious tourists from spring through fall.

[11]Epistle to Salmon Macrin, *Poésies complètes*, 124–25.

[12]L'Hôpital's testament does not specify when he left for Toulouse. Maurice Taillandier, *Des Projets de réforme du chancelier de L'Hospital et de quelques réformes actuelles* (Arras: Imprimerie de la Société du Pas-de-Calais, 1903), 3, contends that he was twelve years old; this of course depends on when he was born.

[13]It is not clear what role Jean de L'Hôpital played in the rebellion of 1523. In August, when Francis I was increasingly suspicious of the constable's movement, Bourbon attempted to screen his rebellious intentions, claiming to be ill. As personal physician of Bourbon, Jean might well have aided him in this particular effort. Pierre Merle, "Jean de L'Hospital, père du chancelier et médecin du connétable de Bourbon," *L'Auvergne littéraire, artistique et historique* 37 (1960): 10, contends that Jean signed a "certificat de complaisance," or false certificate of ill health. Bourbon's illness seems, however, to have been genuine; see R. J. Knecht, *Francis I* (Cambridge: Cambridge University Press, 1982), 153.

and his properties were confiscated.[14] The Parlement of Toulouse arrested Michel under the suspicion of previous knowledge of his father's treachery and threw him into jail. Michel's uncle Georges, concerned about his young nephew, came to see him. The Parlement arrested and interrogated this priest from Aigueperse, but he denied any knowledge of the conspiracy.[15] Michel remained imprisoned in Toulouse until early 1526, when he was released "by the commandment of the king as it was found that there was nothing against me."[16] It does not seem that young Michel knew of his father's treason. In later life, he vehemently protested his innocence, asking the plaintive question: "Why should I always be punished for my father's fault? Are the sins of the fathers to be visited on the honest children?"[17] Yet L'Hôpital defends his father's action on the ground of excessive devotion to his master: "My father ...remained loyal to the party which heaven abandoned. He was wrong, I admit it, but, at least, he did not take up arms, and he simply gave the benefit of his knowledge to the enemy, who for thirty years protected him as friend."[18]

L'Hôpital emphasized that his father never forgot his fatherland, even in exile, and that after Bourbon's death in May 1527 he was most anxious to come back to France. Yet it appears that instead Jean de L'Hôpital was an expatriate in active service of the duc de Bourbon, who led the Habsburg troops against the French in Italy. In 1525, Bourbon bestowed upon Jean "in consideration of his service of twenty years" the domains and the lordship of La Tour de La Bussière in Auvergne, along with La Roche and the villages of Bans and Croiset.[19] On August 18, 1526, Charles V appointed Jean to the office of the general of finance in Milan.[20]

---

[14]Roger Doucet, *Etude sur le gouvernement de François Ier dans ses rapports avec le Parlement de Paris* (Paris: E. Champion, 1921–1926),1:300–301; L. Cimber and F. Danjou, eds., "Charles, duc de Bourbon, connestable de France, et de ses complices, 1523," in *Archives curieuses de l'histoire de France depuis Louis XI jusqu'à Louis XVIII* (Paris: Beauvais, 1834–1840), 2:203–49.

[15]Doucet, *Gouvernement de François Ier*, 1:277–78, 289. Georges was still in prison in December 1526; Merle, "Jean de L'Hospital," 11.

[16]*Testament, Oeuvres complètes,* 2:516. L'Hôpital was probably acquitted after February 1526, when Francis I came back to France from captivity in Madrid.

[17]Epistle to Pierre du Chastel, *Poésies complètes,* 79.

[18]Epistle to Pierre du Chastel, *Poésies complètes,* 81. This apology for his father, written in 1546, is remarkable in that it testifies to his eager efforts to erase or at least diminish the grave impact of his father's treason.

[19]*Lettres patentes* dated March 5, 1525, issued at Saragossa, Spain. The text was printed in P.D.L., *Eclaircissements,* 141–46; see also Guillaume Chabrol, *Coutumes générales et locales de la province d'Auvergne* (Riom, 1790), 4: 4; Duchesne, *Histoire des chanceliers,* 636; Anselme, *Histoire généalogique,* 6:489.

[20]Dupré Lasale, *L'Hospital,* 1:50 (the text is printed in appendix 1, pp. 1:267–68).

After Michel's release from prison in 1526, he joined his father, but soon left Milan for Padua. In his testament Michel described how he, disguised as a muleteer, escaped the French siege of Milan in June of that year.[21] He studied law at the University of Padua for the next six years, a period he later recalled as the happiest of his life. At Padua, this son of an exile in the imperial service registered himself as Burgundian. He was elected twice "consiliarius" of the Burgundian nation at the university, and in 1531, while still a student, was nominated instructor of civil law, as "schola secunda juris civilis inter extraordinarias."[22] Besides his legal studies, Michel devoted himself to research of ancient authors. Classical parallels and allusions, frequent in his Latin poems, bear witness to such studies.[23]

In 1533, Michel went to the University of Bologna, where he received the degree of doctor during his brief stay before he departed for Rome.[24] His father, having followed Charles V to Rome after the death of the duc de Bourbon, procured Michel a post in the Curia, the pontifical tribunal, as one of the twelve "auditores de rota."[25] But Michel did not actually take up the position, because he received a more attractive offer from Cardinal Gabriel de Gramont, one of the French envoys present at the imperial court.[26] Noticing Michel's talents, the cardinal promised him a career in France and guaranteed his father the restoration of citizenship. Gramont's offer prevailed with the L'Hôpitals. Michel decided to forego the duties of auditor in Rome and, accompanied by his father, followed the cardinal to Avignon. In Avignon, on September 2, 1533, Gramont, in accordance with his pledge, obtained a royal declaration that reinstated Jean in all his

---

[21]Testament, *Oeuvres complètes*, 2:517.

[22]Dupré Lasale, *L'Hospital*, 1:59.

[23]In his later life he lamented in one of his poems that he "wasted time meaninglessly imitating Latin authors" instead of spending more time on the study of the scriptures and theology; see Epistle to Jacques Corbinelli, *Poésies complètes*, 330–31.

[24]Testament, *Oeuvres complètes*, 2:517. According to Dupré Lasale, *L'Hospital*, 1:60–61, n. 2, the library of the University of Bologna preserved a manuscript in which L'Hôpital's name was listed among the doctorates conferred by the university.

[25]Testament, *Oeuvres complètes*, 2:518.

[26]It seems that Jean, and possibly Michel, met the cardinal of Gramont around March 1525. The letter of Saragossa suggests that Jean was in Spain at that time: "… ne voullant estre repris de vice d'ingratitude ains luy satisfaire auculnement comme bien le mérite à icelluy présent et acceptant, etc."; see Epistle to Pierre du Chastel,*Poésies complètes*, 81. Henri Amphoux, *Michel de l'Hôpital et la liberté de conscience au XVIe siècle* (Paris, 1900; Geneva: Slatkine Reprints, 1969), 49–50, contends that Michel went to Madrid, where he was introduced to the Cardinal. Michel himself did not mention in his testament this alleged trip to Spain.

rights, titles, and property, thereby granting him the amnesty promised to the constable's followers by the Treaty of Madrid in January 1526.[27]

Michel's hopes of a brilliant future in France appeared doomed, however, when Gramont died suddenly in March 1534 near Toulouse. Having lost his benefactor, Jean did not dare to enter Paris, and retired to the county of Lorraine under the protection of the duchess of Guise, Antoinette de Bourbon, sister of his old master the constable of Bourbon.[28] Deprived of any protection or connection in Paris, Michel was thus left to his own resources. Apparently bemoaning his having spurned the post at the tribunal in Rome, Michel registered for the bar of Paris. No records tell us about his activities during the next three years.[29] It appears, however, that he was already gaining a solid reputation as a poet and scholar.[30]

Since his return to France, L'Hôpital was painfully aware of the serious consequence of his father's rebellious involvement in 1523. He knew of the stigma attached to his family name, which proved even more of a detriment when he tried to establish himself as a public servant. The first serious repercussion befell him in 1537. L'Hôpital had found a patron in Pierre Le Filleul, governor of Paris and archbishop of Aix, who had served the constable of Bourbon while he was lieutenant of Languedoc. Filleul warmly received the son of his old master's councillor, and placed him under protection. Eventually, the archbishop recommended L'Hôpital to Jean Morin, *lieutenant criminel* at the Châtelet, as a possible spouse for Morin's eldest daughter, Marie. Upon learning about Jean de L'Hôpital's implication in the rebellion of 1523, Morin balked at the idea of marrying his daughter to a traitor's son. His apprehension prompted him to write to Chancellor Antoine Dubourg in order to ask his opinion: "I am very much

---

[27]Anselme, *Histoire généalogique*, 6:489; Duchesne, *Histoire des chanceliers*, 648. The declaration was registered at the Parlement of Paris on December 18 of that year. Its text is printed in Dupré Lasale, *L'Hospital*, appendix 2, 1:288–90.

[28]Pierre Bayle, *Dictionnaire historique et critique*, 4th ed. (Amsterdam: P. Brunel, 1740), 2:804; Dupré Lasale, *L'Hospital*, 1:64. Jean de L'Hôpital died in January 1547. L'Hôpital's poem written in 1544 implied that his father was still alive: "I would accept punishment willingly, if it would reduce the punishment of my father..."; Epistle to Pierre du Chastel, *Poésies complètes*, 79.

[29]L'Hôpital wrote "je feus frustré en mesme temps de l'espérance que j'avois d'une part et d'aultre; car l'estat d'auditeur feut donné à ung aultre, et estant demeuré en arrière par la mort du cardinal de Grammont, qui m'avoit fait revenir en mon pays soubs cette espérance, je me mis à suyvre le palais..." in Testament, *Oeuvres complètes*, 2:518. Roland Delachenal, *Histoire des avocats au Parlement de Paris, 1300–1600* (Paris: Librairie Plon, 1885), does not mention the name L'Hôpital.

[30]L'Hôpital's reputation is attested in a Latin verse written by his friend Jean Voulté: "Is there anything more pleasant than the language of L'Hôpital? / Anything purer than the poems of L'Hôpital? / Anything more impressive than the face of L'Hôpital? / Anything more saintly than the life of L'Hôpital?" quoted in Dupré Lasale, *L'Hospital*, 2:67.

aware of L'Hôpital's reputation; but as soon as I heard that he is the son of the doctor of Bourbon, great fear took me over. I would prefer the death of my daughter and myself to provoking the least suspicion of the king and jeopardize the royal favor and the good will you bear me."[31]

Chancellor Dubourg, who happened to be an Auvergnat himself, may have been particularly sympathetic to the plight of his young compatriot.[32] The chancellor's express endorsement of the proposed marriage dissipated the worries of Jean Morin, and the wedding took place in September 1537. Through his marriage into the Morins, a family long known and respected in Paris, L'Hôpital entered into the Parisian elite.[33]

His wife brought as dowry, acknowledged L'Hôpital in his testament, the office of conseiller at the Parlement of Paris, a post L'Hôpital could not have purchased on his own.[34] Nonetheless, L'Hôpital's installation at the Parlement was not without difficulties. First, the question remained whether the king would tolerate a traitor's son sitting in his highest court. Guillaume Poyet, *premier président* of the Parlement of Paris and future chancellor, felt it necessary to solicit personally royal approval of L'Hôpital's appointment. He wrote a letter to Chancellor Dubourg requesting to "find the opinion of the king whether he would mind having L'Hôpital in the office, because he is a man strongly qualified for the job."[35] The office that Marie Morin had brought was that of *conseiller clerc*, a position theoretically reserved to a member of the clergy. It was not unprecedented for a layman or married person to be sworn as conseiller clerc, but in such cases, still regarded as irregular, the Parlement specified in its registers that the admission was granted by exception.[36] L'Hôpital's case appears to have rekindled some controversies about the practice. The *procès-verbal* of the Parlement of Paris of August 8, the day L'Hôpital was sworn into the court, reads:

---

[31]BN, Dupuy 194, fol. 21, June 20 [1537]. This letter is printed in "Lettre de Guillaume Poyet relative au mariage de Michel de l'Hospital," *Bulletin historique et scientifique de l'Auvergne* 12 (1882): 130, n.

[32]Hélène Michaud, *La grande Chancellerie et les écritures royales au seizième siècle (1515–1589)* (Paris: Presses Universitaires de France, 1967), 24. Le Filleul and Dubourg's support shows that L'Hôpital significantly benefited from the "solidarité auvergnate," i.e., the concerted support from his compatriots; see *La Cour des Comptes* (Paris: CNRS, 1984), 141.

[33]Jean Morin was a longtime councillor to the Hôtel de ville de Paris.

[34]Testament, *Oeuvres complètes*, 2:518.

[35]Guillaume Poyet to Antoine Dubourg, June 18, 1537, "Lettre de Guillaume Poyet," 132.

[36]Félix Aubert, "Recherches sur l'organisation du parlement de Paris au XVIe siècle (1515–1589)," *Extrait de Nouvelle revue historique du droit français et étranger* (Paris: Sirey, 1912), 239.

L'Hospital was provided with an office of *conseiller clerc*; it was noted that he was soon to marry the daughter of the *lieutenant criminel* of the *prévosté de Paris*, M. Jehan Morin, but the letter of exemption of L'Hospital was granted in consideration of the great expectation that the court has of him, and without further deliberations, M. Michel de L'Hospital was received, and he took the oath.[37]

Following this somewhat conspicuous entry, L'Hôpital's career at the Parlement falls into two periods. During the first ten years, from August 1537 through August 1547, he mostly devoted himself to his duties as judge and kept a relatively low profile. It was not until after he spent the next fifteen months at the Council of Trent, then sitting at Bologna, that he became actively involved in political issues. In 1544, Francis I vetoed L'Hôpital's appointment to the presidency of the Parlement of Turin, which the king had created after his occupation of Piedmont in 1537. Although the reasons for the royal disapproval were not made public, it was widely understood that L'Hôpital's background dissuaded Francis from appointing him to the post.[38]

Deeply disappointed, L'Hôpital poured out his frustration in a bitter epistle to Pierre du Chastel, bishop of Mâcon and *grand aumônier* of the king: "Exiles, once pardoned, served their countries well; then, why should the children of exiles be denied such opportunities?" Protesting his innocence from his father's fault, L'Hôpital stresses his devotion to the royal service: "For almost nine years, sitting among the judges at the court, I have entirely dedicated myself to the public good. Why should I not be treated better? Why should my innocence be clouded by my father's fault?" L'Hôpital pleads for clemency to his father and justice to himself and pledges his loyalty to the king: "Oh, King François, your clemency is far greater than your rigorousness. I would accept the punishment willingly, if it would reduce the punishment of my father.... I do not want to reach the highest rank. But let fair Apollo rest his eyes upon me and count me as one of his subjects."[39] His Apollo was, however, too hard-hearted to be moved by this ardent plea for mercy. Denied royal favor,

---

[37]The text is printed in Dupré Lasale, *L'Hospital*, 1:76., n. 1. L'Hôpital's letters of provision were originally issued at Fontainebleau on June 14, 1537; see Anselme, *Histoire généalogique*, 6:488.

[38]Dupré Lasale, *L'Hospital*, 1:112, 306–8. Francis I occupied Piedmont in 1536 and created a parlement at Turin in 1537. Ironically, the presidency went instead to René de Birague, who later succeeded L'Hôpital as chancellor of France.

[39]Epistle to Pierre du Chastel, *Poésies complètes*, 83, 84.

L'Hôpital had to remain in his "obscure position" at the Parlement of Paris, as he once called it, tormented by a deep sense of misfortune.

The registers of the Parlement of Paris contain only a few scattered records of L'Hôpital's activities during the reign of Francis I. Far more abundant and important are L'Hôpital's copious epistles written during this period. He was a prolific writer of Latin verses;[40] his exuberant versification often invited accusations from his colleagues that writing poems was not an activity worthy of magistrates and that he wasted public time toying with the Latin lines. L'Hôpital defended himself by asserting that his poems were "chaste and honorable enough to be read by children." They were written in his leisure time, he retorted, and the accusers spent no more minutes at their work than he did.[41] L'Hôpital's poems written in the 1540s reveal increasing disillusionment with his work. L'Hôpital did not like his duties as judge and abhorred the constant wrangling of litigants. He complained that his post rendered him "odious" because his verdicts never satisfied both parties. L'Hôpital compared his work to the labor of Sisyphus, and he would rather do anything than spend his days "rolling the eternal rock of disputes from dawn to dusk and watching a father suing his son-in-law or spouses suing one another."[42] In one verse, L'Hôpital describes how justice was swayed by the vain eloquence of lawyers arguing at trials. "The trials now proceed," writes L'Hôpital, "through the abuse of mental talent to attain shameful victories. Such wrongdoings must not sully the French tribunals."[43]

L'Hôpital vocally criticizes the corruption of magistrates, especially those who were prone to the *épices*, free gifts given to judges by litigants. He loftily professes, "I held gold and wealth in contempt, and I proudly refused the gifts and honors with which people often wanted to shower me."[44] Since payment of judges' salaries was frequently delayed, any refusal to accept such perquisites as the épices meant financial hardship for those without other sources of income. Judge L'Hôpital complains in a letter written in 1542 to an unknown cardinal: "I am like a day laborer: I did not inherit any fortune from my ancestors. The pittance that I earn

[40]His numerous poems claim attention not just for their literary elegance, but also for their historical value. Written over a period of more than thirty years, they chronicle L'Hôpital's public as well as private life, and they allow the reader to peruse his thought in progress.

[41]Epistle to Jean Morel, *Poésies complètes*, 144–45. He knew that he was being called a "judge turned poet"; see Epistle to Olivier, *Poésies complètes*, 9. He justified his versification by saying that many sage ancients wrote poems; see Epistle to the cardinal of Tournon, *Poésies complètes*, 16.

[42]Epistle to Tournon, *Poésies complètes,*13.

[43]Latin poem, "Litium exsecratio," written to Jacques du Faur, conseiller at the Parlement of Paris. The text is translated in Taillandier, *Nouvelles Recherches*, 348–59.

[44]Epistle to Olivier, *Poésies complètes*, 153.

barely suffices to nourish me and my family. It is far from enriching me.…
It takes all my time and efforts to provide meager means of subsistence.
This is the situation I have been forced into during the last five years, and
where I remain."[45]

L'Hôpital's economic hardship is not surprising considering that as
conseiller clerc he was paid only about half the salary of lay members.[46] In
the letter quoted above, he fails to mention that he had received La Roche
from his father at the time of his wedding. Apparently, any income from
the land was not of much help to his tight financial situation.[47]

As an outspoken critic of the practice of selling judicial offices,
L'Hôpital deplored the fact that venality of offices saturated the Parlement
with unqualified youngsters who should be sent back to school.[48] Increasingly pervasive venality and the heredity of offices at the Parlement
allowed a few prominent, closely connected families to monopolize many
offices. The rise of the robe nobility was clearly discernible in the sixteenth
century. Since L'Hôpital was independent of any interests vested in the
Parlement's "parenté"—alliance networks between families developed to
consolidate their respective positions—L'Hôpital was free to voice openly
his criticism against the system as a major corruption of the judicial system. L'Hôpital once vehemently protested being discriminated against
because of his lack of influential background. In 1542, when assessed two
hundred écus that was to be his share of a loan which the king demanded
from the magistrates, L'Hôpital asked why this disproportionate sum
should be levied on him while his richer colleagues escaped rather
easily.[49]

L'Hôpital's verses that derided the corruption and ignorance of his
colleagues did not exactly amuse them, but instead brought on their
"incessant hostility." His frequent clashes with the Parlement of Paris
during his chancellorship were partly an outgrowth of the distressful relations begun during this period. L'Hôpital was not unaware of the growing
antagonism of some of his colleagues. He preferred, though, to remain
aloof from their attacks, assuring himself that he alone in the court, except

---

[45]BN, Dupuy 491, fol. 29. The original Latin text is translated in Dupré Lasale, *L'Hospital*, 1:84–89.

[46]The wages attached to clerical offices were not more than one-half those paid to lay
members; see Gerald Francis Denault, "The Legitimation of the Parlement of Paris and the
Estates General of France, 1560–1614" (Ph.D. dissertation, Washington University, 1975), 151.
L'Hôpital was conseiller clerc as late as 1547.

[47]On August 22, 1543, L'Hôpital, seigneur of La Roche, paid homage to the duc de
Montpensier; see P.D.L., "Dénombrement de la terre et seigneurie de la Roche in 1543," in
*Eclaircissements*, 147–50; Anselme, *Histoire généalogique*, 6:488.

[48]Epistle to Tournon, *Poésies complètes*, 20.

[49]BN, Dupuy 491, fol. 29.

for a few old judges, was committed to restoring the honor of the judiciary. In his own account, L'Hôpital's "austere conduct often aroused critical jealousy, which was dissipated amidst universal eulogies."[50]

L'Hôpital's epistles written in the 1540s bear witness to his burgeoning political ambitions. He aspired to a political career, finding endless legal squabbles increasingly distasteful. Mindful of his tarnished background, he was anxious to solicit favors from highly placed friends and patrons. Literary achievement was L'Hôpital's best asset, and he did not fail to employ carefully his talent to bring himself to the notice of powerful figures. Many of his poems were dedicated to influential people, including Cardinals Jean du Bellay, Georges d'Armagnac, François de Tournon, and Odet de Châtillon.[51] L'Hôpital's epistle to the cardinal of Tournon illustrates his efforts to appeal to his benefactor: "I do not get upset to see myself left out and other people instead called to important positions. It seems to me that everything is for the best result, and I tell myself that person was more capable, or that he took the position thanks to his old friend, or"—he adds quickly—"that you must have a better position prepared for me." L'Hôpital was aware that his eager efforts to obtain protection and patronage invited accusations of his being an inveigler and an opportunist. Yet he denied that his ability to use the patronage system to advantage should compromise his loyalty or sincerity. In a letter to Cardinal Odet de Châtillon, L'Hôpital divulges his ambitions: "To me it seems desirable to associate with all the parties and benefit from them regardless of their differences. Yet, one must not pursue them all for the same reason; some have their positions, some have their virtue, while others, and these are the best people, have sincere affection which makes possible the exchange of loyalty.... You know my ambitions; I do not want to commit myself to any single party. Perhaps I look like a flatterer, but I am no less loyal, sincere, and truthful than anyone."[52] This seems to be more than

[50]Epistle to Tournon, *Poésies complètes*, 20.

[51]Jean du Bellay, a trusted councillor of Francis I, was made cardinal by Pope Paul III in 1535. It is said that du Bellay's advice crucially affected the decision of Francis I to establish the Collège de France in 1529. Georges d'Armagnac, made cardinal in 1541, patronized many contemporary humanists. Cardinal François de Tournon actively participated in the government of Francis I. After a prolonged stay in Italy during the reign of Henry II, Tournon returned to the French political scene in 1559, having been appointed by Pope Pius IV as the doyen of the college of the cardinals. The friction between Cardinal Tournon and Chancellor L'Hôpital at the Colloquy of Poissy is discussed in chap. 3 below. Odet de Coligny, cardinal of Châtillon, is best known as elder brother of both Admiral Gaspard de Coligny and François d'Andelot.

[52]Epistle to Cardinal Odet de Châtillon, *Poésies complètes*, 165. Maurice Taillandier, *Des projets de réforme du Chancelier de L'Hospital et de quelques réformes actuelles* (Arras, 1903), 21, indicates that the poem was written probably around his appointment to the chancellorship of the duchy of Berry.

mere self-justification; indeed it is a manifesto of the philosophy underlying L'Hôpital's politics. Discernible in these lines is an expression of incipient pragmatism, which underpinned the so-called politics of conciliation that was to characterize his chancellorship.

L'Hôpital found a particularly sympathetic supporter and protector in François Olivier, then the premier président of the Parlement of Paris, and chancellor of France from 1545 to 1560. Michel de Montaigne acclaimed Olivier and L'Hôpital as "able men of uncommon virtue."[53] Olivier was almost a father figure for L'Hôpital. L'Hôpital often confided his frustrations as well as his aspirations in epistles to Olivier, who returned solace and encouragement to his young protégé. In particular, Olivier complimented L'Hôpital's elegant Latin verses and praised him as one of the best Latin poets of the time. It was Olivier who acquired for L'Hôpital most of the distinctions he enjoyed at the Parlement. L'Hôpital was assigned to many important commissions; most notably he was delegated to the *Grands Jours* in Moulins in 1540 and again in Riom in 1542.[54] In July 1547, the Parlement of Paris selected L'Hôpital again to serve at the Grands Jours to be held at Tours from September through October.[55] On the recommendation of Chancellor Olivier, Henry II discharged L'Hôpital from the commission and appointed him as one of the delegates to the Council of Trent, then in session in Bologna.[56] Thus shortly after the death of Francis I, Olivier allowed L'Hôpital to realize at last his long-cherished dream of launching a political career. The accession of Henry II to the throne in

[53]*The Complete Essays of Montaigne*, tr. Donald M. Frame (Stanford: Stanford University Press, 1958), book 2, chap. 17, pp. 501–2.

[54]Grands Jours is a special legal commission staffed by parlementaires, delegated to the provinces to investigate irregularities, abuses, and disorders of the lower courts. During this period, L'Hôpital also presided over the criminal case of the admiral de Brion in 1540, judged in collaboration with the Parlement of Burgundy a litigation between Charles de la Baume and Nicolas de Bauffremont in 1541, judged the case of Rothelin in 1543, joined the Chambre des Comptes in a criminal case of the trésorier Loppier in 1545, and participated in the reform project of hospitals in 1546; see Dupré Lasale, *L'Hospital*, 1:118; Aubert, "Recherches sur l'organisation du Parlement," 45.

[55]Edouard Maugis, *Histoire du Parlement de Paris de l'avènement des rois Valois à la mort d'Henri IV*, 3 vols. (Paris: Picard, 1913–1916), 1:440, n.

[56]*Lettres patentes* of August 5, 1547. The list of August 3 included L'Hôpital's name among the *commissaires* to be delegated to Tours; see *Catalogue des actes de Henri II, Collection des ordonnances des rois de France* (Paris: Imprimerie Nationale, 1979), 1:229, 235. The Parlement's register of August 6 is printed in Lasale, *L'Hospital*, 1:120. Other delegates were Claude d'Urfé, ambassador to Rome, Claude d'Espence, doctor of theology, Antoine Filhol, archbishop of Aix, and Claude de La Guiche, bishop of Mirepoix; see "Lettre du Roy, envoyant M. Claude Despence au Concile à Boulogne avec ses ambassadeurs, 15 août 1547," in Pierre Dupuy, ed., *Instructions et lettres des rois très-chrestiens, et de leurs ambassadeurs, et autres actes concernant le concile de Trente* (Paris, 1654), 18–19.

March 1547 was for L'Hôpital more than just a change of regime. Francis I, whose ego was deeply hurt by Bourbon's rebellion, was never quite willing to forgive this son of a traitor. Under the new reign, L'Hôpital seemed finally to have freed himself from the unfavorable legacy of his father's transgression. L'Hôpital must have been happy to be relieved of the legal duties that were becoming increasingly unbearable for him.[57]

Once he arrived in Bologna in October 1547, however, L'Hôpital found his first diplomatic mission rather disconcerting. It is not clear what role he played at the Council, which had been transferred from Trent in March, but L'Hôpital's letters to his friends in Paris during his yearlong sojourn testify to his deep disillusionment with the Council of Trent. Boycotted by the imperial delegates, the Council faltered from the beginning, with its legality contested by Charles V.[58] Henry II, seeing no point in involving France in the quarrels of others, had instructed his ambassadors to assert above all the Gallican liberties of the French church.[59] To avoid a threatened schism, the pope decreed in February 1548 the suspension of discussions at Bologna. Thus reduced to inaction and disappointed at what he perceived as a useless conclave, L'Hôpital solicited his recall to France. He was afflicted by a severe case of gout and by indigestion, and it appears that he suffered from debilitating depression and stress during this period. L'Hôpital rather enigmatically wrote to Olivier:

> Ill physically and mentally, a letter of the king will cure me immediately.... My aspiration to return was not caused by my desire for any better position or by homesickness. Do not ask me what troubles my soul so much; [here] I have no one to divulge the secret sorrow which agitates me. Oh! if I could spend just one day with you, I would bring out all the agony I have hidden so far, the agony that has stifled me for so long.[60]

L'Hôpital was deeply disappointed by the theological quarrels and controversies at the Council, which he found as wearisome as the pleadings in the Parlement. His disillusionment with the Council bears witness to his aversion to abstract theoretical discussions. His experience in Bologna led to his critical view of the papacy and its abuses. He poured out his

---

[57]"Fatigué des procès et de leur lenteur, ennuyé de la capitale, je me suis occupé, malgré mon âge avancé, des affaires publiques. C'est alors que par tes soins le roi m'a envoyé en Italie pour le représenter à Bologne." Epistle to Olivier, *Poésies complètes*, 155.

[58]Hubert Jedin, et al., *History of the Church*, Vol. 5, *Reformation and Counter Reformation*, tr. Anselm Biggs and Peter W. Becker (New York: Seabury Press, 1980), 473–76.

[59]Lucien Romier, *Les Origines politiques des guerres de religion* (Paris: Perrin, 1913), 2:199–201.

[60]Epistle to Olivier, *Poésies complètes*, 11.

criticisms against the political ambitions and the corruptions of the popes in his letter to Cardinal du Bellay:

> Give the name of one pope who does not try to make his nephews equal to the kings, to establish at the center of Rome the name, arms and insignia of his family, bringing all the people of Europe to their arms. It is not the way that Saint Peter and the first torch of faith sowed, in Europe and Asia, the seeds of the true religion.[61]

L'Hôpital's sojourn in Bologna was not devoid of its benefits. Intellectually, it provided him with an opportunity to associate with humanists in Italy and to catch up on his old school days at Padua.[62] More important, L'Hôpital entered the powerful patronage of the Guises, who were to exercise perhaps the most significant influence on his subsequent career.

While in Bologna, L'Hôpital visited often with Renée, the duchess of Ferrara and daughter of Louis XII, who was patroness of the French scholars in Italy. The profound trust the duchess and her husband, Ercole II, had in L'Hôpital led to their appointing him guardian of their daughter Anne for her upcoming marriage to François, duc d'Aumale and the future duc de Guise. Apparently L'Hôpital had already been introduced to the duke's brother Charles, the cardinal of Lorraine, either through literary fame or through his father's connection with the duchess of Lorraine.[63] In a letter to François de Guise, L'Hôpital expressed his gratitude for the opportunity to serve at the coming marriage: "I assure you that I will continue to be in your services for the rest of my life; my seigneur the cardinal will be the witness to my pledge to you."[64]

The marriage contract was signed by proxy in Ferrara on September 28, 1548, while François de Guise was away suppressing the revolt of Saintonge.[65] L'Hôpital was relieved of his ambassadorship in time to escort the bride to Paris. He and the young duchess formed an enduring friendship during this trip, which played an important role in building up the Guises' trust in L'Hôpital, and the friendship continued even after L'Hôpital's open estrangement from the cardinal of Lorraine in the early

[61]Epistle to Cardinal Du Bellay, *Poésies complètes*, 41–42.

[62]He exchanged Latin verses with Italian poets and scholars, including Antonio Vacca and Achille Bocchi; Epistle to Vacca, *Poésies complètes*, 332–36; Epistle to Bocchi, *Poésies complètes*, 52–54.

[63]Jean de L'Hôpital probably died sometime before January 1547. A contract of January 5, 1547, by which Michel ceded the land and lordship of La Roche to his brother Pierre mentions their father's recent death; see *Minutier Central*, ET/VIII/73.

[64]BN, Collection Clairambault 341, fol. 203 (March 18, 1548).

[65]BCF, MS 740, fols. 25–45; fol. 33v contains L'Hôpital's name.

1560s.[66] L'Hôpital assured the young bride, "Your husband and your brother-in-law can do anything."

L'Hôpital perceived that the Guises were in the ascendant under the new king Henry II and he hoped to improve his political fortune through their influence. A letter written to Secretary of State Claude de L'Aubespine testifies to L'Hôpital's enthusiasm for the changed political climate under the new regime.[67] For L'Hôpital, it seemed that France had suddenly emerged out of darkness. He congratulated the cardinal of Lorraine that his reform programs were quickly implemented, restoring order to finance and rebuilding dignity in the judicial system.[68] No doubt L'Hôpital felt relief by the lifting of the cloud that hung over his career during the life of Francis I, and his successful introduction to the Guises gave him good reason to anticipate a bright future.

In November 1548, L'Hôpital returned to Paris full of hope, expecting some mark of royal favor in recognition of his services at Bologna. He must have awaited some dispensation of favor from his new patrons, the Guises, especially a promotion to a post other than the one at the Parlement of Paris. While complaining to Chancellor Olivier about being stuck at Bologna, he had confessed his abhorrence of the idea of resuming his legal duties at the Parlement: "I would rather do anything else than judging cases of despicable disputes of chicanery."[69] To his extreme disappointment, however, no advancement was forthcoming: "Instead of rewards which I had hoped for," wrote L'Hôpital in his testament, "I found great struggles and conflicts among the princes and nobles who surrounded the king, for rising virtue encounters, as is often said, many ambushes and obstacles."[70] After sixteen months of absence, L'Hôpital thus grudgingly returned to his old seat in the Parlement, to fulfill duties he "had almost forgotten."[71]

---

[66]During the St. Bartholomew's Day massacre in 1572 L'Hôpital asked Anne to protect the safety of his daughter, who happened to be in Paris. In his letter of gratitude he recalled their old friendship which had begun in Ferrara; Epistle to Anne d'Este, *Poésies complètes*, 360–63.

[67]Epistle to L'Aubespine, October 6, 1548, written in Parma; BN, *Manuscrits Français* (hereafter MS Fr.) 6620, fol. 5.

[68]It seemed to him to "sortir d'un songe, tant les prophéties et les voeux du cardinal s'étaient promptement réalisés, tant la France était transformée en si peu de temps"; cited in Dupré Lasale, *L'Hospital*, 1:128.

[69]Epistle to Olivier, *Poésies complètes*, 12. He instead wanted to devote himself to affairs of state, serving as ambassador to Rome for instance, and to compile a cohesive body of law to provide a simple and easy reference to law.

[70]Testament, *Oeuvres complètes*, 2: 519.

[71]"Je renonce à une espérance que j'avais caressée l'année précédente. Me voici de nouveau sur mon siège au Palais, me livrant à des exercices presque oubliées." Epistle to Olivier, *Poésies complètes*, 156.

Not long after his return to Paris, L'Hôpital was called to take a part in a commission closely related to the current political issues. In 1549, Henry II appointed him to the special tribunal set up to judge certain charges of the former commander of Boulogne, Jacques de Coucy-Vervins, and his father-in-law, the maréchal Oudart du Biez. In 1544, Henry, then dauphin, was ordered by his father, Francis I, to relieve Boulogne, which was under siege by Henry VIII. On the way to Boulogne Henry learned, to his great dismay, that the town had suddenly surrendered to the English. He had hoped to gain his father's favor by a military feat. Instead, the dauphin found himself blamed for not having taken swift action; with the loss of the important frontier town, France was forced to sign the unfavorable Treaty of Crépy.[72] Five years later, in January 1549, Henry II ordered the trial of Vervins and Biez. L'Hôpital was chosen, with seven other conseillers of the Parlement of Paris, to compose in part the commission of twenty-three judges, presided over by Pierre de Rémon, *premier président* of Rouen. According to the memoirs of the maréchal de Vieilleville, Henry II had specifically directed the commission to condemn the accused to death in order to redress the humiliation he had suffered as dauphin.[73] The proceedings continued for several months at Melun behind closed doors. On June 21, the tribunal delivered the verdict, declaring Vervins guilty of having traitorously rendered Boulogne to the English. Vervins was sentenced to death and executed shortly thereafter. Biez, whose death sentence was not declared until two years later, was pardoned by the king on account of his old age and previous military exploits.[74]emories de Monluc

L'Hôpital has been mistakenly believed to have been the *rapporteur* of the trial. He indeed drafted the evidence bearing upon the accused in the preliminary stages of the trial, and fragments of his own notes are

[72]Frederic J. Baumgartner, *Henry II: King of France 1547–1559* (Durham: Duke University Press, 1988, 37; Knecht, *Francis I*, 370–71. The townspeople of Boulogne accused their commanders, Vervins and Biez, of treason for the decision to surrender against popular wishes to hold out. Francis I refused to listen to the petition to punish them.

[73]*Mémoires de la vie de François de Scepeaux, sire de Vieilleville*, in *Nouvelle collection des mémoires pour servir à l'histoire de France*, ser. 1, ed. Michaud and Poujoulat (Paris, 1838), 9: 64.The political nature of this trial is discussed in detail in David L. Potter, "A Treason Trial in Sixteenth-Century France," *English Historical Review* 105 (1990): 595–623.

[74]In 1575, twenty-six years after the initial verdict, the son of Vervins appealed to Henry III to review the case, disputing the veracity of testimony by some witnesses. He succeeded in having the original trial declared void by the king and obtained decrees rehabilitating both Vervins and Biez. The commission of 1549 was condemned as a travesty of justice, and the magistrates who served at the tribunal were blamed for having obsequiously suited the wish of the king; *Mémoires de Vieilleville*, 9:66; *Mémories de Monluc*, ed. Michaud, 7:73, 276.

extant.[75] But L'Hôpital's role in this trial was rather a limited one. L'Hôpital resigned from the commission soon after the execution of Vervins in July, and did not participate in the trial of Biez, who was not sentenced until 1551. L'Hôpital explained his removal from the tribunal by saying, "My presence there was offensive [to others]."[76] It is likely that he was pressured to disqualify himself from the commission because of his relationship with François de Guise, who was a close friend of Biez.[77] It is also plausible, although speculative, that L'Hôpital held some dissenting opinion about the verdict. His own fragmentary notes do not provide sufficient information to show to what extent his position differed from that of the rapporteur, whose brief reveals that the testimony of witnesses was overwhelmingly unfavorable to the defendants.

L'Hôpital's brief involvement in the Vervins trial attests to his clientage to the house of Guise during these days. He carefully cultivated other political connections as well. On November 29, 1550, L'Hôpital asked to be excused from a case involving the prince of La Roche-sur-Yon and the constable of Montmorency. He cited, among other reasons, that his father was an old servant of the constable of Bourbon, uncle of the prince of Roche-sur-Yon, and that he was himself a native of the duchy of Montpensier.[78] By this public affirmation of his family's ties to the house of Bourbon, L'Hôpital renewed his old connection with one of the most powerful families in France.

During these days, L'Hôpital seemed to have been increasingly weary of his presence at the Parlement and worried about his slow advancement. The promotion, which his meritorious work as a judge could not obtain

[75]BN, Collection Dupuy 38, fols. 58–61, "Pièces relatives aux procès de lèse-majesté ou procès analogues intentés à Jacques de Coucy, seigneur de Vervins, 1549, de la main du chancelier Michel de l'Hospital"; copies in MS Fr. 3876, fols. 327–33v, "Extraict des informations (écrit de la main du chancelier de l'Hôpital), faictes contre Mre. Jacques de Coucy, Seigr. de Vervin, accusé d'avoir rendu par intelligence la ville de Bouloigne à l'Anglois, 1549." Apart from these manuscripts, there remain in the Bibliothèque Nationale a volume of notes kept by the *rapporteur* of the trial; *Collection Dupuy 475, Extraicts des procès faicts aux Sieurs de Vervins et Du Biez.* Dupré Lasale, *L'Hospital,* 1:136–44, ascribes the manuscripts to L'Hôpital, and Shaw, *L'Hospital,* 49–54, and appendix, follows Dupré Lasale's attribution. Recently Potter, "A Treason Trial," 596, n. 2, refuted L'Hôpital's authorship of this volume since its hand was quite different from L'Hôpital's own notes.

[76]Epistle to Olivier, *Poésies complètes,* 155–56. Nalèche incorrectly identified the situation, saying that L'Hôpital was in charge of the misappropriation cases during the wars in Italy; ibid., 155, note.

[77]Biez and François de Guise had collaborated in the battles around Boulogne in 1545. According to Potter, "A Treason Trial," 599, the duchess of Guise (François' mother) and Vervins were close, but these acquaintances failed to rescue Vervins or Biez.

[78]The king, by the letter of November 29, 1550, removed L'Hôpital from the proceedings; Dupré Lasale, *L'Hospital,* 1:14, 158; Taillandier, *Nouvelles Recherches,* 18–19.

for him, was procured thanks to his literary expertise, when he "least expected it."[79] L'Hôpital had never ceased to cultivate the classics, devoting his vacations from legal duties to literary pursuits. His literary talents gained him the attention of the king's sister, Marguerite de Valois. L'Hôpital was probably introduced to her through her literary tutor, Jean Morel, seigneur de Grigny, soon after he returned from Italy in late 1548.[80] Marguerite's first act upon becoming the duchess of Berry in April 1550 was to appoint L'Hôpital as chancellor of her duchy.

Marguerite was one of the three Valois women who exerted tremendous influence on L'Hôpital's career; the other two were Catherine de Médicis, under whose regency he served as chancellor of France, and Anne d'Este, through whom he solidified his relationship with the Guises. Marguerite was among the most frequent recipients of L'Hôpital's verses. His many poems dedicated to her are filled with lofty affection and loyal attachment. L'Hôpital mostly freely disclosed to her his concerns and aspirations:

> Often, children playing before your palace see me wandering about, uncertain whether I should go in or not. It was not because I was afraid of the guards ... but because I was overwhelmed by my deadly timidity and false shame, those [qualities] that also paralyze me in the presence of the king.[81]

Marguerite understood well the dilemma of the timorous poet-judge, who, despite his growing aspirations, still saw it as obsequious to chase publicly after political favors. His gratitude for his appointment as her chancellor was unbounded: "When I was tossing around, the prey of wind

---

[79]"Au moment où je m'y attendais le moins, la princesse royale me relève de ma chute et, me prenant la main, me dit de ne pas perdre courage"; Epistle to Olivier, *Poésies complètes*, 156.

[80]"J'ai…, au retour de la mission qui m'avait conduit en Italie, jugé, par moi-même, de la bonté de ton coeur pour tout ce qui t'approche; depuis ce moment tu m'as permis de compter au nombre de tes familiers"; Epistle to Olivier, *Poésies complètes*, 65. Jean Morel, a friend of Erasmus, was a prominent humanist scholar of the sixteenth century. Catherine de Médicis entrusted Morel with the education of her son, the future Henry III. Shaw, *L'Hospital and His Policy*, 57–58, argues that his poem to Pontronius, tutor of Marguerite, asking about the study of his royal pupil, drew the favorable attention of Marguerite. But the poem in question apparently was written after she was invested with the duchy of Berry, which had been held by the queen of Navarre until her death in April. "Que fait-elle des superbes villes dont le roi l'a dotée, de ces vastes campagnes que laboure le paysan du vieux Berry." Epistle to Pontronius, *Poésies complètes*, 28.

[81]Epistle to Marguerite de Valois, *Poésies complètes*, 64–65.

and wave, she alone, that blessed maiden Marguerite, the sister of Henry our King, rescued me."[82]

Marguerite, one of the most learned women of the sixteenth century,[83] was called "the patroness of the learned," a title she had taken over from her aunt Marguerite, queen of Navarre. As her chancellor, L'Hôpital dispensed patronage in her stead to many literary figures and built a large literary clientele around himself. His association in this capacity with many prominent scholars in the sixteenth century—the so-called Bourges connection—indeed reveals a little-known aspect of L'Hôpital as a great patron of intellectuals. Among his protégés were Pierre de Ronsard, Joachim du Bellay, and Scévole de Sainte-Marthe. L'Hôpital also wielded extensive influence at the University of Bourges, one of the finest legal institutions in Europe during the sixteenth century, where he was actively involved in the administration. He particularly exercised strong influence over the nomination of professors, bringing distinguished legal minds to its law faculty.

When L'Hôpital first came to Bourges in 1550, the University of Bourges already boasted a dazzling list of its law faculty, including François le Douaren, François Baudouin, and Hugues Doneau.[84] A conflict with Douaren caused Baudouin's departure for Geneva in early 1555. L'Hôpital subsequently nominated another renowned legal scholar, Jacques Cujas, for the vacant chair.[85] Doneau opposed Cujas' appointment, but he was rebuked by L'Hôpital in a missive written August 3, 1555. In this interesting letter, L'Hôpital severely criticizes Doneau for contesting the decision of the duchess and himself: "[You believe] one cannot appoint a successor to Baudouin without asking your opinion? ...[If so,] you judged me quite wrong."[86] A year later, L'Hôpital nominated the Calvinist François Hotman to a new chair of jurisprudence, thus significantly enhancing the university's strong reputation as a center of legal studies. In the 1560s, L'Hôpital maintained his relationship with Hotman (author of *Francogallia*) as his protector and patron. According to Donald Kelley, L'Hôpital gained Hotman's admission into the royal library at Fontaine-

---

[82]Testament, *Oeuvres complètes*, 2:519.

[83]Baumgartner, *Henry II*, 8.

[84]Donald Kelley, *François Hotman: A Revolutionary's Ordeal* (Princeton, N.J.: Princeton University Press, 19770), 76–77.

[85]L'Hôpital's letter to the échevins of Bourges, July 21, 1555, recommending Cujas' appointment; see Dupré Lasale, *L'Hospital*, 1:203, n. 1.

[86]*Oeuvres de Doneau*, 1762, quoted from Dupré Lasale, *L'Hospital*, 1:204–205.

bleau in 1563 and again in 1567, and apparently had Hotman appointed royal historiographer.[87]

During the 1550s, L'Hôpital energetically performed his various duties. Despite his appointment as chancellor of the duchess in April 1550, he retained his seat as conseiller of the Parlement until January 1554. The king specifically requested the Parlement to excuse L'Hôpital from legal duties when he needed to travel to Berry.[88] Even after he gave up the judgeship at the Parlement, L'Hôpital kept a position in the municipal government of Paris, as conseiller de l'Hôtel de ville de Paris. The registers of the Bureau de la ville de Paris contain scattered records of L'Hôpital's career as councillor, extending from February 1546 through November 1561.[89] L'Hôpital probably had been nominated to this office through the influence of his father-in-law, Jean Morin, long a city councillor himself and *prévot des marchands* at the time of L'Hôpital's entrance into the council.[90]

A discussion of L'Hôpital's early life cannot be complete without a few words about his wife, Marie Morin. After all, it was thanks to her dowry that L'Hôpital entered the Parlement of Paris, which allowed him to launch his unusual rise to power. Unfortunately, not much is known about Marie except L'Hôpital's sporadic references to her in his poems. In one account, L'Hôpital regretted that she had to give up the study of Greek and Latin, which he had encouraged her to take up after their marriage, when their first child was born.[91] She gave birth to three daughters: Madeleine was born in 1538, Jeanne in 1541, and Charlotte in 1542, but the last two had died by 1543.[92] L'Hôpital often spent vacations with his family in his father-in-law's estate in Paroy.[93] L'Hôpital's devotion to and trust in his wife is evident in his testament, in which he named her, instead

[87]Kelley, *Hotman*, 293; idem, *The Beginning of Ideology: Consciousness and Society in the French Reformation* (Cambridge: Cambridge University Press), 206, 240.

[88]Dupré Lasale, *L'Hospital*, 1:159.

[89]*Registres des délibérations du Bureau de la ville de Paris*, ed. François Bonnardot, et al. (Paris, 1883–1893), vols. 4 and 5. L'Hôpital's municipal councillorship is examined by Barbara Diefendorf, *Paris City Councillors in the Sixteenth Century: The Politics of Patrimony* (Princeton, N.J.: Princeton University Press, 1983). It was not until over a year after his appointment as chancellor of France that L'Hôpital finally gave up this municipal office. He resigned on November 18, 1561, in favor of Denis Tanneguy, avocat at the Parlement of Paris; *Registres des délibérations de la ville de Paris*, 5:105.

[90]Jean Morin died in 1548.

[91]Cited in Dupré Lasale, *L'Hospital*, 1:132–33.

[92]Dupré Lasale, *L'Hospital*, 1:82–83, n.; Amphoux, *Michel de l'Hôpital*, 69. The name Madeleine given to his first daughter seems to indicate that L'Hôpital did have a sister named Madeleine; see n. 4 above.

[93]Epistle to Tournon, *Poésies complètes*, 17.

of his daughter and son-in-law, as the administrator of all his possessions.[94]

L'Hôpital's appointment as the chancellor of the duchess of Berry in
1550 marked a crucial turning point in his career. He seems to have finally
liberated himself from the onus of being an exile's son, and he obtained a
fair opportunity to bring his political wisdom and abilities into full bloom.
He enjoyed the absolute confidence of Marguerite throughout his life.[95] It
appears that Marguerite, who was very close to her brother Henry, exerted
considerable influence on L'Hôpital's advancement in the government. In
L'Hôpital's own account, the princess's efforts to acquire the king's favor
for him aroused criticisms that it was "unworthy of the sister of the king
to have so much influence on him."[96] But L'Hôpital was quick to add that
those critics should rather learn not to resist the king or his sister. One can
presume that his devotion to the princess took rather exaggerated forms
in compensation for the lack of royal favor in his earlier career. At any rate,
under the unfailing protection of Marguerite and the powerful patronage
of the rising Guises, L'Hôpital was ready to accelerate his climb to the top
of the royal administration.

[94]Testament, *Oeuvres complètes*, 2:525–26.
[95]L'Hôpital, on his deathbed, entrusted his wife and his daughter to Marguerite's
benevolence and protection.
[96]Epistle to Marguerite de Valois, *Poésies complètes*, 218.

# CHAPTER 2

# A Judge Turned Etatiste Minister

J ULES MICHELET WROTE THAT when Michel L'Hôpital was appointed to the chancellorship of France in 1560, he was a figure "absolutely unknown in the magistracy who had plodded on in obscurity."[1] Michelet exaggerated; it is true that L'Hôpital, with his unpropitious background, followed an exceptional route to the top ranks of government. By 1560, however, L'Hôpital had held such important offices as conseiller at the Parlement of Paris, chancellor of the Duchess of Berry, *maître des requêtes*, and *premier président* of the Chambre des Comptes, and since 1559 had been a member of the Conseil Privé. Yet Michelet's comment does underscore the need for a careful reexamination of L'Hôpital's political career before 1560, a period which has been largely overlooked because it seems to bear little relevance to his policy of religious tolerance. On the contrary, the ten years prior to his chancellorship marked a crucial phase in his career and demonstrated remarkable continuity in his attitudes towards religious tolerance. Investigation of the formative years of the first minister will provide an important addition, and corrective, to the traditional portrait of Chancellor L'Hôpital.

One intriguing theme in the study of L'Hôpital is his relationship to the house of Guise. L'Hôpital owed his rapid rise in the government to extensive and generous patronage by the Guises. L'Hôpital himself once declared that his political fortune grew as the power of the Guises increased.[2] L'Hôpital's conflicts with Charles de Guise, the cardinal of

---

[1]Jules Michelet, *Oeuvres complètes*, ed. Paul Viallaneix (Paris: Flammarion, 1980), vol. 8, *Histoire de France au seizième siècle: Guerres de religion,* 158–59.

[2]"Never did your influence, and that of your brother, fail me. My position advanced as you two rose; my honor grew along with yours"; Epistle to the cardinal of Lorraine, *Poésies complètes*, 293.

Lorraine—especially their differences over religious issues during his chancellorship—have been discussed amply. But L'Hôpital's rapport with the Guises before 1560 has been virtually ignored, perhaps because L'Hôpital's position as a client of the Guises seems inconsistent with the well-established portrayal of Chancellor L'Hôpital as a heroic foe of the fanaticism that is often believed typical of the Guise faction. L'Hôpital's later estrangement from the cardinal is well known, but it needs to be balanced against a better understanding of his early clientage to the Guises. L'Hôpital himself is responsible in part for this incomplete picture of his relationship to the Guises because he kept silent in his later life about his earlier political debts to them. There is no single mention of the cardinal of Lorraine in L'Hôpital's testament—actually a short autobiography— even though the cardinal had such enormous influence on his career. L'Hôpital instead ascribed each of his advancements to the patronage of Marguerite de Valois. Yet, for nearly twenty years, L'Hôpital wrote numerous verses of appreciation to the cardinal. His failure to make proper acknowledgment to the cardinal in his testament should be interpreted not as an indication of ingratitude, but as a reflection of the dilemma of a statesman driven into conflict with his old patron by the exigencies of the religious wars.

Following his return from Italy in November 1548, L'Hôpital began to work in close collaboration with the cardinal of Lorraine on important political issues. In early 1551, François Olivier was about to give up his duties as chancellor. Olivier was one of the few high officials of Francis I who managed to hold onto office through the change on the throne. The circumstances surrounding his stepping down are not clear, and historians are not in agreement as to whether it was a disgrace or a voluntary decision because of his deteriorating eyesight and health.[3] The situation was complicated since the chancellor had received his appointment for life. Before Christmas 1550, the Parlement of Paris had assembled "to discuss if one could depose [Olivier] from the office."[4] The cardinal of Lorraine convened an ad hoc committee of parlementaires, including L'Hôpital and others regarded as being among the cardinal's men, to bypass the opposition of the Parlement, which remonstrated against the removal of the seal from Olivier on the grounds that it was a violation of the irremovability of the chancellor. The committee's decision to create the office of *garde des sceaux* incurred criticism from the Parlement, and the court demanded that the conseillers who participated in the committee

---

[3]Baumgartner, *Henry II*, 53, argues against the view that Olivier had been disgraced.
[4]Cited from Duchesne, *Histoire des chanceliers*, 619; Michaud, *La grande Chancellerie*, 26.

resign from the Parlement.[5] It is not easy to sort out L'Hôpital's personal stance in this seemingly arbitrary breach of the chancellor's irremovability, a fate that was to befall L'Hôpital himself seventeen years later. At the least, L'Hôpital's later relationship with Olivier and in particular L'Hôpital's letters written shortly after Olivier's retirement make it unlikely that he consented to the ousting of the chancellor against his will.[6] Nonetheless, this incident clearly shows L'Hôpital's close collaboration with the cardinal and his open defiance of the Parlement to which he belonged.

In October 1553, the cardinal of Lorraine procured for L'Hôpital the office of maître des requêtes. That office was another important step to higher appointment in the government.[7] L'Hôpital sincerely thanked the cardinal for finally rescuing him from his "obscure position" as a conseiller at the Parlement: "If you had not broken my chains, I would still have been there [in the Palais] when my hair and my beard turned white."[8]

L'Hôpital's close relationship with the Guises during this period is attested by the many poems he dedicated to them.[9] L'Hôpital always took time to thank his patrons profusely. In his mostly extravagant displays of affection and appreciation, L'Hôpital praised the political leadership of the cardinal of Lorraine and celebrated the military feats of the duc de Guise. He acclaimed the Guise brothers as "the hope of France," and urged all poets to "sing eternal hymns in honor of their great deeds."[10] L'Hôpital declared after the duc de Guise's conquest of Thionville in June 1558: "One can never praise too much the two brothers of Lorraine; one [Charles] will always be the special object of my cult; the other [François] saved the country, [and] restored France to its ancient frontiers."[11]

L'Hôpital's poems are indeed a laudatory chronicle of the military exploits of the duc de Guise, who "sustains with his arms our nation, as Atlas supported the sky on his shoulders."[12] After the duke's successful defense of Metz in the winter of 1552, L'Hôpital wrote: "The entire nation is grateful to you, for it acknowledges that you are the guardian of its

---

[5]Dupré Lasale, *L'Hospital,* 1:146–48.

[6]Epistle to Chancellor Olivier, *Poésies complètes,* 96–99.

[7]Epistle to the cardinal of Lorraine, *Poésies complètes,* 189–90. A document of the Trésor des Chartes bears L'Hôpital's signature; see AN, JJ 262, no. 341.

[8]Epistle to the cardinal of Lorraine, *Poésies complètes,* 247.

[9]Between 1550 and 1560, L'Hôpital wrote more than twenty poems for the Guises.

[10]"Sur la prise de Thionville," *Poésies complètes,* 182.

[11]Ibid., 185. Comparing L'Hôpital and Machiavelli, Marcel Jardonnet, "Michel de L'Hospital: poète néo-Latin et humaniste," *L'Auvergne littéraire* 158–59 (1958): 1–127, suggests that the Guises were to L'Hôpital what Cesare Borgia was to Machiavelli.

[12]Epistle to Jean de Morvillier, *Poésies complètes,* 230.

peace and safety."[13] The disastrous defeat of the constable of Mont-morency at Saint-Quentin in the summer of 1557 confirmed L'Hôpital's belief that François de Guise was the only savior of the country: "The victory calls you, our greatest captain.... To whom else could the king entrust our safety [when] threatened by the powerful enemy? It is the destiny of your family to reprimand the insolence of the House of Burgundy. As the sun shines again after the storm ... so will you rekindle the courage of the terrified people and of the defeated noblemen, filling their hearts with new hope."[14]

More important than the effusive adulation in these poems is their revelation of the degree to which L'Hôpital was integrated into the political network of the Guises. L'Hôpital was most vocal in support of the war policy of the Guises, who were the leading advocates of continuing the war in Italy. In a long epistle to Jean de Morvillier, bishop of Orléans, written shortly before the peace settlement with Spain at Cambrésis, L'Hôpital vehemently protested against concluding the peace. Endorsing the contention of François de Guise, L'Hôpital denied that royal finances were on the brink of bankruptcy; sound management, he asserted, would still allow France to maintain a powerful front. L'Hôpital was not indisposed to peace, he said, but he did oppose a disgraceful peace. He was afraid that "excessive desire for peace would cause people to be seduced by the pretended sincerity of the enemy; thereby they could be led, not to peace, but into a series of wars that would be more horrible than ever before."[15] For L'Hôpital, the moment for peace was yet to come. People were exhausted by the war and especially by recent defeats. But if France concluded peace, asserted L'Hôpital, France would have to make enormous concessions to Spain.

It is notable that L'Hôpital, in his advocacy of continuing the war, completely equated the interests of the Guises with those of the state. L'Hôpital denounced those at the court who argued for peace, charging that they were only concerned about their popularity and merely appealing to the people's wishes without caring for the future of the kingdom. The Guises, asserted L'Hôpital, wished to serve the best interests of the state. L'Hôpital was hardly discreet when he declared in his letter to Morvillier: "True pacifiers are the victorious generals," such as the duc de Guise, "and not the peace-seekers who sell themselves to the enemy," such as the Constable of Montmorency.[16] This letter of L'Hôpital's almost

[13]"Ode sur la prise de Metz," *Poésies complètes*, 113.
[14]Epistle to François de Lorraine, duc de Guise, *Poésies complètes*, 171–72.
[15]Epistle to Morvillier, *Poésies complètes*, 222–36.
[16]Epistle to Morvillier, *Poésies complètes*, 235.

sounds, as Dupré Lasale appropriately points out, as if it had been dictated by the Guises.[17] It is indeed an excellent apology for their war policy. But L'Hôpital's support for continuing the war was more than a mere echo of the politics of the Guises. In fact, his several verses on war and peace seem to be a manifesto of his little-known political views. Acclaimed for his policy of moderation and his denunciation of violence during the religious wars, L'Hôpital has been regarded as a Christian humanist in pursuit of pacifism. Christian humanists' moral objection to war is considered to be best represented by Erasmus, who believed that the Christian people would be spared many wars if the gospel were truly preached.[18] L'Hôpital shared with the Christian humanists their fundamental pacifism, but his faith in peace did not deter him from idealizing military glory and patriotism. Both before and after he became chancellor, L'Hôpital frequently turned to patriotic enthusiasm, which he hoped would generate a strong sense of national unity and cut across the polarization within the kingdom. The Guises apparently personified that unifying force during the reign of Henry II through successive victories at Metz, Calais, and Thionville. Yet L'Hôpital's support for the war reveals too much of his keen understanding and preoccupation with the dynamics of power to be a mere reflection of his association with the politics of the Guises.

L'Hôpital had already expounded a philosophical apology for war in a letter to a colleague at the Parlement of Paris, Pierre Grassin, composed probably sometime between 1547 and 1550.[19] His main contention was that war was necessary for a nation to sustain the morality of the citizens: "War is not less useful than peace: it refines human passions more forcefully than words, reason, and laws." People always talk about peace and repose. But in peacetime," luxury and affluence give rise to faulty utopias, shameful waste,... endless dispute, discord, suits, sentences, appeals, informers, avaricious judges, citizens unjustly chased away from their property.... War keeps us from those disasters, and thus has desirable effects which would not please the enemy." While prolonged peace inevitably corrupts morals and drags empires into decadence, war makes

---

[17]Dupré Lasale, *L'Hospital*, 2:127.

[18]James D. Tracy, *The Politics of Erasmus: A Pacifist Intellectual and His Political Milieu* (Toronto: University of Toronto Press, 1978), 4.

[19]Epistle to Pierre Grassin, *Poésies complètes*, 105–8. The original editors of L'Hôpital's poems claimed that they arranged them in chronological order, which Duféy followed in his edition of L'Hôpital's poems; see also Jacques-Auguste de Thou, *Histoire universelle* (Basle: Jean Louis Brandmuller, 1742), 6:79. This particular poem is placed in Duféy's edition between the one written when L'Hôpital was on his way to Bologna, in late 1547, and the one composed in 1550; see "Ad Crassinum, senatorem," *Oeuvres complètes*, 3:143–46. But the chronology of L'Hôpital's poems in Dufey's collection is often unreliable.

everyone wiser. The sound of arms sobers people down: "The powerful and rich reach out towards the weak and poor. They no longer despise the populace, and ask them to respond to common good; they submit themselves humbly to the most painful vows." L'Hôpital thus argued that the common fear of unknown terror and danger created and strengthened solidarity in society. Therein, according to L'Hôpital, lay the usefulness of war, perhaps far superior to its peril. War had destroyed and would destroy many towns. But, asked L'Hôpital, "does it matter if such a catastrophe is beneficial to us?" No, he exclaimed: "Better die honorably than drag in a long and miserable existence in shame!"[20]

L'Hôpital's verses on war reveal a surprisingly broad scope of perspectives. Like many of his contemporary humanists, he opposed France's involvement in Italy. Yet his criticism is based on realistic consideration of national interests rather than moral scruples.[21] L'Hôpital's view of the wars in Italy is indeed highly reminiscent of that of the great Hellenist scholar and legal humanist Guillaume Budé. Budé, who served Francis I as maître des requêtes, opposed the French expeditions in Italy because they contributed little to the French national interest.[22] Likewise, L'Hôpital criticized the French campaigns in Italy not because they were morally wrong but because they were useless. France had crossed the Alps many times, but always retreated in defeat and humiliation. For L'Hôpital, this occurred not because the French troops were weak but because the Italian allies, violating all their promises, abandoned French forces in the face of the enemy. In fact, the French involvement in Italy was a mistake to start with because, according to L'Hôpital, it was supposed to help the papacy. The French were proclaimed saviors of Rome, but "what prize do we get for our services?"[23] The pope was corrupt and the Church divided into a thousand sects. But France repeatedly "took the trouble to go all the way down to Italy, only to enrich the family of the Latin pope."[24] The French were therefore in service of a cause which "God disapproved." What could be a more daring attack against the papacy?

---

[20]Epistle to Grassin, *Poésies complètes*, 105, 106, 108.

[21]The Bibliothèque Nationale has two copies of L'Hôpital's poem "De Postrema Gallorum in Italiam expeditione carmen, scriptum anno 1557" in BN, Yc. 11259, and Rés. p. Yc. 1193 (6). The 1732 edition of L'Hôpital's poems contains only the first half of the poem; see *Michaelis Hospitalii, Carmina: Editio a prioribus diversa et auctior*, ed. P. Vlaming (Amsterdam: B. Lakeman, 1732), 462. Its French translation is found in Lasale, *L'Hospital*, 2:105–6, and in Coupé, *Essai de traduction*, 108. The boldness of the poem led Dupré Lasale to presume that it was published after L'Hôpital's death. The second half of the Latin poem is printed in Dupré Lasale, *L'Hospital*, 2:251–53.

[22]For Budé's view of the Italian expeditions, see Tracy, *The Politics of Erasmus*, 41–42.

[23]Quoted in Dupré Lasale, *L'Hospital*, 2:105.   [24]Dupré Lasale, *L'Hospital*, 2:106.

Like Budé, L'Hôpital made a distinction between wars that might serve the French national interest and those that did not. Aware of the futility of French involvement in Italy, L'Hôpital nonetheless regarded the wars in Italy as inevitable reality. "We all want to pursue peace," emphasizes L'Hôpital, but "we are forced to fight." The king of France made due efforts to end the war. But, "Philip [of Spain] refused [the peace], and we were forced to take up our arms again, believing in Providence, which lowers the noble and raises the humble." L'Hôpital deplores the fact that Christians, "the children of the same God, united by the same religion and cult," go to war because they belong to different countries and different masters. When war becomes inevitable, we should not forget that "we battle against our own brothers."[25] But, "God alone is the dispenser of peace and war,"[26] and it was God's will that the French fought despite their wishes. Therefore, concludes L'Hôpital, France rightfully deserves divine compensation.[27]

This is indeed a stunning justification of the French cause in the war. L'Hôpital carefully blended his astute observation of the political circumstances with philosophical speculation about God's will. Thus L'Hôpital's poems on war reveal a unique mélange of Christian ideals and political realism, which can be justly called Christian Realpolitik. Contemplation of the laws of God is a major undercurrent of his Latin poems, in which his Christian belief imparts a decisive tone to his interpretation of the given political situations. Nevertheless, L'Hôpital's advocacy of the French cause in Italy is not a mere self-serving or irrational argument invoking Providence. It is firmly based on his reasoned patriotism and keen understanding of the dynamics of power. He asks those who argue for a quick conclusion of the war: "Are you so naive as to believe that a powerful empire [like France] can remain in peace forever?" He opposes the peace treaty because, historically, two neighboring powers rarely live long without violating peace treaties. The victor, unable to check his desire, "will attack his adversaries, whomever he thinks less powerful, and make new enemies." L'Hôpital flatly concludes: "This is how many empires have been ravaged and lost, because kings, too much inclined to peace and too afraid of war, have made more concession than necessary to the enemy." L'Hôpital could hardly be more straightforward in his solemn warning of the illusions of peace, when he reminds that "peace does not depend on

[25]"Sur la prise de Thionville," *Poésies complètes*, 184–85.
[26]Epistle to Morvillier, *Poésies complètes*, 228.
[27]Epistle to Henry II, *Poésies complètes*, 118.

wishes alone." After all, he asks, "Why should we seek dishonorable peace and give up our rights?"[28]

L'Hôpital's profound pragmatism, carefully theorized in his Latin verses, also found expression in his political activities. His political career during the decade prior to 1560 was marked by continuous conflicts with the Parlement of Paris. L'Hôpital was above all a politician, whose practical consideration of the interests of the state dictated his politics. L'Hôpital's characteristic pragmatism led him to identify the interests of the state with those of the crown and thus to defend unlimited royal power. But his assertion of unchallenged royal authority inevitably clashed with the constitutional assumptions of the chief law court, and as a consequence, almost every initiative of Chancellor L'Hôpital encountered bitter resistance from the Parlement. It has been argued that L'Hôpital's chancellorship was unsuccessful because his policy of toleration was incompatible with the orthodox mentality of the Parlement of Paris. Yet the remarkable lack of collaboration between the magistrates and the royal government that L'Hôpital headed requires an examination of the full ramifications of the Parlement's opposition, not just from the religious angle but also from the perspective of separate interests and conflicting constitutional pretensions. Clashes between L'Hôpital and the Parlement in the 1560s were a product of their distressed relationship which had begun in the early 1550s. It is difficult to estimate to what extent such deep-seated animosity affected L'Hôpital's chancellorship. But the absence of support from the Parlement proved most damaging to the implementation of his policies and eventually led to the failure of his efforts to prevent the religious wars.

L'Hôpital's outspoken criticism of the Parlement while he was still a conseiller and his attack against unprincipled magistrates earned him much hostility from his colleagues. While L'Hôpital was emerging as a prominent political figure under the powerful patronage of the Guises and Marguerite de Valois, friction with the parlementaires increased as he confronted them over important political issues. In 1554, L'Hôpital faced fierce accusations from the Parlement of Paris in connection with his role in the Edict of the Semester.[29] A device proposed mainly to increase the

---

[28]Epistle to Morvillier, *Poésies complètes*, 220, 228, 230–31.

[29]Etienne Girard and Jacques Joly, *Trois livres des offices de France* (Paris, 1658), 1:19–20; François André Isambert, et al., *Recueil général des anciennes lois françaises* (Paris: Belin-Leprieur, 1828), 13:373. The edict was registered at the Parlement of Paris on April 28, after numerous remonstrances, under the title "Edit du semestre et règlement nouveau des épices et jugemens des procès par commissaires." According to *Discours pour la majorité de Charles IX et trois autres discours*, ed. Robert Descimon (Paris: Imprimerie Nationale, 1993), introduction, 16, the Semester reform was one of the worst rounds the Parlement of Paris was to suffer before the abolition of the law court by Chancellor Maupeau in 1771.

number of offices available for sale, the semester system required that each office at the courts have two incumbents who exercised its functions for six-month terms. Henry II justified the system by alleging that it would reduce the épices and make fraud more difficult by establishing mutual control between the two semestral sections.[30] But the edict met with fierce opposition from the parlementaires, who feared the change would reduce the prestige and income of their offices.[31] The Parlement held L'Hôpital responsible for having masterminded the system in collaboration with the cardinal of Lorraine. The Parlement was even more furious with L'Hôpital because it felt he betrayed his colleagues at the Parlement to favor his own political ambitions. When the king presented the edict for registration in January 1554, it was revealed that several parlementaires had already been consulted secretly and that they provided their signatures in consent to the new measure.[32] It seems likely that L'Hôpital functioned as a kind of lobbyist at the Parlement in order to undermine opposition. But L'Hôpital declined to assume responsibility for the system:"I will never usurp the credit for having brought this result [abolishing épices]; I will simply take pride in having been the first who brought the abuses to light. I approved the idea … in order to reform and purify the morals of the judiciary. You magistrates, how could you pursue your old colleague with curses and accusations?"[33] The edict was registered on April 28, 1554, and the new

[30]The épices originated as free gifts in kind by the disputants to the judges in charge of their cases. By the sixteenth century they had been converted into a standardized money payment to the judges.

[31]Edouard Maugis, *Histoire du Parlement de Paris de l'avènement des rois Valois à la mort d'Henri IV*, 3 vols. (Paris: Alphonse Picard, 1913–1916), 1:197–98; Romier, *Royaume de Catherine de Médicis*, 2:16. Baumgartner saw the semester system as the biggest point of contention between the king and the judges during Henry's reign. Baumgartner, *Henry II*, 88–89.

[32]Maugis, *Parlement de Paris*, 1:193, 197. On April 27, avocat général Pierre Séguier condemned those parlementaires as "betrayers" and "authors of the schism." In May 1553, Séguier reported that he saw "messieurs de Mesmes and de L'Hospital" sitting with the cardinal of Lorraine at the Conseil Privé. Since it was not until October that L'Hôpital was appointed maître des requêtes, Séguier's report indicates that L'Hôpital assisted the cardinal at the royal council while he was still a conseiller at the Parlement; see Dupré Lasale, *L'Hospital*, 1:225.

[33]Epistle to Chancellor Olivier, *Poésies complètes*, 153. L'Hôpital made no mention of the semester system while he acknowledged his responsibility for the suppression of the épices. De Thou, *Histoire universelle*, 2:247, affirms that L'Hôpital was in charge of drafting responses article by article to refute the Parlement's remonstrances. L'Hôpital congratulated the cardinal on his reforms of the épices in his poem; see Epistle to the cardinal of Lorraine, *Poésies complètes*, 247.

system came into effect at the Parlement on the first day of July.[34]

Squabbles surrounding L'Hôpital's resignation from the Parlement reflect the uncongenial relations within that body, which were exacerbated by the semester system. In October 1553, L'Hôpital resigned his office of conseiller in favor of Philippe Hurault, the future chancellor Cheverny, to become a maître des requêtes. The following January, the Parlement opposed the installation of Hurault on the grounds that he had purchased the post in contradiction to prohibition against the sale of judicial offices.[35] The Parlement contended that the receipt for 8,000 livres, the amount which Hurault was taxed for the office, had been forged, and that the money had not reached the royal treasury but had instead lined L'Hôpital's pocket.[36] In his accusations against L'Hôpital, Pierre Séguier, the avocat général, admitted that "similar practices have been made lately in a few judicial offices."[37] In fact, more than "a few" royal offices had been sold by parlementaires, and the Parlement's scruples against venality indicated its ambivalent attitude since the interests of its members were seriously affected by the practice. L'Hôpital was accused of having illegally appropriated a royal tax payment, but the imposition of a financial levy on a new incumbent was a fiction frequently employed to disguise a transaction that had been tacitly approved by the king.[38] Hence the Parlement could hardly disclaim the charge that it deliberately targeted L'Hôpital because it had felt outflanked over the semester system. The opposition of the Parlement was rendered ineffective when the king ordered prompt installation of Hurault, but this incident irreparably

[34]The system newly created offices for four presidents and thirty-seven conseillers. The old members of the Parlement were not happy when new officials demanded admission. The king sent lettres de jussion on April 26 and again on May 29, 1555, ordering Parlement not to discriminate against new magistrates; see Felix Aubert, "Recherches sur l'organisation du Parlement de Paris au XVIe siècle (1515–1589)," *Extrait de Nouvelle revue historique du droit français et étranger* (Paris: Sirey, 1912), 61–62. The system never functioned in a satisfactory manner, however, and was abolished by the edict of January 1558.

[35]*Mémoires du Chancelier Cheverny*, in *Nouvelle collection des mémoires*, 1ère série, ed. Michaud and Poujoulat, 10:456–66.

[36]AN, X1a 1577, fols. 173, 17, Jan. 16 and 19, 1554; Maugis, *Parlement de Paris*, 1:226; Dupré Lasale, *L'Hospital*, 1:225–31.

[37]AN, X1a 1577, fol. 173; Taillandier, *Nouvelles recherches*, 23.

[38]AN, X1a 1577, fol. 212, Jan. 27, 1554. Various subterfuges were employed to hide the fact that often the offices were venal. The Parlement admitted that "there had been some derogations," but rather maladroitly maintained that those were committed "for the necessity for the affairs," and that no one received profit from them. But in the current case, the Parlement alleged, the receipt was forged and money was actually paid to the resignant, which constituted a clear "fraud"; see Maugis, *Parlement de Paris*, 1:226–27.

soured L'Hôpital's relationship with the Parlement of Paris.[39]

In 1556, L'Hôpital and the Parlement were once again pitted against each other over the right of resignation from royal offices. In November 1554, at the request of Marguerite de Valois, Henry II had promised to L'Hôpital the first office of conseiller to be vacated in the Parlement or Cour des Aides, which he could dispose of as part of his daughter Madeleine's dowry in her marriage to Robert Hurault, seigneur de Belesbat.[40] When one Jacques Potier, a conseiller at the *grand' chambre*, died in March 1556, the office became vacant, but the Parlement contested the king's will, and declared that it was a "pernicious thing" to promise an office to someone even before the incumbent was dead. The deceased magistrate had already resigned his office in favor of a Jean Dauvet. But Potier died only five days after the resignation, and the office would normally have been subject to the "quarante jours" regulation, since, according to the rule, no resignation in favor of another was valid unless the resigning party survived forty days after the completion of the transaction.[41] The Parlement insisted that the forty day rule should not be applied to the office in question since the right of resignation had already been infringed.[42] In his vehement response to the Parlement's contention, L'Hôpital condemned the Parlement for not binding itself to the "quarante jours" rule, and refuted its assumption that offices carried the same right as that of private property.[43]

This incident illustrates L'Hôpital's abhorrence of venality—notwithstanding his having sold his own position in the Parlement—which was to become a major point of contention between Chancellor L'Hôpital and the chief law court. L'Hôpital was opposed to the trend that high judicial offices passed from generation to generation within a single family, thus creating a highly privileged quasi-hereditary noblesse de robe. If public offices were monopolized by a few men with great fortune, asserted

[39]"The hideous figures [8,000 livres] followed him till his death"; P.D.L., *Eclaircissements*, 86.

[40]The register of the secretary of finance specified:"The first office to be vacated in the Parlement or Cour des aides will be offered to L'Hôpital, before anyone else who might have a similar promise from the king"; see Dupré Lasale, *L'Hospital*, 2:72–73. The Huraults were one of the oldest families prominent in the legal profession, and L'Hôpital had reason to feel pleased with the marriage alliance with the Huraults. L'Hôpital had resigned his councillorship at the Parlement for Philippe Hurault de Cheverny, cousin of his future son-in-law, Robert Hurault; see Henri de Vibraye, *Histoire de la Maison Hurault* (Blois: J. de Grandpré, 1929), 146, 165–66.

[41]For the "quarante jours" rule, see Roland Mousnier, *La Vénalité des offices sous Henri IV et Louis XIII*, 2d ed. (Paris: Presses Universitaires de France, 1971), 44–46.

[42]Dupré Lasale, *L'Hospital*, 2:78–83.

[43]Epistle to Marguerite de Valois, *Poésies complètes*, 249–50.

L'Hôpital, people would desert studying , and would not make an honest living. This altercation was a prelude to the heated battle between Chancellor L'Hôpital and the Parlement over the king's right over royal offices. L'Hôpital already made his constitutional stance clear in 1556: "All offices are at the king's disposal and only the king has the right to distribute offices, which return to his hands when the incumbent deceases. Offices are not supposed to be transmitted to descendants like private property: we enjoy the dignities of royal offices only during our lifetime." Furthermore, the king's wishes that were solemnly declared at the royal council "must be obeyed in any circumstances." Then he asked, "Why do [my adversaries] dispute the office which the king had the right to dispose of and granted to me?"[44]

This incident, while attesting to the increasing discord between L'Hôpital and the Parlement, also bears witness to the royal favors he enjoyed thanks to his relationship to the king's sister, a situation which the parlementaires apparently found repugnant. Henry II finally ordered that Dauvet be installed in the office, but Dauvet agreed to pay L'Hôpital a certain sum toward his daughter's dowry.[45] L'Hôpital wrote a letter to Marguerite thanking her for having backed him up in this irritating conflict with the Parlement: "This time the fight was fierce, and your victory was all the more brilliant. By this incident, the people who, boasting of their wealth, dare to traffic honors and dignities against the royal order, will learn that they should not challenge the king and his noble family." His enemies murmured about Marguerite's influence on her brother. But, L'Hôpital pronounced triumphantly, "they were soundly punished for being so stupid."[46]

Hostility between L'Hôpital and the Parlement had already been escalating into institutional conflict when the king appointed him to the newly created first presidency of the Chambre des Comptes in February 1555.[47] The Chambre des Comptes judged cases relating to the king's finances. It also registered fiscal edicts and the audit of taxes. The cardinal of Lorraine, who was in charge of finance, might well have wished to appoint to the post someone on whom he could rely. As the war in Italy progressed, there was great need for efficient control over war expenditures and, in particular, for tighter supervision of tax officials to reduce the pervasive corrup-

---

[44]Epistle to Marguerite de Valois, *Poésies complètes*, 249.

[45]Dupré Lasale, *L'Hospital*, 2:83.

[46]Epistle to Marguerite de Valois, *Poésies complètes*, 248–49.

[47]Many historians incorrectly dated L'Hôpital's appointment 1554 instead of 1555, probably because of confusion over the old calendar style in use until 1564; see Anselme, *Histoire généalogique*, 488; Dufey, introduction to *Oeuvres complètes de Michel de L'Hospital*, 1:77; Michaud, *La grande Chancellerie*, 27.

tion within the fiscal system. L'Hôpital's appointment was by any standard an irregular, not to say arbitrary, political measure. The edict of January 1555 created the new office of the premier président at the Chambre, in addition to the existing six presidents, in order to impose effective supervision over the two semestral sections.[48] The innovative measure was a serious blow to the entire Chambre and in particular to Antoine de Nicolay, then président clerc. The président clerc at the Chambre traditionally functioned as the chief president who supervised the others, and the position had been occupied by the members of the same family, the Nicolays, without interruption from 1506.[49] Antoine de Nicolay did not dare to resist the king's will. The edict was registered on February 6, 1555, despite remonstrances from the Chambre, and the same day L'Hôpital was appointed to the position.[50]

L'Hôpital soon proved his worth to the king and the cardinal of Lorraine. As a self-proclaimed "scrupulous guard of the royal treasury," L'Hôpital exerted rigorous surveillance over the collection of taxes and the expenditures of public funds. He gained a reputation for being particularly severe in meting out punishment to fraudulent officials. It is said that L'Hôpital refused to pay from the treasury Henry II's gift of 20,000 livres to Diane de Poitiers, reminding the king that "such an amount equals the revenues from twenty villages."[51] L'Hôpital's severity in guarding the royal treasury inevitably incurred wrath from many quarters. L'Hôpital complained to Olivier in 1558: "The care with which I protect the royal purse makes me widely detested by thieves.... It must be painful for them not to be able to pillage [the royal treasury] any longer as they did in the past."[52]

---

[48]BN, Dupuy 854, fol. 126, Letters of Henry II, "Création d'un office de premier président en la Chambre des Comptes, en faveur de Michel de L'Hospital, maître des requêtes," issued in Saint-Germain-en-Laye.

[49]The Nicolays continued to hold this office until 1791.

[50]Dupuy 846, fol. 379v; Dupuy 854, fol. 128. See also the Procès-verbal at the Chambre des Comptes, *Archives Nicolay*, 3/AP/14, dossier C12. His appointment was prompted and justified by the semester system he favored. L'Hôpital was theoretically in charge of both semestral sections, but the lettres patentes of September 8, 1555, excused him, "in order to treat him fairly," from sitting throughout the year, requiring instead that he serve only six months (November–January and May–July). He was to serve the other six months as long as his health would permit. The position of the premier président, which was created in this irregular manner almost tailor-made for L'Hôpital, was left unfilled after he became chancellor, and it was permanently abolished by the edict of September 24, 1563; *Actes royaux, supplément 1554–1572*, BN, *Imprimé*, F. 23740 (242). See *La Cour des Comptes*, 141–46.

[51]*Bibliographie universelle*, 459.

[52]Epistle to Chancellor Olivier, *Poésies complètes*, 157.

L'Hôpital also played an important role in expanding the jurisdiction of the Chambre at the expense of the Parlement of Paris. Changes introduced by Francis I had enhanced the status and authority of the fiscal courts and thus brought them into conflict with the Parlement, which sought to preserve its traditional authority over the other sovereign courts.[53] The Parlement maintained that it had cognizance, as the supreme court of the realm, over cases judged at the Chambre, but the Chambre did not recognize the appellate jurisdiction of the Parlement. Under the presidency of L'Hôpital, the Chambre proved more adamant than ever in asserting its prerogative as a sovereign court against the pretensions of the Parlement.

Jurisdictional disputes between the two courts were rekindled only a few months after L'Hôpital's appointment to the Chambre. This time the principal point of contention was whether a case regarding the falsification of accounts by a financial commissaire at the Parlement of Rouen was of a purely fiscal nature, for which the Chambre had the last appeal, or of criminal nature, which could be heard by the Parlement.[54] When the official obtained permission from the Parlement to appeal against the decision made at the Chambre, the Chambre refused to turn over the trial records. The Parlement remonstrated to the king, alleging that the competency of the Chambre was limited to the operations of public finance and that the Parlement retained higher jurisdiction over the Chambre. After some scuffles between the two bodies, L'Hôpital succeeded in procuring an arrêt dated July 7 from the Conseil Privé, which denied the appellate jurisdiction of the Parlement and ordered that the case be reviewed by a commission at the Chambre, attended by judges from both courts.[55] The contention between the Chambre and the Parlement was an inevitable result of ill-defined jurisdictional boundaries, and similar conflicts kept resurfacing as each body claimed its respective domains. The king had a crucial interest in these jurisdictional frictions since the demand for more efficient control over royal finance inclined him to limit the right of convicted officials to appeal to the Parlement. By making fiscal officials more

---

[53]Martin Wolfe, *The Fiscal System of Renaissance France* (New Haven: Yale University Press, 1972), 269–78.

[54]Maugis, *Parlement de Paris*, 1:387–396. R. Doucet, *Les Institutions de la France au XVIe siècle* (Paris: Picard, 1948), 1:195.

[55]*Cour des Comptes*, 53; Maugis, *Parlement de Paris*, 1:395; Lasale, *L'Hospital*, 1:245–46. The arrêt confirmed the Ordinance of Vivier of 1408, which stipulates that grievances against the verdicts of the Chambre were to be reviewed by a commission called "Chambre du Conseil lez la Chambre des Comptes." The Chambre du Conseil conferred a certain edge to the Chambre des Comptes because proceedings were held at the Chambre des Comptes, "assisted" by delegates from the Parlement; see *Cour des Comptes*, 38–39.

responsible to the crown, L'Hôpital thus defended royal interests and protected the king's rights over his revenues.

Competition between the Parlement and the Chambre led to their intransigent attitudes towards each other. Each court jumped at any opportunity to undermine its rival's authority. In one case, for example, the Chambre issued an ordinance in October 1556 declaring that it would no longer recognize the *debentur,* a payroll form attesting to a parlementaire's regular attendance, unless it was endorsed by the president of the Parlement.[56] The rationale behind the innovation was that frequent absences of conseillers from their seats made it necessary for some conseillers to work during both semesters, causing a considerable loss to the royal treasury for their salaries. Appalled by the audacious action of the Chambre, which the Parlement perceived as a direct challenge to its authority, the magistrates remonstrated that the double service of some conseillers was required not because of the unauthorized absences of conseillers, as the Chambre alleged, but because of the slow sale of newly created posts to fill the two semestral courts.[57] The Parlement invited L'Hôpital and other presidents of the Chambre to the Parlement to discuss the matter, but L'Hôpital refused any negotiation, staunchly upholding the Chambre's decision on account of the financial exigency of the royal treasury.

The incident unfolded in quite a remarkable way. After hearing the remonstrances by the Parlement that the Chambre's action was merely an ill-spirited vendetta aimed at jeopardizing the magistrates, the Conseil Privé issued *lettres patentes* deciding the issue of debentur in favor of the Parlement, and confirmed the Parlement's superiority over the Chambre.[58] Within days, however, L'Hôpital obtained from the king a second declaration, much to the surprise of the Parlement, which revoked the preceding declaration and proclaimed the equality of the Parlement and the Chambre. This famous edict of December 27, 1556, confirmed the Chambre des Comptes as a sovereign court and forbade the Parlement to assert

[56]Maugis, *Parlement de Paris,* 1:396–400.

[57]The Parlement's rebuttal was a convincing argument against the semester system. When the system came into effect on July 1, 1554, only two conseiller posts among thirty-seven newly created jobs had been sold. The king allowed the provisional filling of empty seats with conseillers off the semester; Maugis, *Parlement de Paris,* 1:202.

[58]Séguier asked how the inferior court could impose a law on the Parlement, which was "delegated the absolute and indivisible sovereignty of the prince." He asserted that "the chambre contested the validity of debentur simply out of maliciousness to jeopardize the magistrates and deprive them of authority and prestige." His contention that the new measure would bring about no impact on royal finance was favorably heard at the Conseil Privé; cited from Maugis, *Parlement de Paris,* 1:398.

any superiority over the Chambre.[59]

Disputes over "precedence" between the two rival courts were almost classical. On March 21, 1557, at the funeral procession of the cardinal of Bourbon, the Parlement ordered the "gens des comptes" to march behind—not beside—the parlementaires as had been the ancient usage.[60] The Chambre resisted. The Parlement obtained a royal declaration in its favor, but the Chambre succeeded in having the declaration revoked within days.[61] The king's being not consistent, protocol disputes between the two bodies ensued without solution.[62]

L'Hôpital's efforts to assert the prerogative of the Chambre des Comptes coincided with the king's attempt to strengthen the authority of other important bodies to counterbalance the power of the Parlement.[63] They were, in effect, part of L'Hôpital's larger programs to prevent the growth of excessive esprit de corps and independence of the law courts, which could compromise royal power. L'Hôpital believed that the unchallenged authority of the crown was most beneficial to the kingdom, and it was this belief that prompted him to restrict the Parlement's jurisdictional claims against the Chambre and, when he became chancellor, to limit the Parlement's rights of remonstrance and registration of royal edicts. L'Hôpital arrived at the Chambre as an outsider—a political appointee. Once installed at the Chambre, however, this former conseiller at the Parlement displayed surprising determination to expand the authority of the Chambre at the expense of the Parlement. Throughout his political career, whether during his presidency at the Chambre or during his chancellorship, L'Hôpital thus consistently pursued policies directed to increase royal power and relied on royal authority as his ultimate appeal.

L'Hôpital's clashes with the Parlement in the 1550s left an indelible imprint on their relations over the next decade. The Parlement felt betrayed by its former member when L'Hôpital led the Chambre's adamant challenges to its authority. In 1560, the Parlement was clearly miffed

[59]"Déclaration concernant les debentur" of December 27, 1556, *Actes Royaux*, BN, *Imprimé*, F. 23740 (211): "Par l'érection des deux Cours, l'une n'a sur l'autre aucune autorité, ains sont toutes deux en leur droit et respectivement connoissantes en dernier ressort." The Conseil Privé's decision on *debentur* remained affirmed; see Arthur Michel de Boislisle, *Chambre des comptes de Paris: Pièces justicatives pour servir à l'Histoire des premiers présidents 1506–1791* (Nogent-le-Rotrou: Imprimerie de A. Gouverneur, 1871), xlvii.

[60]In public ceremonies, members of the two bodies were to march "in pair," side by side, as confirmed by the king in 1523; see Gaston Zeller, *Les Institutions de la France au XVIe siècle*, 2d ed. (Paris: Presses Universitaires de France, 1987), 291–92.

[61]*Cour des Comptes*, 47.

[62]Félix Aubert, *Le Parlement de Paris au XVIe siècle: Extrait de la Revue des études historiques* (Paris, 1905), 352, 493; Isambert, *Recueil général*, 13:483.

[63]Doucet, *Les Institutions de la France au XVIe siècle*, 1:195.

at the king's selection of President L'Hôpital of the Chambre des Comptes as chancellor, because he had not previously been the president of the Parlement as had his predecessors.[64] Once he became chancellor, L'Hôpital launched sweeping judicial reforms that seriously limited the privileges of the magistrates. Fresh from past humiliations, and now with their interests threatened, the Parlement stood as one of the most antagonistic opponents of L'Hôpital's chancellorship, not only thwarting the execution of his judicial reforms but also obstructing the implementation of his religious policies. They deprived the chancellor of support, when he needed it most, by opposing his toleration edicts. Historians have noted the diversity of parlementaire opinion concerning heresy in the Parlement in the late 1550s and early 1560s.[65] Conseiller Anne du Bourg, although he met his unfortunate fate of being burned at the stake in 1559, is one illustration of the existence of a tolerant spirit within the law court, which was a traditional champion of the orthodox religion. It is possible to conjecture, therefore, that the Parlement could have been less hostile to L'Hôpital's toleration policy if its relations with the chancellor, all too often emotionally tainted, had been more harmonious. By the 1550s, however, their relationship had already been seriously impaired.

L'Hôpital's obstinate attitude toward the Parlement was largely due to the powerful backing he held in the royal council through the cardinal of Lorraine. By the late 1550s, L'Hôpital was doubtless among the cardinal's primary confidants. In January 1557, shortly before the battles of Guines and Calais, the cardinal launched a large campaign to raise money and L'Hôpital, as président of the Chambre des Comptes, presided over a special assembly that voted for the funds requested by the duc de Guise. The concerted efforts of the cardinal and L'Hôpital were amply redeemed by the duke's glorious victory.[66] In April 1558, L'Hôpital dedicated to the

[64]L'Hôpital's predecessors, Antoine Duprat, Antoine Dubourg, and François Olivier, were all premier président of the Parlement of Paris when they were appointed chancellor. Guillaume Poyet was président of the Parlement of Paris.

[65]See, e.g., Linda Taber, "Royal Policy and Religious Dissent within the Parlement of Paris, 1559–1563" (Ph.D. dissertation, Stanford University, 1982); idem, "Religious Dissent within the Parlement of Paris in the Mid-Sixteenth Century: A Reassessment," *French Historical Studies* 16 (1990), 684–99.

[66]Epistle to the cardinal of Lorraine, *Poésies complètes*, 178: "When the treasury was empty because of long war, God gave you, Charles, resources in the form of your intelligence and patriotism of compatriots.... You raised within two days the subsidies of good citizens of Paris; soon money gave vigor to the soldiers and prepared them to obey you." L'Hôpital's active role in raising taxes and forced loans was prompted by not only his official duties as president of the Chambre des Comptes but also his relationship to the Guises. See L'Hôpital's letter to the cardinal of Lorraine, June 10, 1558, in Guillaume Ribier, *Lettres et Mémoires d'Estat, des roys, princes, ambassadeurs, et autres ministres, sous les règnes de François premier, Henry II & François II* (Paris, 1666), 2:743–44.

cardinal of Lorraine an ode celebrating the wedding of Mary Stuart and the dauphin François. Mary Stuart was the daughter of James V of Scotland and Marie de Guise (the sister of François de Guise and the cardinal of Lorraine). L'Hôpital congratulated the cardinal that his niece and her husband would some day govern France, Scotland, and England, and would share the whole world—a rather hasty prediction.[67] As if returning such unswerving loyalty, in May 1558, the cardinal of Lorraine served as godfather to L'Hôpital's first grandchild, Charles Hurault de L'Hôpital.[68]

At court, the constable of Montmorency's argument for peace prevailed with the king. L'Hôpital's position in favor of pressing on with the war was more than a reflection of his blind support of the Guises. L'Hôpital's philosophical justification of war served, nonetheless, as a brilliant theoretical apology for the politics of the Guises, glossing over their misgivings that the truce would diminish their dominance at court. One must wonder why L'Hôpital, who had composed poems on almost every important event during the war, remained silent at the conclusion of the war.

In March 1559, L'Hôpital and his son-in-law, Robert Hurault, conseiller at the Grand Conseil and maître des requêtes, went to Cateau-Cambrésis to sign the marriage contract of Marguerite de Valois and Philibert-Emmanuel, the duke of Savoy, as a part of the peace settlement.[69] L'Hôpital stayed in Cateau-Cambrésis at least until late May. It seems likely that

[67]In Francisci, illustriss. Franciae delphini, et Mariae, sereniss: Scotorum reginae, nuptias, viri cujusdam ampliss. BN, Rés. p. Yc. 1465. The English translation of L'Hôpital's poem is in Francis Wrangham, An Epithalamium on the Marriage of Francis of Valois and Mary Stuart (London, 1837), 29: "The hour will come, when a refulgent race / Of gallant boys our royal halls shall grace: / To each a separate throne assign'd shall be / Gaul to the first, the second Lombardy / From the peak'd Alps to far Tarento's tide / And this shall Scotland, that Britannia guide; / While other sceptres other sons shall bear / So shall one house the world's vast empire share."

[68]Buisson, Michel de L'Hôpital, 85. L'Hôpital wanted their grandchildren from Madeleine (the couple's only child, who was married to Robert Hurault) to bear the surname L'Hôpital. L'Hôpital specified his wish in his testament: "The eldest named Charles writes also his name: Charles Hurault l'Hôpital"; see Testament, Oeuvres complètes, 2:526. According to Vibraye, Histoire de la Maison Hurault, 146, it figured into the marriage settlement of Madeleine in 1557. L'Hôpital hoped this arrangement would distinguish his grandchildren from the Huraults, "who are in too great number."

[69]Giovanni Michiel, the Venetian ambassador, to the doge, March 16, 1559, Calendar of State Papers and Manuscripts Relating to English Affairs, Existing in the Archives and Collections of Venice (hereafter CSP Venice), ed. Rawdon Brown, et al. (London, 1864–1947), 7:49; Trivultio, the cardinal-legate, to A. Carafa, March 19 and March 21, 1559, Acta Nunciaturae Gallicae, vol. 14, Lenzi et Gualterio, légation du Cardinal Tribultio (1557–1561), ed. J. Lestocquoy (Rome: Université Pontificale Grégorienne, 1977), 189–90; Romier, Origines des guerres de religion, 2:338.

L'Hôpital during this time had an audience with Philip II, king of Spain.[70] L'Hôpital, a trusted councillor of Marguerite, also enjoyed the confidence of her husband. Shortly after their marriage in July, the duke of Savoy requested that L'Hôpital supervise the reorganization of the judicial system in Piedmont and Savoy.[71] We do not know what, if any, role L'Hôpital played in the project.

By the middle of that year, the situation at court was changing rapidly. After the unexpected death of Henry II, Francis II was enthroned on July 10. The following day, the Guises, now the unchallenged masters at court, recalled Olivier to his duties of chancellor and reconstituted the royal councils. The newly organized Conseil Privé included President of the Chambre des Comptes L'Hôpital.[72] On November 18, L'Hôpital left Blois to escort the duchess to her husband in Turin. He arrived in Nice in early February 1560.[73] In early April, L'Hôpital learned of the death of Chancellor Olivier on March 30, and of his own appointment to the chancellorship. L'Hôpital hastened his return to Paris to assume his new duties as the first minister of the kingdom. He was not doubtful about who had procured the honor to him. On April 23, on his way back to Paris, L'Hôpital pledged his loyalty to the cardinal of Lorraine:"I will try to emulate and follow suit [of the deceased chancellor] as far as I can, and I believe I can do it with more ease when I follow you in all my actions as my *chef, patron,* and *conducteur.*"[74]

[70]Marguerite wrote to Philip II: "j'ay donné charge au président de l'Hôpital vous faire entendre sil vous plaist luy faire tant d'honneur de l'escouter de ce quil vous dira de ma part"; May 17, 1559, *Archivo documental Español, Francia, 1559–1566 (Archivo general de Simancas)* (Madrid: Real Academia de Historia, 1950–1954), 1:8.

[71]"… with entire confidence I have in you, I ask you to advise me what should be done to begin and complete the enterprise"; letter of the duke of August 18, 1559, quoted in Dupré Lasale, *L'Hospital,* 2:131–32.

[72]Giovanni Michiel to the Doge, July 30, 1559, *CSP Venice,* 7:113; Fournier de Flaix, "L'Hospital, son temps et sa politique," *Comptes-rendus de l'Académie des Sciences Morales et Politiques* 153 (1900), 443. According to the list in Noël Valois, *Le Conseil du roi aux XIVe, XVe, XVIe siècles* (Paris, 1888), 178–79, the Conseil des Affaires of Francis II consisted of: Antoine de Bourbon, king of Navarre, the cardinal of Lorraine, duc de Guise, Constable Anne de Montmorency, the Marshal of Brissac, the Marshal of Saint-André, duc de Montpensier, and the prince of la Roche-sur-Yon; the Conseil Privé included nineteen members: Antoine de Bourbon, the Cardinals of Lorraine, Tournon, Bourbon, Guise, and Châtillon, the prince of la Roche-sur-Yon, duc de Guise, duc d'Aumale, duc d'Etampes, Michel de L'Hôpital, the marshal of Brissac, the marshal of Saint-André, Admiral Coligny, André Guillard (sieur du Mortier), Jean de Morvillier (bishop of Orléans), Jean de Monluc (bishop of Valence), Nicolas de Pellevé (bishop of Amiens), and Jacques de Saint-Marcel (sieur d'Avanson).

[73]L'Hôpital received a letter from the cardinal requesting that he explain to the duchess of Savoy that she no longer held the right to appoint officials in the duchy of Berry; see cardinal of Lorraine to L'Hôpital, February 2, 1560, BN,MS Fr. 15871, fol. 204.

[74]Epistle to the cardinal of Lorraine, April 23, 1560, written from Saint-Vallier, BN, Dupuy 31, fol. 62.

# Chapter 3

# L'Hôpital à Outrance

L 'HÔPITAL ARRIVED IN PARIS in early May 1560 to assume his duties as chancellor.[1] He found, to quote his own account, "the court full of disturbances following the tumult at Amboise, an incident that was not in itself so dangerous as the movement of parties which followed it."[2] The so-called Tumult of Amboise was a conspiracy of disaffected noblemen in early 1560 to destroy the dominance of the Guise faction at court. The ill-fated plot was ruthlessly stamped out by the Guises in March near Amboise.[3] Yet, it had the significant repercussion of aligning different groups and elements together in their common opposition to the government. Superimposed on the already serious religious conflicts between Catholics and Protestants, the political turbulence at Amboise fueled the increasing polarization in the kingdom. Strong feelings of bitterness remained in the aftermath of its violent suppression, in which several hundred conspirators were executed. Such was the situation which allegedly brought down Chancellor François Olivier, who died shortly after the conspiracy's repression, and awaited Chancellor-elect L'Hôpital upon his return to court.[4]

[1]Taillandier, *Nouvelles recherches*, 40; Lucien Romier, *La Conjuration d'Amboise* (Paris: Perrin, 1923), 181. L'Hôpital was still in Saint-Vallier, Dauphiné, on April 23, 1560.The Spanish ambassador Chantonnay confirmed on April 29 that L'Hôpital had not yet arrived at Amboise; Chantonnay to Philip II, April 29, 1560, *Archivo documental Español, Francia, 1559–1566 (Archivo general de Simancas)* (Madrid: Real Academia de Historia, 1950–1954), 1:279.

[2]Testament, *Oeuvres complètes*, 2: 519–20.

[3]According to contemporary Catholic sources, one-third of the conspirators were Calvinist and the remainder were malcontents or "political" Huguenots; see J.H.M. Salmon, *Society in Crisis: France in the Sixteenth Century* (New York: St. Martin's Press, 1975), 124.

[4]According to Vieilleville, Chancellor Olivier "fell ill of extreme melancholy caused by remorse" after the execution of the conspirators, and died of chagrin; *Mémoires de Vieilleville*, 188.

The Tumult of Amboise marked the beginning of a long series of factional disputes between the pro- and anti-Guise parties, one of the important themes of the French religious wars. L'Hôpital's stance in this struggle is of particular interest, because of his seemingly ambivalent position as a client of the Guises and at the same time as an opponent of his patrons' ultraconservative religious policy. Representing the myth that L'Hôpital was a sworn enemy of the Guises, Agrippa d'Aubigné alleged L'Hôpital's secret complicity in the anti-Guisard conspiracy of Amboise. In his *Mémoires*, d'Aubigné asserted that he found in his father's collection a document bearing L'Hôpital's signature among those of the conspirators. This evidence would have proved L'Hôpital's secret implication in the plot, if only, contended d'Aubigné, he had not burned it because some people were attempting to blackmail Chancellor L'Hôpital.[5] D'Aubigné did not elaborate about the source of the document, nor did he explain how L'Hôpital, who was away from court from November 1559 accompanying Marguerite de Valois in her trip to Nice, could have possibly signed a document drawn up in Nantes in February 1560.[6] The Calvinist historian's allegation hence should be viewed rather as an affirmation of his passionate partisanship, perhaps illustrative of the Huguenot propaganda effort to enlist the new chancellor in its cause. That L'Hôpital launched his chancellorship as a foe of the Guises has too often been uncritically accepted by historians, obscuring as a consequence L'Hôpital's position in the political network at court during this period.[7] Nothing could be farther from the truth than portraying L'Hôpital at this time as an opponent to the Guises.

Historians have not quite agreed on the situation surrounding L'Hôpital's selection as chancellor. Jaques Auguste de Thou ascribed the credit to Catherine de Médicis, who decided on L'Hôpital at the recommendation of the duchess of Montpensier, Jacqueline de Longwy.[8] The

---

[5]*Mémoires de Théodore Agrippa d'Aubigné*, ed. Ludovic Lalanne (Paris: Charpentier, 1854), 24–25; also Agrippa d'Aubigné, *Histoire universelle*, ed. André Thierry (Geneva: Librairie Droz, 1981), 1:280. D'Aubigné contended that Jean Salviati, sieur de Talcy, suggested that he sell the document for 10,000 écus either to L'Hôpital or to his enemies. D'Aubigné's allegation had already been effectively refuted by Dupré Lasale, *L'Hospital*, 2:177–88.

[6]*Mémoires de Michel de Castelnau*, in *Nouvelle collection des mémoires pour servir à l'histoire de France*, ser. 1, ed. Michaud and Poujoulat (Paris, 1838), 9:415.

[7]In the nineteenth century, H. Forneron, *Les Ducs de Guise et leur époque* (Paris: E. Plon, 1877), 1:299, contended that L'Hôpital collaborated with the conspirators of Amboise to establish a new government of the royal princes to replace that of the Guises.

[8]De Thou, *Histoire universelle*, 2:775–76. Anselme, *Histoire généalogique*, 6: 488, also ascribes the suggestion to the duchess, wife of Louis de Bourbon. Until her death in August 1561, the duchess exerted strong influence over Catherine; see Ivan Cloulas, *Catherine de Médicis* (Paris: Fayard, 1979), 130.

post had initially been offered to Jean de Morvillier, bishop of Orléans, but Morvillier declined it on account of his health. Then the office was offered to L'Hôpital.[9] But De Thou's account appears predisposed towards a fundamental anti-Guise sentiment, because he contends that Catherine had been persuaded by the duchess of Montpensier, who "did not see without pain the power of the Lorraines increasing day by day," to choose L'Hôpital, "a man of courage opposed to the Guises." It is hard to believe that the cardinal of Lorraine, who was "both the pope and the king" during this period, would have accepted the queen mother's choice of L'Hôpital had he held any suspicion about L'Hôpital's loyalty to his family.[10] More plausible is the interpretation that L'Hôpital was regarded as a candidate mutually satisfactory to Catherine de Médicis and the cardinal of Lorraine. It is likely that L'Hôpital, having studied at the University of Padua, was familiar with Italian ways, and that he was thereby more appealing to Catherine de Médicis.[11] Catherine later told L'Hôpital that she had been favorably influenced by Chancellor Olivier's recommendation of L'Hôpital as his successor.[12] The seventeenth-century historian François Duchesne perhaps most appropriately commented that L'Hôpital was recommended both "by his own singular merits and rare capacities" and "by the favor of the cardinal of Lorraine."[13] L'Hôpital's elevation to the chancellorship was warmly accepted throughout the court circle. The cardinal of Tournon, who was at Rome, expressed satisfaction with the news.[14] Few people seemed to think that there was much to fear from this

---

[9]Giovanni Michiel to the Doge and Senate, March 31, 1560, *CSP Venice*, 7:181. Morvillier cited "his delicate constitution, which was unsuited to so important a charge." Both the English and Spanish ambassadors confirmed that Morvillier was the original candidate for the office; Throckmorton to the queen, April 6, 1560, *Calendar of State Papers, Foreign Series of the Reign of Elizabeth* (hereafter *CSP Foreign*) (London, 1861–1950), 2: 505; Chantonnay to Philip II, April 22, 1560, *Archivo documental Español*, 1:270.

[10]The quotation is the Tuscan ambassador's; Leone Ricasoli to Cosimo I, August 27, 1559, *Négociations diplomatiques de la France avec la Toscane, Collection de Documents inédits sur l'histoire de France*, ed. Abel Desjardins (Paris, 1859–1886), 3: 404. De Thou's assertion seems also based on the simplistic assumption that Catherine de Médicis was necessarily intent on diminishing the political power of the Guises during the reign of Francis II. But the queen mother's dislike of the cardinal of Lorraine rested less on political reason than on personal antipathy; Henry Outram Evennett, *The Cardinal of Lorraine and the Council of Trent* (Cambridge: Cambridge University Press, 1930), 235.

[11]Jean Héritier, *Catherine de Médicis*, tr. Charlotte Haldane (New York: St. Martin's Press, 1963), 127; L'Hôpital was, moreover, a compatriot of Catherine through her mother's side.

[12]*Lettres de Catherine de Médicis*, ed. Hector de La Ferrière (Paris, 1880–1940), 1:273.

[13]Duchesne, *Histoire des chanceliers*, 636, 640.

[14]François de Tournon to François de Noailles, bishop of Dax, May 4, 1560, *Correspondance du Cardinal François de Tournon, 1521–1562*, ed. Michel François (Paris: Champion, 1946), 415–16.

gentle and respectable judge, who was a writer of excellent hexameters. Yet there must have also been certain expectation, it seems safe to assume, that this new chancellor, who had already revealed his staunch royalist position as the president of the Chambre des Comptes and who enjoyed the confidence of the king's uncles, would have his voice heard at the royal council more frequently, and more assertively, than his predecessors.

Before he accepted the nomination, L'Hôpital demanded the deposition of Garde des sceaux Jean Bertrand, archbishop of Sens, who had exercised the duties of chancellor during Olivier's disgrace. The edict of August 1551, appointing Bertrand as garde des sceaux, had promised him the office of chancellor in case of Olivier's death. The king accepted L'Hôpital's request to resolve this awkward situation. L'Hôpital's letters of provision, signed on June 30 at Saint-Léger and registered at the Parlement of Paris two days later, indicated that Bertrand, "in order to prevent all the difficulties," had relinquished voluntarily his claim to the chancellorship.[15] Even before his official appointment, L'Hôpital had been exercising his duties as chancellor since his return to court in May. A receipt of L'Hôpital's salary dated July 30 shows that his remuneration as chancellor began retroactively effective April 1.[16]

L'Hôpital's appointment has generally been seen as reflecting a shift in royal policy from the extremism of Henry II to one of moderation. The new religious policy of the government, in the aftermath of the Tumult of Amboise, was to find a mean between persecution and toleration by drawing a line between political offenses and religious misbelief. The cardinal of Lorraine held the view that it was necessary to distinguish between the "Huguenots d'état" and "Huguenots de religion," that is, rebellion and sedition ought to be punished, but leniency should be shown to simple misbelief.[17] He was keenly aware of the need not to alienate further the powerful nobles who had embraced the Protestant cause. L'Hôpital seems to have been an important instigator of this conciliatory and more realistic direction of the government's religious policy. Chancellor L'Hôpital's principal concern was to preserve law and order in the midst of widespread sedition. He unreservedly regarded the maintenance of law as the most important duty of the king. In a discourse dedicated to

---

[15]Letters of provision, BN, MS Fr. 23159, fol. 63. Its text is printed in P. Bondois," Catalogue des actes de François II" (thesis, Ecole des Chartes, January 1908), pièces justificatives, no. 3. Also see De Thou, *Histoire universelle*, 2:776; Abraham Tessereau, *Histoire chronologique de la Grande Chancellerie de France* (Paris, 1710), 124, 134; Isambert, *Recueil général*, 14:33–35.

[16]Text in P.D.L., *Eclaircissements*, 88.

[17]Evennett, *Cardinal of Lorraine*, 235–36. Contemporary observers frequently made a distinction between the "Huguenots of state" and "Huguenots of religion"; see, e.g., Norris to Cecil, May 31, 1568, *CSP Foreign*, 8:470.

Francis II in 1559, L'Hôpital had urged the king above all to "observe laws and have them observed."[18] Anything proven as being in conflict with laws of the state, such as sedition and crime concealed beneath a cloak of religion, ought to be punished. In the same discourse, the king was exhorted to follow the guidance of his uncles, the Guises, "whose wisdom is the most solid mainstay of France." Strict distinction between politics and religion constituted the basis of the government's policy, under the leadership of L'Hôpital who remained in close collaboration with the cardinal of Lorraine.[19]

L'Hôpital's first task as chancellor was to solicit registration of the Edict of Romorantin at the Parlement of Paris.[20] The edict, drawn up in

---

[18]*De Sacra Francisci II, Galliarum regis, initiatione, regnique ipsius administrandi providentia* (Paris, 1560). BN, Res. p. Yc. 1468, and translated in *Poésies complètas*, 256–67. Written shortly after the coronation of Francis II in September 1559, the eloquent Latin poem is a collection of judicious advice on how to govern the kingdom, and it is a remarkable illustration of the "mirror of princes" literature of the sixteenth century. The tract was translated into French the same year; see Joachim du Bellay, *Discours au roy contenant une brefve et salutaire instruction pour bien et heureusement régner: Oeuvres de J. Du Bellay*, ed. Ch. Marty-Laveaux (Paris: Alphonse Lemerre, 1867), 2:477–511. In this tract, L'Hôpital specifically advises the king to be "slow in punishing the faults not demonstrated," but to be "without pity for positive crimes"; *Poésies complètes*, 257; thus he wrote: "May he not intervene in things once judged according to proper procedures; may he not be lenient to the guilty; may he let the laws follow their course."

[19]In 1559, Joachim du Bellay composed a discourse, *Ample discours au Roy sur le faict des quatre états du royaume de France, composé par Joachim du Bellay, ... à l'imitation d'un autre plus succinct au paravant faict en vers latins, par Messire Michel de L'Hospital, ... et après mis en François par ledict Du Bellay* (Paris, 1567), in BN, Ye. 20562. Authors such as Dupré Lasale and Albert Buisson suspected that this was in fact a longer expository version of L'Hôpital's lost Latin poem, on the grounds that the ideas expressed in this discourse closely resembled those of L'Hôpital. Dupré Lasale, *L'Hospital*, 2:154; Buisson, *Michel de L'Hôpital*, 261–62. It seems probable, however, that the model of Du Bellay's lengthy poem was L'Hôpital's discourse written for Francis II, cited above (n. 18), and not another poem of his which is supposed to have been lost. In this tract, the author argues that the solution to differences in religion is not persecution but moral reforms, because "the fatal monster [of heresy] cannot be suppressed by fire or iron; it can be suppressed only by sobriety, humble modesty, and chastity, by fulfilling Christian duties, and by leading a saintly life." The author urges the pastors to follow a perfect model, the cardinal of Lorraine, who, "at the same time as he sustains France on his strong shoulders, just as Atlas holds up the sky, also fulfills the duty as a faithful pastor ... preaching, admonishing, and showing perfect examples." He thus exhorts the king: "Sire, this is the way to lull to sleep the beast whose throat, when God wills, you will cut off.... It will be aided by this great Cardinal ... and the princes of the Guises, who seem to have been born to defend the church." The author, like L'Hôpital, reveals genuine faith in the Guises' capacity to pacify and resolve religious dissensions.

[20]Isambert, *Recueil général*, 14:31; Antoine Fontanon, *Les Edits et ordonnances des rois de France* (Paris, 1580), 4:229–30.

May, was a manifesto of the government's new religious policy.[21] It removed heresy trials from the secular into the ecclesiastical courts by separating secular and spiritual jurisdiction. Heresy jurisdiction had been predominantly secular, the most active court against heresy being the notorious *Chambre ardente* at the Parlement of Paris.[22] In accordance with the new edict, however, cases concerning heresy were prescribed to diocesan prelates, and cases of sedition arising out of heretical beliefs to secular judges. No civil court, including the parlements, was to have competence in cases of "pure" heresy. The edict was based on the government's judgment that religion was less the cause than the excuse of the current violent disturbance in the kingdom. By distinguishing heresy from sedition, the edict was thus geared to suppress the "huguenots d'état," but pacify "huguenots de religion" whose differences with Catholics were to be resolved by rational discussions.[23] The edict inevitably aroused concern about the vagueness of the boundary between secular and spiritual crimes and the consequent likelihood of disputes. But the equivocal way the edict was drawn up was a deliberate choice of the royal council. The edict granted *prévôts* and judges of the *présidiaux* the right to decide "sur le genre de crime," giving almost entire jurisdictional disposition to these courts, which were directly under the control of the chancellor and far less hostile to Protestants than the notoriously Catholic parlements.[24] It was also a milder way of combatting the Huguenots, because the ecclesiastical tribunals were only competent to inflict "canon-

[21]Henri Martin, *Histoire de France depuis les temps les plus reculés jusqu'en 1789* (Paris: Furne, 1855–1860), 9:45, acclaimed the edict as L'Hôpital's first great service to France. The fact that L'Hôpital did not take up his duties as chancellor until around May 20 inclined some historians to argue against his role in the formulation of the edict, which was drawn up in Romorantin. There is reason to believe, however, that L'Hôpital, already a member of the Conseil Privé and chancellor-elect, assisted at the discussions in Romorantin. Furthermore, his eager defense of the edict and efforts for its registration at the Parlement show his endorsement of its stipulations.

[22]The 1540 edict of Fontainebleau gave cognizance of heresy to lay judges; Salmon, *Society in Crisis*, 83–84. The 1549 edict of Saint-Germain and the 1551 edict of Châteaubriant attempted to introduce for lay judges the procedures of the inquisition; Fontanon, *Edits et ordonnances*, 4:249–50; J. H. Shennan, *The Parlement of Paris* (Ithaca: Cornell University Press, 1968), 206; N. M. Sutherland, *The Huguenot Struggle for Recognition* (New Haven: Yale University Press, 1980), 43, n. 12.

[23]Cloulas, *Catherine de Médicis*, 146–47.

[24]The *présidiaux* were created in 1552 as the courts next to the parlements in the judicial hierarchy, and these new courts were the most easily controlled by the crown. Judges of *présidiaux*, *prévôtés*, and *bailliages* were often Protestant converts or sympathizers; see Salmon, *Society in Crisis*, 134.

ical punishment," without being able to impose capital punishment.[25] Furthermore, the relative inefficiency of the ecclesiastical courts seemed to favor the Huguenots' lot in general. By punishing all acts of public disorder but ending prosecution by civil courts on purely religious grounds, the Edict of Romorantin clearly revealed the preoccupation of the chancellor with law and order rather than with religious issues. The edict was submitted to the Parlement of Paris on June 19, but the Parlement was far from eager to register measures that would substantially reduce its jurisdiction. Chancellor L'Hôpital was given the task of inducing the magistrates to register the edict without further delay.

L'Hôpital's address at the Parlement of Paris on July 5 can be regarded as his inaugural speech. On his first official appearance as chancellor, L'Hôpital told the parlementaires that he was full of deep emotion to see his old colleagues in the court where he had spent so many years. Apparently not unmindful of the conflicts with the Parlement during his presidency at the Chambre des Comptes, L'Hôpital emphatically pleaded with the magistrates for cooperation and support for his ministry. The chancellor assured them that he would do everything in his power to augment the greatness and authority of the illustrious corps, at which remark the speech was interrupted by loud applause.[26] L'Hôpital then disclosed the new direction in the government's religious policy. He argued that religious disorder was mainly due to the corruption of the clergy. The Church had lost its guiding role. Absenteeism of the bishops from their churches was common, and, as a result, the people turned a ready ear to those "*qui quaerunt res novas.*"[27] Experience had shown, however, that persecution was powerless to check the growth of heresy. The king was like a doctor who, realizing that the remedies he had used to cure the disease did not work, would try a new treatment. But the "maladies of spirit" were different from physical disease, for "when a man who holds false views recants, and repeats the shibboleth of another faith, he does not thereby change his heart." Religious opinions were thus to be changed not by constraint but by persuasion and the exemplary life of good pastors. The chancellor pointed out, however, that religion was being used merely as a cloak for rebellion. The Edict of Romorantin was proposed to distinguish clearly heresy from sedition, and allow the secular courts to concentrate on repressing sedition. "Force was necessary to combat force," emphasized the chancellor. The magistrates should not consider themselves deprived

[25]The edict was a result of careful deliberation to prevent the introduction of the Inquisition into France by clearly demarcating the jurisdiction of the Gallican church.
[26]De Thou, *Histoire universelle*, 2:791–92; idem, *Mémoires de Condé, pour servir à l'histoire de France, & d'éclaircissement à celle de M. De Thou* (The Hague, 1743), 1:542–47.
[27]*Oeuvres complètes*, 1:323.

of their ancient and honorable privileges. They were still the sole judges over the questions of illegal and seditious assemblies, but simply not the judges in matters which lay outside the pale of civil law and had only to do with conscience. The "fait politique" should be debated by the Parlement, in conjunction with the Conseil Privé, but the "mérite de la religion" should be dealt with in an episcopal synod summoned for that purpose. L'Hôpital finally declared that one "must try to live peaceably" until "the hand of God and a universal council" would find a remedy for the religious problems.

The Edict of Romorantin can be seen as a part of L'Hôpital's extended program during his chancellorship designed to delineate jurisdictional boundaries by clarifying lines of authority. This particular edict proposed separation of royal and ecclesiastical justice. The Parlement objected to the measure, however, asserting that the jurisdiction attributed to the church courts would override royal jurisdiction and debar subjects from the king's justice.[28] It is noticeable that the magistrates based their contentions on the sovereign's judicial independence from the spiritual authorities, and that they claimed that the new edict would prevent them from asserting the king's authority. For the chancellor, however, royal authority would be better served, rather than compromised, when peace was promoted in the kingdom by loosening persecution of simple heresy and concentrating instead on the suppression of sedition. After repeated remonstrances, the Parlement reluctantly proceeded with the provisional registration of the edict on July 16. The Parlement's resistance to the Edict of Romorantin revealed the differences in the priorities of the law courts and the government in dealing with the current situation. It also foreshadowed the difficulties the new chancellor was to face in the years to come in registering edicts of pacification.[29]

L'Hôpital was keenly aware of the fundamental vulnerability of the regime: the king was an inexperienced sixteen-year-old boy. L'Hôpital's frequent reference to the king's uncles as the powerful guardians of the throne was more than a vain tribute to his patrons. Seeing that the government desperately needed to restore public confidence, L'Hôpital judged that rallying great families and prestigious members of the kingdom around the crown was crucial to enhancing royal authority. No other means appeared more effective than convoking an assembly of notables. Assemblies of notables had often been used to seek advice or, at least, to

---

[28]Maugis, *Parlement de Paris*, 2:25–26; Shennan, *Parlement of Paris*, 209.

[29]Less than a month later, on August 7, a royal declaration clarified the Edict of Romorantin by adding a clause that the edict had not been intended to deny Parlement cognizance of illicit assemblies and armed gatherings; Sutherland, *Huguenot Struggle*, 350–51.

provide a semblance of consent in times of national emergency.[30] Usually much smaller in size than the Estates General, and with their membership selected by the royal council, they were relatively easy to control and could bestow weight and credibility to the policies adopted.[31] At the Assembly of Fontainebleau which was duly convoked on August 21, 1560, the majority opinion endorsed the programs of the government.[32] François Marillac, archbishop of Vienne, and Jean de Monluc, bishop of Valence, strongly upheld the chancellor's policy, voicing their opposition to religious persecution and sharply criticizing the abuses of the Church. Both requested the pope to reconvene an ecumenical council to settle the differences in religion. If he were unwilling to do this, they argued, a national council must be held.[33] The cardinal of Lorraine urged that the bishops be summoned within two months to advise the king concerning calling a general or a national church council. The cardinal stated his belief that the disturbers of the peace of the realm should be severely punished, especially those who resorted to arms, but he also expressed his regrets that persecution had been meted out in the past to sincere misbelievers who simply participated in heretical services.[34] At the closing session on August 26, the assembly agreed on the convocation of the Estates General on December 10 and, in default of a general council, a national council on January 20. The Venetian ambassador Giovanni Michiel had reported in March that the government already seemed determined to bypass a

---

[30]Salmon, *Society in Crisis*, 65.

[31]D'Aubigné, *Histoire universelle*, 1:277; *Mémoires de Castelnau*, 432. Catherine wrote to Sébastien de L'Aubespine, the bishop of Limoges and the French ambassador in Madrid, on July 28: "Et maintenant nous sommes venus en ce lieu de Fontaynebleau pour prendre une bonne résolution en tous noz affaires, et y establir quelque bon ordre et règlement, ce qui n'est pas, comme vous pouvez très bien penser, ung oeuvre d'ung jour, ny d'ung mois...."; *Lettres de Catherine de Médicis*, 1:143.

[32]Chantonnay reported that L'Hôpital advised that Francis II hold the assembly, despite opposition from the Guises; Chantonnay to Philip II, June 27, 1560, *Archivo documental Español*, 1:322–23. Once the convocation was decided upon, the notables were chosen at will by the Guises; Georges Picot, *Histoire des Etats Généraux* (Paris: Hachette, 1888), 2:12. In his opening speech, the chancellor returned to his favorite analogy of a patient and his physician; *CSP Foreign*, 3:245. The text of L'Hôpital's discourse at the beginning of the assembly is not extant; an excerpt is in *Oeuvres complètes*, 1:339–42; De Thou, *Histoire universelle*, 2:796–97.

[33]The address of Monluc is printed in *Mémoires de Condé*, 1:555–68; Marillac's address is printed in Pierre de La Place, *Commentaires de l'estat de la religion et république soubz les rois Henry et François seconds et Charles neufième*, in *Choix de chroniques et mémoires sur l'histoire de France*, 1565, ed. J. A. C. Buchon (Paris: 1836), 13:58–66.

[34]One should continue to punish the "séditieux et perturbateurs," the cardinal argued, but one should no longer inflict the punishment of justice on those "qui sans armes, et de peur d'être damnés, iraient au prêche, chanteraient les psaumes et n'iraient point à la messe"; La Place, *Commentaires de l'estat*, 67–68.

general council, "the decision of which would be tardy," and convene instead a national council to solve the religious problems, "which admit of no delay."[35] In the meantime, the government ordered that bishops and curates reside at their churches. Leniency was to be shown toward heretics not involved in seditious activities. Protestants were not to be molested, as long as they remained peaceful.[36]

L'Hôpital took precautions lest the promise of convoking the Estates General and the national council should give the false impression that the king granted the "liberty to introduce a new sect," or allowed "impunity of that sect."[37] The chancellor pointed out at the Parlement of Paris on September 7 that there were some people who "interpret everything improperly." It had been decided at Fontainebleau that punishment would not be inflicted on "religionnaires" until the Estates General and the council would convene, in hopes that everyone would behave reasonably and moderately. But some people willfully stretched this decision, complained the chancellor, and behaved as if they were allowed to live in full license, "chascung à sa façon et appétit." L'Hôpital stressed that one must restrain oneself to live "in accordance with the ways which have been upheld till now, in this kingdom." The chancellor was aware that, in the aftermath of the prolonged wars in Italy, the Protestant cause was embraced by many idle and discontented men, whose motives had little in common with those of the religious movement. "The Frenchmen who once had been at the war no longer have a job," L'Hôpital pointed out, "and they join seditious groups, which *se couvrent du manteau de religion.*"[38] Religion did not teach men to take up arms. If they still would not lay down arms, he flatly

[35]Michiel to the Doge and the Senate, March 28, 1560, *CSP Venice*, 7:177.

[36]The decision was announced by a royal edict dated August 31. But the discovery of a Protestant conspiracy overshadowed the chancellor's effort to minimize the threat from "pure" Protestantism. A Basque nobleman named Jacques de La Sague was arrested in Lyon and brought to Fontainebleau while the assembly was still in session. He alleged that a vast conspiracy was in preparation among the Protestants, involving Anthony of Bourbon and the prince of Condé; see *CSP Venice*, 7, no. 193 (August 30, 1560), 249–51; *Négociations, lettres et pièces diverses au règne de François II*, ed. Louis Paris (Paris, 1841), 486–90; La Place, *Commentaires de l'estat*, 68–69. La Sague recanted his confession, however, saying that it was made only "to please the cardinal of Lorraine and the grand chancellor"; *Despatches of Michele Suriano and Marc Antonio Barbaro, Venetian Ambassadors at the Court of France, 1560–1563*, ed. Henry Layard (Lymington, 1891), 29. This incident illustrates that L'Hôpital was definitely considered to belong to the camp of the Guises, in opposition to the Bourbons.

[37]L'Hôpital's address at the Parlement of Paris on September 7, 1560, *Discours pour la majorité de Charles IX*, 50; *Oeuvres complètes*, 1:352. The text of this address is also printed in *Mémoires de Condé*, 1:574–78.

[38]*Discours pour la majorité de Charles IX*, 48–49; *Oeuvres complètes*, 1:350.

declared, they could not deny that they had wicked desires other than religion.[39]

The year 1560 witnessed a rapid polarization of the kingdom, with the intermingling of religious and political affiliations. The two rival camps were the Catholic Guises, the unquestionable masters at court under Francis II, and the Bourbons, the prince of Condé being the leader of the Calvinist force in France, aside from the third force of the Montmorency/Châtillon group. The power contest between the first two families culminated in the arrest of the prince of Condé in Orléans in November, on charges of his complicity in the Amboise conspiracy. This incident is of particular interest, because it provides an important clue to estimating L'Hôpital's stance in the political network at court during this period. Chancellor L'Hôpital was appointed to lead a special commission to interrogate the prince of Condé.[40] When he went to Orléans to begin proceedings on November 13, however, Condé refused to answer to the chancellor, asserting that he, being a prince of the blood, was supposed to give account of himself to the king alone and be judged only by the Parlement of Paris and twelve peers of France. The chancellor replied that he had not been sent by His Majesty to adjudicate Condé's case, but only to draw up the indictment, which would then be referred to competent judges. The prince retorted that he knew very well that the chancellor and the other commissioners were henchmen of the Guises, who sought to deprive him of his honor and of his life.[41] The contemporary observer

[39]*Discours pour la majorité de Charles IX*, 48; *Oeuvres complètes*, 1:349. At the end of his speech, L'Hôpital specifically referred to a Desjardins, lieutenant of Paris, who had recently been dismissed from office. The king wanted Desjardins restored, although he was a convinced Protestant magistrate and accused of some misappropriation. It certainly seemed an irregular act, but was done for some good reason. The chancellor would not explain further in detail, but assured his listeners that this exception would not be perpetual. The premier président St.-André responded that Desjardins was dismissed according to the terms of the edict because he was a convinced Protestant, although he had since obtained lettres patentes from the king that allowed him to exercise his office. If the edict was not observed, the president asserted, it should be revoked. Finally, St.-André requested the payment of the magistrates' salaries that had been delayed for several months. The chancellor answered that, although there was no budget available for their salaries, the judges would be the first to be paid when funds were available; *Discours pour la majorité de Charles IX*, 57–58; *Oeuvres complètes*, 1:362–66.

[40]De Thou, *Histoire universelle*, 2:829, asserted that L'Hôpital signed Condé's arrest warrant "à regret, et ne pouvant faire autrement."

[41]Suriano to the Doge, November 22, 1560, *Despatches of Suriano*, 4; *CSP Foreign*, 3:409; *CSP Venice*, 271; Chantonnay to Philip II, November 28, 1560, *Archivo documental Español*, 1:491; De Thou, *Histoire universelle*, 2:830. An arrêt of November 20 ordered Condé to answer to the commissioners; A. de Ruble, *Antoine de Bourbon et Jeanne d'Albret* (Paris, 1881–1886), 2:412.

Michel de Castelnau, seigneur de Mauvissière, contended that, when
Condé was condemned to death on November 26, L'Hôpital refused to
sign the execution warrant.[42] But Castelnau's account, which has been
uncritically repeated by many historians, appears unreliable.[43] The Venetian ambassador reported on November 22 that proceedings against
Condé had already been suspended until the meeting of the Estates General, or "perhaps even longer."[44] Castelnau's assertion, which seems to
have been predisposed to portray L'Hôpital as an enemy of the Guises by
highlighting his seeming defiance of them, was effectively refuted by De
Thou. Citing his father Christophe de Thou, who assisted the chancellor in
the commission as first president of the Parlement of Paris, de Thou
argued that the sentence had been drawn up but not signed at all.[45] It is
likely that L'Hôpital did recoil from the idea of executing Condé, yet not
because he wanted to oppose the Guises but because he knew the serious
ramification of killing a prince of the blood, which would provoke unnecessary opposition to the government. More important, the chancellor
feared the death of Condé might trigger full-fledged strife between the
Bourbons and the Guises.[46]

The sudden death of Francis II on December 5 changed everything at
court "literally overnight."[47] The cardinal of Lorraine was forced to retire
from the court. What was L'Hôpital's position in the course of this court
coup? L'Hôpital wrote in his testament: "The faction which dominated the
government during the reign of Francis could not stand the fact that
others would be managing the state affairs. Departing from court, they
provoked the king of Navarre and other princes (who complained that

---

[42]*Mémoires de Castelnau*, 435–38; Louis Regnier de La Planche, *Histoire de l'Estat de
France, tant de la république que de la religion, sous le règne de François II*, ed. Mennechet (Paris,
1836), 2:91.

[43]Many historians repeat Castelnau's account: see, e.g., Cloulas, *Catherine de Médicis*,
150; Diefendorf, *Paris City Councillors*, 76, n. L'Hôpital reportedly said: "Je sais mourir, mais
non me deshonorer"; *Biographie universelle*, 457.

[44]Suriano to the Doge, November 22, 1560, *Despatches of Suriano*, 4; *CSP Venice*, 271–72.

[45]De Thou, *Histoire universelle*, 2:835–36; De Thou, ibid., 834, wrote that L'Hôpital dismissed the idea of executing Condé, asking "Qui n'a eu nulle part aux troubles & aux factions, qu'on reproche au Prince de Condé?" Romier concluded that the "condemnation" of
Condé was the fiction of historians sympathetic to the house of Bourbon; *Conjuration
d'Amboise*, 279. The Parlement of Paris declared Condé's innocence on June 13, 1561. BN, MS
Fr. 3952, fols. 138–39.

[46]L'Hôpital reportedly told Catherine: "Il faut suspendre le jugement rendu contre le
Prince de Condé, & ne pas répandre le sang de nos Rois, pour favoriser la passion de ceux
que leur haine rend aveugles"; De Thou, *Histoire universelle*, 2:834. L'Hôpital further warned
the queen against the revenge of the king of Navarre, which would follow the execution of
the prince of Condé; Taillandier, *Nouvelles recherches*, 55.

[47]Sutherland, *Huguenot Struggle*, 119.

their power and authority were diminished by that of *a mere mother*) to take up arms under the pretext of religion."[48] It should be borne in mind, however, that this harsh comment about the Guises was made in 1573, not in 1560. At the end of 1560, there is no evidence that L'Hôpital had broken with his patron, the cardinal of Lorraine. That he was widely looked upon by his contemporaries as a protégé of the cardinal of Lorraine is attested by the fact that the deputies of the estates in Paris in March 1561, following the cardinal's retirement from court in January after Francis II's death, demanded the chancellor's resignation, since he was a creature of the Guises.[49]

In the wake of the cardinal's departure, L'Hôpital had to cope with the new situation at court. The Venetian ambassador Michiel observed that L'Hôpital, although he was a "creature" of the Guises, was a "man very skillful and well-informed in the affairs of his office," and that "as a *nouveau venu*," he had "of necessity to obey the queen and, as a consequence, the king of Navarre."[50] L'Hôpital was keenly aware of the need for balancing the power of the two rival families. He reportedly advised Catherine: "Protect the Bourbons against the Guises, and defend the Guises against the Bourbons."[51] Witnessing the eclipse of the Guises, L'Hôpital judged that an alliance between the crown and the royal princes was indispensable. According to a contemporary source, L'Hôpital told Catherine de Médicis that, with the Guises now discredited, the only way she would preserve power and prevent civil wars was to collaborate with the king of Navarre.[52] It was decided at the Conseil Privé on December 6 that

---

[48]*Oeuvres complètes*, 2:521 (L'Hôpital's emphasis).

[49]They demanded that "the chancellor suspend the exercise of his office because he has not been appointed by the princes nominated to the Council by the said Estates"; BN, Collection Moreau 740, fol. 32; "Délibérations des états tenus à Paris 15 mars 1560 [old style]," in *Négociations de François II*, 833–84; *Registres des délibérations du Bureau de la ville de Paris*, V, 84, n.; Paul Van Dyke, "The Estates of Pontoise," *English Historical Review* 28 (1913): 487. The same demand was presented at the national synod of Poitiers; J. Aymon, *Tous les synodes nationaux des Eglises réformées de France* (The Hague, 1710), 1:13; Noël Valois, "Les Etats de Pontoise," *Revue d'Histoire de L'Eglise de France* 24 (1943): 243, n.

[50]M. N. Tommaseo, *Relations des ambassadeurs vénitiens sur les affaires de France au XVIe siècle* (Paris, 1838), 1:437.

[51]De Thou, *Histoire universelle*, 2:832; L'Hôpital continues: "C'est ainsi que vous les dominerez; et, à la faveur de leurs divisions, vous régnerez entre les partis et au-dessous des partis." The Venetian ambassador Suriano reported the day after Francis II's death that the queen mother would still "favor the House of Guise as much as she can; because from them she has derived the whole or the greater part of the repute enjoyed by her hitherto."

[52]"Le crédit des Guises tombant avec la personne du roi, il falloit qu'elle se fortifiat en s'unissant aux princes, qu'en leur donnant de l'autorité elle conserveroit la sienne, et qu'elle empêcheroit ainsi que le régne qui alloit s'ouvrir ne fut troublé par les guerres civiles"; *Négociations de François II*, 734.

Catherine de Médicis was to be entrusted with "the care of the king's person and property," although without the title of regent. The king of Navarre was named *lieutenant-général* of the kingdom, in return for waiving his rights to the regency.[53] L'Hôpital defended Catherine's assumption of power: "what could be more equitable than giving the charge and tutorship of the son to his mother?"[54] L'Hôpital wrote in his testament: "The queen often complained to me about the circumstance that she was almost excluded from the administration of the kingdom. I had nothing to tell her but to reassert the authority of Her Majesty; if she could do it wisely, she could easily counterattack and weaken the ambition and stupidity of her adversaries...."[55]

After the departure of the cardinal from court, L'Hôpital was ready to support single-mindedly the queen mother, who was left to pacify the agitated kingdom. He hoped to fill the power vacuum at court with the reasserted power of the crown, which would guarantee him full support in tackling the problems in the realm.

In the midst of the change of reigns, the Estates General opened on December 13 at Orléans. In his keynote address, the chancellor justified the royal decision to convene the Estates, which had not been held for nearly eighty years.[56] It has been argued that L'Hôpital resolved to resort to the authority of the Estates General after he experienced resistance from the Parlement of Paris to registering the Edict of Romorantin. Émile Dupré Lasale contended that L'Hôpital's excessive, and unrealistic, expectation for the Estates General, which had not been summoned since 1484, contributed to driving the Parlement further away from the chancellor.[57] At any rate, the chancellor emphasized to the deputies that the king had not forgotten the beneficial functions of the Estates General. The king lost no

[53]BN, MS Fr. nouv. acq. 7225, fol. 31; nouv. acq. 7236, fol. 45; Pierre Dupuy, *Traité de la majorité de nos rois et des régences du royaume, avec les preuves tirées tant du Trésor des Chartes du roy que des registres du parlement, ensemble un traité des prééminences du Parlement de Paris* (Paris, 1655), 347–49; *Négociations de François II*, 731.

[54]Testament, *Oeuvres complètes*, 2:520

[55]Testament, *Oeuvres complètes*, 2:521.

[56]The chancellor began his address by praising the king of Navarre for having set an example to others by yielding his own interests to the good of the kingdom. L'Hôpital announced as a fait accompli the decision of the Conseil Privé concerning the organization of the new government, ignoring the murmurs among the deputies that they had not been consulted at all; Gustave Baguenault de Puchesse, *Jean de Morvillier: Evêque d'Orléans, Garde des Sceaux de France 1506–1577* (Paris, 1869; Geneva: Slatkine-Megariotis Reprints, 1977), 133–34. The text of L'Hôpital's address at the Estates General is printed in *Discours pour la majorité de Charles IX*, 71–89; *Oeuvres complètes*, 1:375–407; De Thou, *Histoire universelle*, 3:2–7

[57]Dupré Lasale, *L'Hospital*, 1:254. The Parlement apparently felt that its authority was overshadowed by that of the Estates General. The Parlement's surly reaction to the Ordinance of Orleans, promulgated at the Estates General, is discussed in chapter 4.

dignity, asserted L'Hôpital, by coming face to face with his subjects, because "there is no act so dignified of the king and so appropriate to him as summoning the estates, giving general audience to his subjects and rendering justice to each one of them."[58] Having cajoled the deputies, L'Hôpital moved to the discussion of more specific issues. The king called the estates together in order to restore peace, union, and order. L'Hôpital resorted to his favorite medical simile: a good doctor would not content himself with curing the disease but would attempt to prevent the disease from recurring by tending to its causes.[59] If he only took care of fever, the disease would surely come back. Likewise, those who only wanted to punish the crimes would be successful for a brief while, but "tost après, c'est à refaire, et pis que devant." One ought instead to find out the causes of the present troubles in the kingdom.[60]

L'Hôpital flatly denied that religion was the cause of the afflictions currently besetting the kingdom. How could it be, asked the chancellor, that sedition was the result of our religion, Christian and evangelical, which commanded above all peace and love between men?[61] Those who incited seditious movements on account of religion were wrong, because "la cause de dieu ne veult estre défendeue avec armes."[62] If they said that they took arms not to attack anyone but to defend themselves, the argument would be valid against foreigners, but not against the king, their own sovereign lord. "It is no more permissible that a subject defend himself against the prince and against his magistrates than a son against his father, whether rightly or wrongly, whether the prince and magistrates be good or bad. Furthermore we are more obligated to obey the prince than our father"[63]

L'Hôpital declared that sedition creating divisions among the subjects of one prince was the biggest evil: "Every sedition is evil and pernicious in

---

[58]*Discours pour la majorité de Charles IX*, 74; *Oeuvres complètes*, 1:380.

[59]Atkinson, *L'Hospital*, 147, presumed that L'Hôpital's frequent use of medical simile had something to do with L'Hôpital's being the son of a doctor; but medical imagery was used commonly by legislators in sixteenth-century France, who likened their role to that of doctors, whose business was to diagnose disorders and prescribe remedies; Donald Kelley, *The Beginning of Ideology: Consciousness and Society in the French Reformation* (Cambridge: Cambridge University Press, 1981), 192.

[60]*Discours pour la majorité de Charles IX*, 78; *Oeuvres complètes*, 1:387.

[61]*Discours pour la majorité de Charles IX*, 82; *Oeuvres complètes*, 1:394–95.

[62]L'Hôpital declared that "si c'est religion chrestienne, ceulx qui la veulent planter avec armes, espées et pistolets, font bien contre leur profession, qui est de souffrir la force, non la faire"; *Discours pour la majorité de Charles IX*, 82; *Oeuvres complètes*, 1:395.

[63]L'Hôpital specifically referred to the idea of tyrannicide: "We Christians should not approve the ideas of the Greeks and Romans that glorify tyrannicide"; *Discours pour la majorité de Charles IX*, 83; *Oeuvres complètes*, 1:396.

kingdoms and republics, no matter whether it has a good and honest cause; because it is better for the author of a sedition to suffer himself all the losses and injuries than to become the cause of such a serious trouble as civil wars in his country."[64]

If men were good and perfect, they would never take up arms for religion. Yet, due to the faults of human beings, religion "gives people passion that nothing can surpass." L'Hôpital's skeptical mind, critical of excessive religious zeal which obscured the true meaning of Christianity, raised a further question. How could one know that his or her religion was the only true belief? "You say your religion is a true one, and I say mine is. Is it any more reasonable that I should adopt your opinion than that you should adopt mine?"[65]

L'Hôpital was aware of the virtue of religious conformity in a kingdom. Nothing divided men so deeply, he declared, as religion. It was a shame that there should be more friendship between an Englishman and a Frenchman of the same religion than between two Frenchmen of different creeds. Religion separated father from son, brother from brother, and husband from wife, and it alienated subjects from the king and drove them to rebellion. Different languages did not cause the division of the kingdom, but different religions and laws divided the kingdom into two. L'Hôpital admitted that "it is folly to hope for peace, repose, and amity between peoples of different religions." Without the unity under the adage of "une foy, une loy, une roy," he declared, it was inevitable for war to follow.[66] Yet L'Hôpital was also keenly aware of the futility, and absurdity, of punishing those of different religious opinions in order to impose religious uniformity. Heresy to him was nothing more than an error. The "errors of spirit" should be tackled with the "arms of charity, prayers, persuasion, words of God," and not with force, since "the knife could do little against the spirit, apart from destroying the soul as well as the body."L'Hôpital regretted that the past persecution policy of the government had driven Protestants to extremity instead of bringing them to the Catholic faith: "If they had been treated more moderately, with paternal admonishment rather than punishment, there would not have been gates destroyed, city walls collapsed, or houses burnt down."[67]

Above all, it was necessary to get rid of all those fiendish terms such as Huguenots and Papists. L'Hôpital loftily declared: "Ostons ces mots diaboliques, noms de parti, factions et séditions, luthériens, huguenots,

[64]*Discours pour la majorité de Charles IX*, 78; *Oeuvres complètes*, 1:387–88.
[65]*Discours pour la majorité de Charles IX*, 83, 85; *Oeuvres complètes*, 1:396, 399.
[66]*Discours pour la majorité de Charles IX*, 84; *Oeuvres complètes*, 1:398.
[67]*Discours pour la majorité de Charles IX*, 86, 87; *Oeuvres complètes*, 1:400, 403.

papistes: ne changeons le nom de Chrestien."[68] Since the dissoluteness of the church was an important cause of the birth of heresy, the chancellor emphasized, the clergy must set an example of a good and upright life to win back the heretics. L'Hôpital assured the estates that the king and the queen mother would try to the utmost of their power to do "better than their predecessors had done so far." The religious questions could only be judged by a holy council.[69] Waiting for a council, stressed L'Hôpital, one should keep watch so that there would not be as many new ceremonies and cults as the number of families or their leaders. The chancellor could not emphasize too much that one ought to obey the king and spare the kingdom from sedition. The pacification policy of the government was far from being a do-as-you-please policy. One should not show any pity to those who resorted to religion as an excuse for sedition. In case of sedition, the king was forced to, and determined to, employ harsh measures for its suppression. Finally, L'Hôpital sincerely pleaded that one should not be so impetuous and reckless as to accept and follow the new opinions, "chascung à sa mode et façon," since changing religion was not a matter of little importance but was a question of the salvation of one's soul.[70]

L'Hôpital's address at the Estates General, which was adjourned on January 31, 1561, reflects the fundamental nature of his approach to religious issues. He assumed that the corruption of the clergy, and not heretical belief, was the most important cause of the current troubles. The chancellor consistently discussed religious problems only in terms of political and administrative matters. While minimizing the threat of heresy, the government headed by L'Hôpital hence devoted its efforts instead to suppressing secular breaches of the peace. The *lettres de cachet* of January 28 and the two *lettres patentes* of February 22 ordered the parlements to release the people imprisoned for the cause of religion. Those pardoned were strictly warned that in the future they should live in accordance with the rules of Catholicism, without committing any scandalous or seditious acts.[71] But the Parlement of Paris did not register these edicts without resistance, publishing them on March 1 with the disclaimer that it did so only because it was the king's will.[72] There was, indeed, increasing

---

[68]*Discours pour la majorité de Charles IX*, 86–87; *Oeuvres complètes*, 1: 402.

[69]L'Hôpital attempted to divert the deputies' attention from religious issues, saying that the pope had already announced the resumption of the Council of Trent for the following Easter. The papal bull convoking the general council had been published on November 29; Donald Nugent, *Ecumenism in the Age of the Reformation: The Colloquy of Poissy* (Cambridge, Mass.: Harvard University Press, 1974), 51.

[70]*Oeuvres complètes*, 1:399.

[71]Cloulas, *Catherine de Médicis*, 159; *Mémoires de Condé*, 2:268, 271.

[72]Maugis, *Parlement de Paris*, 2:27.

discrepancy between the religious policy of the government and conservative opinion in the Parlement. While the chancellor was seeking to relax the persecution on the grounds of religion, the Parlement was strengthening its crackdown on heretics. The Parlement ordered local officials to pursue every report of illicit assemblies, and Châtelet officials were threatened with loss of office if they failed to investigate heretical assemblies.[73]

The spring of 1561 was marked by violent conflicts between Protestants and Catholics. That Easter, which fell on April 6, numerous clashes and disturbances occurred both in Paris and in the provinces.[74] On April 17, L'Hôpital told the Parlement that the disorder was so widespread that some firm and swift action was needed.[75] Two days later, the king issued a declaration, banning the use of the names "Papist" and "Huguenot." The public prohibition of those derogatory epithets was proposed by the chancellor, who was aware of the disastrous psychological effect of the terms offensive to either party. The edict forbade the two sides to "disturb the security, tranquility, and liberty of each other," and prohibited anyone to enter others' houses under the pretext of enforcing previous edicts.[76] The edict was a confirmation of the government's policy to separate religious and judicial offenders. The chancellor strictly instructed royal officials in the provinces to make a clear distinction between seditionists and simple worshippers. This policy of the chancellor was eagerly supported by the queen mother and the king. When troubles were reported in Guyenne, a letter was sent under the signature of Charles IX to the lieutenant général, sieur de Burye: "You will make it understood to the leaders of the rebels that you did not come to chastise them for the religion they hold, and that you were sent and have commission from me only to punish those who abuse the name of religion to cause an infinity of scandals, violence, murders and sedition."[77] The government wanted to assure the Protestants

[73]Taber, "Royal Policy and Religious Dissent," 139.

[74]De Thou, *Histoire universelle*, 3:51–52.     [75]*Mémoires de Condé*, 2:352.

[76]The king again commanded that prisoners previously arrested on account of religion be set free. Those who had left the country were allowed to return, provided they would live quietly ("Catholiquement et sans scandale"). Those who did not wish to conform to these conditions would be allowed to sell their property and leave the kingdom. Illicit assemblies remained strictly forbidden.

[77]Charles IX to M. de Burye, September 4, 1561, St.-Germain-en-Laye, BN, MS Fr. 15875, fol. 207. Amphoux, *Michel de l'Hôpital*, 175, incorrectly ascribes this letter to L'Hôpital; see A. de Ruble, *Jeanne d'Albret et la guerre civile* (Paris, 1897), 1:98. Charles IX's letter to the duc de Montpensier in November 1562 also reveals his deep concern about imposing harsh measures on Huguenots, who are "still my subjects." The king was afraid that efforts to make them "good Christians" might instead make them "bad Frenchmen"; *Dokumenty po istorii grazhdanskikh voin vo Frantsii, 1561–1563 (Documents pour servir à l'histoire des guerres civiles en France)*, ed. A. Lublinskaya (Leningrad, 1962), 195–97.

that they would not be molested for their religion, "if on their part they behave with discretion and modesty."

The declaration of April 19, according to the Spanish ambassador, Perrenot de Chantonnay, drove all Catholics into panic.[78] What was particularly remarkable about the declaration was that, to ensure prompt execution, the chancellor dispensed with its registration by the Parlement of Paris and sent it directly to the *baillis* and *sénéschaux*, not to the parlements.[79] The chancellor's action was a testimony to his growing impatience with the Parlement's chronic procrastination in registering pacification edicts. L'Hôpital was protesting against the Parlement for its lack of cooperation in maintaining order in the kingdom. L'Hôpital's position in this matter was based on the legislative authority of the Estates General: his contention was that since every decree in the declaration had already gone through lengthy discussions at the Estates General it did not need further deliberations at the Parlement. It is likely that L'Hôpital was fully aware of the grave implication of bypassing customary legal procedure. His action indeed amounted to explicit negation of the main constitutional claim of the Parlement of Paris that no edict or ordinance had the force of law if not deliberated on and registered by the court.[80] The chancellor's move seriously aggrieved the magistrates, who could not but perceive it as blatant disregard of the Parlement's authority. This incident must have reminded the magistrates of the earlier conflicts with President L'Hôpital of the Chambre des Comptes. The Parlement had already been unhappy, after L'Hôpital became chancellor, with his affirmation of the Estates General's higher status over the Parlement in the constitutional hierarchy.[81] L'Hôpital's acts caused some parlementaires, in exasperation, to go so far as to demand the suspension of the chancellor on charges of flouting traditional procedure. After the queen mother's interventions to placate the magistrates' fury, the Parlement confined itself to petitioning the king to confirm that registration of edicts by the Parlement was required for an ordinance to take the force of law.[82] As for the edict itself, the law court complained that its provisions seemed to imply that "the

[78]Quoted in Sutherland, *Huguenot Struggle*, 125.

[79]*Mémoires de Condé*, 1:27.

[80]De Thou. *Histoire universelle*, 3:52, argues that the queen mother, who was at Fontainebleau, was aware of the chancellor's action.

[81]The Parlement asserted that the chancellor's action "serait placer l'autorité des Parlements au-dessous de celle des Etats-Généraux, ce qui est évidemment opposé aux principes de nostre droit public, aux premiers éléments de nos lois fondamentales"; *Oeuvres complètes*, 1:413; 2:17–18; Taillandier, *Nouvelles recherches*, 67–68.

[82]Shennan, *Parlement of Paris*, 212–13. Duféy, *Oeuvres complètes*, 1:414–45, contends that the cardinal of Lorraine wrote a letter concerning the issue to the queen mother in favor of the position of the Parlement of Paris.

diversity of religion is approved in this kingdom," which was against "what has been stated and prescribed in the previous edicts, and also in all the laws and the ancient constitutions."[83] By an *arrêt* of May 11, the Parlement of Paris forbade the publication of the edict in the capital as being contrary to the fundamental law of the kingdom.[84] Faced with this fierce opposition, L'Hôpital allowed the edict to lapse.

Chastised, but undaunted, L'Hôpital appeared before the Parlement on June 18. Faced with increasing religious troubles, the government decided to call for an enlarged council, consisting of members of the Conseil du Roi and the Parlement of Paris, for the discussion of a new pacification edict. The king decided to send his councillors to the Parlement, declared L'Hôpital, because the parlementaires "are his councillors, not only in judging cases, but also in the greatest affairs of the state, when it pleases him to request it."[85] With the memory of the conflict in April still fresh among the magistrates, the chancellor consciously tried to convince them that the government looked forward to cooperation with the Parlement, instead of forcing the registration of edicts. The idea of joint deliberation was, in fact, a new strategy of the chancellor. The magistrates' participation in the discussion of the proposed edict was expected to preempt the Parlement's resistance in its registration process. Declaring that "we have to acknowledge the truth," L'Hôpital pointed out the deficiency of the past three kings' attempts to punish those who had fallen to the error of the new religion. Heresy was, maintained the chancellor, God's punishment for our own faults and sins. One should therefore turn to "divine and spiritual remedies," not "human remedies."[86] According to the chancellor, some of those who adopted the new religion were atheists hiding behind the cloak of religion. They took up arms, and attacked "not the church but what was inside the church." Sedition and disobedience to royal authority became more serious than the new religion itself because, for religious diseases, "the accidents are more perilous than the principal evil." The joint treatment of religion and politics, though traditional, had only led to confusion. By separating the religious issues from the political

[83]For the Parlement's remonstrance, see Taber, "Royal Policy and Religious Dissent," 147–50.

[84]De Thou, *Histoire universelle*, 3:53.

[85]*Oeuvres complètes*, 1:419. The text is also printed in *Mémoires de Condé*, 2:396–401. The deliberations at the Parlement were attended by notables of the realm: the chancellor; the first president; the other presidents; the cardinals of Lorraine, Châtillon, Bourbon, and Guise; the king of Navarre; the prince of Condé; the prince of Roche-sur-Yon; the dukes of Guise and Nivernois; the constable of Montmorency; the marshals of Saint-André and Montmorency; the bishop of Paris; and seigneurs of Dumortier, Avenson, and Selve. The list is from *Mémoires de Condé*, 1:402.

[86]*Oeuvres complètes*, 1:421.

ones, the government hoped to secure some permanent and stable measures. The Edict of Romorantin had not been successful, because it was not strictly enforced. The royal decrees remained dead letters when the administration did not function, due to the negligence of some judges, who were, in turn, not well served by *baillis* and *sénéchaulx*.[87]

Unable to "govern," declared the chancellor, the king had to "negotiate."[88] L'Hôpital clearly knew that religion was not a subject on which men were prepared to bargain. When religious compromise appeared out of the question, therefore, political compromise seemed inevitable. L'Hôpital took pains to defend the government's fluctuating, seemingly often contradictory, religious policies. When some edicts and ordinances did not work, one ought to change them. Edicts were drawn up for specific situations; hence it would not be strange to change them as the times changed. Government was like a ship, explained L'Hôpital, which oscillated as the wind blew. Human laws and politics could not always be in the same state and must be changed "selon que le peuple est." The chancellor went on to say: "Sometimes a severe law is good, sometimes a lenient law, and sometimes a neither-severe-nor-lenient law.... The true duty of a king and governors is to observe the times and to tighten or loosen laws accordingly."[89]

The king should make alterations in law as were required from time to time, just as a seaman trimmed his sails to the wind. It was therefore necessary to watch and advise remedies for the current problems, either executing, loosening, reinforcing, or changing edicts. The chancellor emphasized that the proposed new edict ought to tolerate poor men who gathered only to pray to God, without doing any harm. No king or equitable judges should find it wrong.

Aware of the usual resistance as well as the procrastination of the Parlement, L'Hôpital specifically pleaded with each magistrate to "rid himself of all passions and affections" and to "be brief in his opinion."[90] But the lengthy deliberation process on the text of the new edict presented by the royal council attested to the Parlement's uncooperative attitudes towards the government's pacification policy. Chantonnay reported to Philip II

---

[87]L'Hôpital warned that the government would no longer have "ni ses pieds ni ses mains," *Oeuvres complètes*, 1:425.

[88]Romier, *Le Royaume de Catherine de Médicis*, 29.

[89]*Oeuvres complètes*, 1:425–26.

[90]L'Hôpital specifically asked the parlementaires that "chascung soit brief, en son opinion, sans répéter ce qui aura esté dict"; *Oeuvres complètes*, 1:428.

that the Parlement "talked nothing but burning."[91] It was only after the
chancellor's repeated call for urgency that the edict was promulgated on
July 11.[92] Yet, when the time came for the Parlement to register this edict,
the delay of the Parlement looked almost willful. The Parlement, although
it had directly participated in the composition of the edict, dragged out its
deliberations, on the grounds that the text had undergone numerous alterations in the intervening weeks.[93] Increasingly impatient with the Parlement's delaying tactics, L'Hôpital demanded that they not stray from the
issues, and not repeat what had already been said.[94] The month of July
went by without any resolution, despite pressure by both the chancellor
and the queen for prompt publication of the edict.[95] At last, the king
issued *lettres de cachet* on July 30, prohibiting any restriction or modifica-
tion of the edict, and required the Parlement to "lire, publier et enregistrer,
entretenir, garder et observer de poinct en poinct, selong sa forme et
teneur."[96] Even so, the parlementaires felt it necessary to register the edict
only *per modum provisionis*, as a concession to "the necessity of the times."

The Edict of July, finally published on July 31, strictly prohibited
preaching, or administration of the sacraments "in any form other than the
usage received and observed in the Catholic church." It forbade the king's
subjects to "molest or provoke one another on any pretense whatever, on
account of religious differences, or for any other reason." The magistrates
were not allowed to pursue people "indiscreetly," or execute the stipulations of the edict in any abusive way. A general pardon was granted to all
who had been persecuted on account of their religion, or who had been
concerned in any seditious proceedings, on the understanding that they
were henceforth to live "paisiblement et catholiquement."[97] The edict
seemed, however, hardly satisfactory to anyone.[98] Protestants regarded it
as a disappointing setback because it forbade all their meetings, whether
public or in private, armed or unarmed. For Catholics, on the other hand,

---

[91]Chantonnay to Philip II, June 19, 1561, *Archivo documental Español*, 2:261. President
Pierre Séguier, in the presence of the royal councillors, wanted to bring forth the issue of the
magistrates' salary, then eighteen months overdue; the chancellor curtly answered: "I am no
longer concerned with bookkeeping and have hardly ever been"; *Oeuvres complètes*, 1:428–29;
*Mémoires de Condé*, 2:401.

[92]L'Hôpital urged the magistrates to occupy themselves with the composition of the
edict, and ordered that "on lût chaque matin le tableau, pour savoir les absents." *Oeuvres
complètes*, 1:429; *Mémoires de Condé*, 2:401.

[93]Shennan, *Parlement of Paris*, 209–10.

[94]On the deliberation of June 26, see *Oeuvres complètes*, 1:430; *Mémoires de Condé*, 2:403.

[95]Aubert, "Recherches sur l'organisation du Parlement de Paris," 117.

[96]The text of the letters of the king and Catherine is printed in *Oeuvres complètes*, 1:432–
34.

[97]Isambert, *Recueil général*, 14:109.        [98]Fontanon, *Edits et ordonnances*, 4:264–65.

the stipulation to live "catholiquement" was not clear enough. The ambiguity of the edict's provisions seemed so apparent that a provincial official complained that "everyone interprets them to favor his own opinion."[99] The Parlement, by registering the edict provisionally, gave it only a temporary character. In fact, the ambiguity of the edict looked to the Venetian ambassador Suriano to be a part of the chancellor's plan. Suriano, one of the few unbiased observers at the French court, and perhaps the most discerning, commented that the chancellor was a "man of very great shrewdness," who desired in this way to mitigate the decree.[100] It is possible to presume that L'Hôpital, by inserting ambiguous clauses, such as enjoining Protestants to "vivre catholiquement," attempted to nullify its intolerant aspects. The Edict of July, along with the Edict of Romorantin in 1560, appears to illustrate L'Hôpital's efforts to lessen the impact of rigorous regulations against Protestants, by drawing on the obscurity of laws.[101]

The government had already announced on June 12 the convocation of the assembly of the Gallican church. It was officially declared on July 25 that there would be a colloquy between Catholic and Protestant theologians during the last part of the meeting.[102] On July 31, the same day that the Parlement registered the edict of July, Chancellor L'Hôpital addressed the opening of the assembly of clergy at Poissy.[103] In this speech, L'Hôpital

[99]Quoted in Sutherland, *Huguenot Struggle*, 128.

[100]Suriano pointed out that the ambiguous stipulation of the edict was "in fact the work of the chancellor whose orthodoxy was suspected"; Suriano to the Doge and the Senate, July 27, 1561, *Despatches of Suriano*, 33.

[101]Salmon, *Society in Crisis*, 134.

[102]The royal letter issued in St.-Germain-en-Laye, printed in Fontanon, *Edits et ordonnances*, 4:364.

[103]The chancellor's speech is recounted in *Diario dell'assemblea de' vescovi à Poissy*, published with a preface by Joseph Roserot de Melin, "Rome et Poissy (1560–61)," *Mélanges d'archéologie et d'histoire* 34 (1921–1922): 91–94. Duféy, *Oeuvres complètes*, I, 485–89, does not include L'Hôpital's speech of this day, but both Evennett, *Cardinal of Lorraine*, 284, n. 1 and 307, n. 3; and Nugent, *Colloquy of Poissy*, 95, n., contend that the speech identified as the one given on September 9 was probably a draft of his speech of July 31. Duféy possibly followed De Thou's *Histoire universelle*, 3:65–67, which prints a speech of L'Hôpital as delivered on September 9, the same one as the speech attributed by Duféy to September 9. Evennett's and Nugent's arguments appear plausible, because the content of the second speech (Duféy's September 9) seems more likely to have been given at the opening of the national assembly in Poissy on July 31. Evennett further argues that the address ascribed by Duféy to September 1 was actually delivered on September 9. He supports his argument by a short account of L'Hôpital's speech of September 9 by La Place, which was similar to the one assigned the date of September 1 in Duféy, *Oeuvres complètes*, 1:469–79; *Commentaire de l'estat*, 158–59. *Histoire ecclésiastique* provided an abstract of L'Hôpital's speech given on September 9, which was identical to that of La Place. *Histoire ecclésiastique des églises réformées au royaume de France*, ed. G. Baum and Ed. Cunitz (Paris, 1883–1889; reprinted by Nieuwkoop: B. de Graaf, 1974), 1:557–58.

defended the convocation of the national council, pointing out that it was impossible to await a general council when affairs in France were daily growing worse. The king could no longer wait for the decisions of a general council, and now would seek a national prescription for national ills. A national synod was expedient for France because, in order to cure such a serious illness, one must use medicines "present and domestic," rather than those "distant and foreign," which might not arrive in time.[104] Waiting for a foreign solution could be compared to the situation of one who, having lost his appetite, went to Egypt and India searching for exotic spices, without even looking into the better-quality herbs growing in his own backyard. L'Hôpital exhorted the prelates to approach the matter in a conciliatory spirit, putting aside any prejudice. They must not "regard as enemies those of the so-called new religion, who are Christians just like themselves and who were baptized."[105] Since diversity of religious opinions was the principal cause of the troubles, the king called Protestants to confer together with Catholics. Protestants must be instructed with no force but persuasion. "One must not close the door to them and to their children but receive them in warm spirit, without harshness and stubbornness."[106] This specific statement of L'Hôpital is noteworthy, because he had said eight months earlier that, if a person was obstinate in his errors, "one must close the church to him."[107] The chancellor attempted to minimize the novelty of the national council. He suggested that, if the prelates shrank from calling the meeting a "council," they designate it an "assembly." L'Hôpital also assured them that all proceedings would be sent to the general council or submitted to the scrutiny of Rome.[108]

The chancellor emphasized that the Gallican council would not circumvent either papal authority or future decrees by the Council of Trent, which had been convoked by the papal bull of November 1560. It would simply provide an immediate remedy for the most pressing evils in the church. It was the government's official position that the national council was not intended to supersede the ecumenical council, and that its discussion would be limited to the preparation for the council at Trent.[109] But many prelates did not perceive as genuine the government's protest of the national council's innocuous nature, and contended that it was merely intended to dispel the suspicions of Rome and to prevent possible papal interference in the colloquy.[110] The cardinal of Tournon, who headed the

---

[104]*Oeuvres complètes*, 1:486.          [105]*Oeuvres complètes*, 1:488.
[106]*Oeuvres complètes*, 1:488.          [107]*Oeuvres complètes*, 1:325.
[108]*Oeuvres complètes*, 1:487.

[109]Dupuy, *Instruction et lettres des rois très-chrestiens*, 79; Valois, "Essais de conciliation religieuse," 240, n..

[110]Nugent, *Colloquy of Poissy*, 60–66.

episcopate, was thoroughly alarmed by L'Hôpital's speech, which he perceived as a virtual repudiation of the Council of Trent. The cardinal sought permission to obtain a copy of L'Hôpital's speech so as to present it for deliberation in the next session of the prelates. But L'Hôpital refused the request, claiming that the speech had been given extemporaneously.[111] According to de Thou, the chancellor said that "everyone heard it well enough," and that the prelates demanded his address in writing only to cause him trouble and delay the conference.[112] Yet a copy of his address was sent to Rome in September, and Pius IV, in exasperation, complained to the French ambassador about the chancellor's defiance of the authority of the universal council.[113] Meanwhile, at Poissy, the cardinal of Tournon, unable to obtain a copy of L'Hôpital's speech, persuaded the prelates to declare the following day that they would confine their consultations to the morals, not the faith, of the Gallican church, and that nothing prejudicial to the pope's authority should be undertaken even in matters of discipline.[114]

The assembly of the clergy at Poissy from July 31 through August 19, was followed by the religious discussion with the Calvinist theologians from September 9 through October 14, known as the Colloquy of Poissy. The convocation of the national council was a clear indication of the government's intention to resolve religious problems on the national level. Mario Turchetti, in his important study of the Colloquy of Poissy, argues that the prime purpose of the colloquy was "concord."[115] According to him, what the organizers of the colloquy attempted to achieve in the summer of 1561 was a Christian church, moderately reformed and capable of reuniting all Christians, through concord. This was, argued Turchetti, a religious program pursued by Catherine de Médicis, Chancellor

---

[111]Chantonnay to Philip II, August 5, 1561, *Archivo documental Español*, 2:322–23; *Correspondance de Tournon*, 409; "Journal du Colloque," ed. Alphonse de Ruble, *Mémoires de la société de l'histoire de Paris et de L'isle de France* 16 (1889): 11–13.

[112]De Thou, *Histoire universelle*, 3: 67, describes this incident as happening after the chancellor's speech on September 9, and not on July 31. It is hard to decide from de Thou's description whether a similar incident happened again on September 9 or it was simply a chronological confusion, although the latter is more likely; see n. 103 above.

[113]M. de l'Isle to the king, September 11 and September 22, 1561, BN, MS Fr. 3955, fol. 29 v, 33 v. Charles IX had to write to the pope on October 24 to explain: "Il n'est rien de ce que l'on dit que mon chancelier a proposé"; Dupuy, *Le concile de Trente*, 97, 103.

[114]They resolved: "ne rien attenter contre le bon vouloir et consentement de N.S. Père le Pape"; Valois, "Essais de conciliation religieuse," 242.

[115]Mario Turchetti, *Concordia o tolleranza? François Bauduin (1520–1573) e i "Moyenneurs"* (Geneva: Droz, 1984); idem, "Concorde ou tolérance? Les Moyenneurs à la veille des guerres de religion en France," *Revue de théologie et de philosophie* 118 (1986): 255–67; idem, "Religious Concord and Political Tolerance in Sixteenth- and Seventeenth-Century France," *Sixteenth Century Journal* 22 (1991), 15–25.

L'Hôpital, and the cardinal of Lorraine at Poissy, and it continued to remain the essential aim of the government throughout the wars of religion.

Turchetti's interpretation is widely considered among historians to have significantly changed our understanding of the history of France on the eve of the religious wars. Turchetti's general thesis is that the ideal of "toleration" was indeed quite rare in the sixteenth century, except for a few theorists such as Sébastien Castellion. A more common ideal was "concord," a kind of forced religious compromise based on mutual concession between Catholics and Protestants, designed to bring them together in one church. Toleration edicts issued by the government in the second half of the sixteenth century were, argued Turchetti, only temporary steps toward the restoration of religious unity in the kingdom. In fact concord had nothing to do with toleration, because if "concord" had been established, the king would have "forced" all his subjects to conform to it. But the Colloquy of Poissy failed, Turchetti concluded, mainly because of the intransigence of Protestants and the intractability of Catholic extremists.

Turchetti's argument provides a significant corrective to the traditional portrayal of L'Hôpital. L'Hôpital has been viewed, from Jacques-Auguste de Thou and Pierre Bayle in the seventeenth century to Albert Buisson in the twentieth century, as an advocate of religious toleration.[116] The eighteenth and the nineteenth-century historians, in particular, proposed to find, retrospectively, the modern concept of secularism and the endorsement of a plurality of religions in the person of L'Hôpital, only to commit a grave anachronism. But what L'Hôpital sincerely wished for, along with Catherine de Médicis and the cardinal of Lorraine, was to stop religious hostilities and safeguard peace in the kingdom. The fiasco of the Colloquy of Poissy brought to an end, however, the royal government's hope that a national synod would provide remedies for France's difficulties by bringing Protestants into communication with Catholics. Its failure seemed to sweep away any opportunities for resolving the troubles in the kingdom and thus convinced the chancellor, already thoroughly disappointed, that toleration of Protestants was the only way of escape from prolonged anarchical confusions and crisis.

On November 12 at the Parlement of Paris, L'Hôpital deplored that "God is still wrathful."[117] The hope for religious uniformity in the kingdom having perished, the government had to devote all its efforts to suppressing rebellious violence. L'Hôpital told the parlementaires that each

---

[116]De Thou, *Histoire universelle*, 2:781–82; Pierre Bayle, "L'Hospital," *Dictionnaire historique et critique* (Amsterdam, 1740), 2:804–807; Buisson, *L'Hospital*.

[117]*Oeuvres complètes*, 2:10.

day he received two dozen reports of sedition across the country.[118] There were complaints, the chancellor added pointedly, that the parlements were obstructing prompt repression of these seditious movements, by interfering with the jurisdiction of the lower courts. The king had ordered in his Edict of July, L'Hôpital reminded the magistrates, that illegal assemblies and sedition be tried without appeal by the judges of *présidiaux*, but the edict was not being observed because of the overzealous parlements' frequent intervention.[119] L'Hôpital was aware of the need for a new edict, which would replace the provisional and rarely observed Edict of July and, above all, one that would define the new situation—*post* Poissy—in unambiguous terms. The failure of the national council and his distrust in the universal council convinced L'Hôpital that France could no longer lose time vainly trying to resolve religious divergences. The question was now how to preserve the unity of the state, notwithstanding religious diversity. L'Hôpital proposed to the queen mother the summoning of an assembly to discuss strictly "administrative" measures for pacification. When Constable Montmorency expressed impatience at another attempt for conciliation, L'Hôpital curtly told him that there was no more time to "gouverner en criant garde! garde!" as the constable always did, but that one ought to "gouverner par raison."[120]

The extended assembly, consisting of the Conseil Privé and two representatives from each of the eight parlements, opened at St.-Germain on January 3, 1562. Once again, L'Hôpital opened the session with his favorite theme that the diversity of religions was God's punishment.[121] What was needed was an effort to please God by reforms of morals and lives. This time, however, L'Hôpital's address was strikingly more outspoken and point-blank than before. The chancellor painfully reminded the delegates of the continuous failure of those religious edicts issued during his tenure. Experience amply showed that punishment of Protestants had done nothing to ameliorate the situation. Some people said that the king must decisively take sides, one way or the other, in order to end religious division. For L'Hôpital, such would be "repugnant not only to the name of

[118]*Oeuvres complètes*, 2:14.

[119]The chancellor was referring to specific complaints: On October 21, an official at the présidiaux of Nîmes complained to the queen that the Parlement of Toulouse frequently interfered with the jurisdiction of the présidiaux courts; *Documents pour servir à l'histoire des guerres civiles en France*, 34–35.

[120]Tornabuoni to Cosimo I, January 3, 1562, *Négociations avec la Toscane*, 3:470–71.

[121]*Oeuvres complètes*, 1:441–53; *Mémoires de Condé*, 2:606–12; De Thou, *Histoire universelle*, 2:118–23. Duféy incorrectly describes this speech as the one delivered at St.-Germain-en-Laye to the joint assembly of the lay and ecclesiastical estates on August 27, 1561. It was a speech given at the same place, but in January 1562; see Joseph Lecler, *Toleration and the Reformation*, tr. T. L. Westow (London: Longmans, 1960), 68–69, n.

Christians we bear but also to humanity." "How could we," he asked, "order the troops to fight against their fathers, sons, brothers, wives, or relatives?"[122] In a civil war, the victory of either side could only result in the ruin of the country: "the victors, whoever that will be, will feel as painful as the defeated, as if one side of the body harms the other."[123] L'Hôpital professed his indifference to doctrinal matters. "I do not want to dispute the doctrines of religion," he flatly declared, "which pertain to the judgment of the *genz d'église* and which were treated in Poissy. I want to discuss only what pertains to the police, in order to maintain people in peace and tranquility." L'Hôpital proposed his policy in unequivocal terms: now that persecution and doctrinal conciliation had both failed, it was time to try a new religious measure, based on toleration and compromise. In individual families, "those who remain Catholic do not cease to live in peace and love with those who adopt the new faith." Likewise, maintained L'Hôpital, "one can live in peace with those of different opinions" in one kingdom.[124]

L'Hôpital was well aware of the novelty of proposing the coexistence of two religions in one state. It would not only mark a departure from the time-honored precept of "one faith" in the kingdom, but also contradict the numerous edicts and ordinances of the past prescribing persecution. It would amount to an open acknowledgment of the criticism that the government was constantly changing its mind with its vacillating religious policy.[125] But "if [the past edicts] were found wanting," cogently argued the chancellor, "it is necessary to correct them."[126] There were two kinds of law:

> Some laws are inviolable and one cannot breach them without contradicting the ordinances of God. Otherwise it will be as if one sends God to the closet for the time being, without knowing how to bring Him out when one needs Him…. Some laws [on the other hand] depend on the grace and beneficence of the prince, and hence can be suspended without danger. One must take into account not only whether the law is just in itself but also whether it is appropriate to the time and people for whom it was made…. One must make sure that the law fits people just as shoes fit their feet.[127]

---

[122]*Oeuvres complètes*, 1: 447–48.       [123]*Oeuvres complètes*, 1: 448.
[124]*Oeuvres complètes*, 1: 452.
[125]The Parlement of Paris contended that the edict of July, composed by an assembly invested with great authority, should remain valid and binding; Shennan, *Parlement of Paris*, 210–11.
[126]*Oeuvres complètes*, 1: 471–72.       [127]*Oeuvres complètes*, 1: 449–51.

The chancellor's message could not be mistaken; the previous edicts of punishment had failed, so a new edict of pacification was necessary. Any objection raised to it on account of the inconsistency of law would be invalid. The deputies at St.-Germain were explicitly reminded that the fundamental question at issue was "not about the maintenance of religion (*constituenda religione*) but about the maintaining of the commonwealth (*constituenda republica*)."[128] The pressing issue was not to decide which of the two confessions was better, but simply whether or not to authorize Protestant preaching. The chancellor went so far as to declare that "many can be citizens who will not be Christians," and that "even the excommunicated does not cease to be a citizen."[129]

This speech is indeed a straightforward and eloquent exposition of L'Hôpital's religious policy.[130] At Orléans a year earlier, he had refused to envisage the possibility of two religions in one state. But in St.-Germain, he boldly proposed the legal toleration of the existence of dissent. L'Hôpital's remark that even a non-Christian did not cease to be a good citizen is conspicuous, because its implication goes a step beyond allowing two kinds of Christians in the realm. Nowhere else did L'Hôpital suggest toleration of differing religious beliefs within the community. This particular statement thus appears to be a result of his efforts to stress the need for the legalization of Protestant worship and the separation of politics and religion, rather than a manifesto of universal freedom of conscience.[131]

The assembly of St.-Germain, overwhelmed by the chancellor's powerful plea for national unity, issued the Edict of January on January 17. It was the most tolerant edict L'Hôpital had drawn up during his regime. Its

[128]*Oeuvres complètes*, 1: 452.

[129]"Plusieurs peuvent estre *cives, qui non erunt christiani*: mesme l'excommunié ne laisse pas d'estre citoyen"; *Oeuvres complètes*, 1: 452.

[130]His speech seems to have stirred many audiences. The Spanish ambassador Chantonnay grumbled that the chancellor, a self-declared humanist and great rhetorician, had tried to persuade people that "all Catholics were very scandalized and had less hope and more fear than before"; see January 5, 1562, *Archivo documental Español*, 3:236–37. Santa Croce testified after the assembly that everyone was talking about the chancellor's speech, in which he "proposed his sentiment with such self-restraint and moderation [towards the Catholic dogmas] that one could easily have taken him for someone else"; see January 17, 1562, Santa Croce to Borromeo, "Lettres anecdotes écrites au cardinal Borromée par Prosper de Sainte-Croix ... nonce du Pape Pie IV," *Archives curieuses de l'histoire de France*, ed. L. Cimber and F. Danjou, 27 vols. (Paris, 1859–1886), 6:29.

[131]Malcolm C. Smith, "Early French Advocates of Religious Freedom," *Sixteenth Century Journal* 25 (1994): 37, n. believes that this statement indicates "an evolution towards liberalism." L'Hôpital's vision of coexistence of Catholics and Protestants was more than a temporary solution. L'Hôpital was, however, neither a believer in individual natural right nor a precursor of modern liberty. Moreover, L'Hôpital's *etatiste* proclivities clearly counterbalance the nineteenth-century liberal biases.

principal significance was that it allowed Protestants to hold synods and to celebrate their liturgy outside the walled cities and towns.[132] Unlike previous edicts, it openly and unambiguously authorized the free exercise of Protestant religion within certain limits, and for the first time legally recognized the existence of the "nouvelle religion." Protestants were ordered to surrender the churches they had seized, and were strictly forbidden to destroy images, or do anything which would trouble public tranquility. No one, Catholics or Protestants, was allowed to attack others on account of religion.[133] It was the culmination of the policy of the separation of "le faict de la religion" and "les affaires politiques," a theme which L'Hôpital had so consistently pursued. The distinction was now clearly drawn between "huguenot de coeur" and "huguenot d'état." Pierre Bayle in the seventeenth century commented that although Henry IV in 1598 by the Edict of Nantes "granted to the Reformed church more than what the chancellor had accorded to it… the Roman religion was exposed to less risk by the Edict of Nantes than by the Edict of January [of 1562]."[134]

The reaction of L'Hôpital's contemporaries to his ideas proposing the coexistence of two religions is best illustrated by the heated resistance from various quarters to the Edict of January. The Sorbonne officially requested that the Parlement of Paris not register the edict, which, it argued, would promote the new religion.[135] The resistance of the Parlement proved more pertinacious than ever. The basis of the *parlementaires'* opposition was twofold. First, the Parlement's reputation as the champion of orthodoxy led them to resist any concessions to Protestants. For the magistrates, the Edict of July offered the best possible solution to the troubles. Further concessions would bring the plurality of religion, which would inevitably result in the dissolution of the state.[136] At the same time, the magistrates' belief that the effectiveness of law depended upon the formality and regularity of their institutions led them to reaffirm emphatically the original text of the Edict of July, which had been legally registered.[137] The new edict contradicted much of what had been solemnly decreed in July. The parlementaires were so ardent in their resistance,

---

[132]Fontanon, *Edits et ordonnances*, 4:267–69; De Thou, *Histoire universelle*, 3:123–24.

[133]Royal officials "de la religion" (except judicial ones) would not lose their offices because of religion.

[134]"The Roman Religion did not run as much risk, when the Edict of Nantes was accorded, as when the Edict of January was issued"; Bayle, "Hospital," in *Dictionnaire historique et critique* (Amsterdam, 1740), 2:805.

[135]Pierre de Paschal, *Journal de ce qui s'est passé en France durant l'année 1562 principalement dans Paris et à la cour*, Société de l'histoire de France, ed. Michel François (Paris: Librairie Henri Didier, 1950), 2.

[136]The Parlement's remonstrance is printed in De Thou, *Histoire universelle*, 2:124–25.

[137]Shennan, *Parlement of Paris*, 211; *Mémoires de Condé*, 3:92.

reported the papal nuncio Santa Croce, that "the king could deprive them of their lives but not force them to consent to such ill-principled acts."[138]

Confronted with stiff opposition from the magistrates, the queen mother tried to appease them by issuing a declaration on February 14, which proclaimed the edict to be "par manière de provision et sans que par nostre dite ordonnance nous ayons entendu approuver deux religions en nostre royaume."[139] The following day, L'Hôpital wrote to the truculent Parlement of Paris, asking them to "follow and execute the royal will, in order to content the people in peace and rest."[140] He did not dispute the Parlement's contention that a republic should ideally be founded upon one religion. But in the current situation, France could only be restored to one religion by two expedients: either exterminating Protestants altogether or banishing them in perpetuity, neither of which was feasible.[141] The chancellor pointed out to the Parlement that the Edict of July, by forbidding Protestants to exercise their religion, had simply been driving them to atheism. Hence it was unavoidable to "establish two religions, until God reunites us in the same will."[142] It was not until March 6, after alternating threats and entreaties from the queen mother and the chancellor, that the Parlement of Paris finally registered the Edict of January. Still, the Parlement attached the reservation that the law court, by registering the edict, "does not pretend to approve the new religion, and the edict will be effective only until His Majesty decrees otherwise."[143] With this clause, the court cast serious doubts upon the validity of the edict, and at the same time sharply criticized the royal government for its vacillating policy.

The Parlement of Paris was not alone in its opposition to the Edict of January. The parlements of Dijon, Rouen, and Toulouse followed its lead and, even after the Parisian court conceded, these provincial courts refused to register the edict. The case of the Parlement of Dijon is of particular interest, because it specifically quoted the danger which the city of

[138]*Archives curieuses*, 6:35.

[139]Fontanon, *Edits et ordonnances*, 4:269–70.

[140]L'Hôpital to the Parlement of Paris, February 15, 1562, St.-Germain, *Mémoires de Condé*, 3:61–62.

[141]Etienne Pasquier, *Lettres historiques*, ed. D. Thickett (Paris, 1966), 84–85, provides a summary of the chancellor's reply to the Parlement's remonstrances.

[142]Pasquier, *Lettres historiques*, 85. On February 19, the queen mother went to Paris to pressure the Parlement to publish the edict. L'Hôpital stayed in Poissy, according to the Spanish ambassador, "feigning illness" It is possible that the chancellor preferred avoiding unnecessary confrontation with the Parlement when its opinion of him was extremely unfavorable. Chantonnay grumbled: "I would have wanted to see him explain himself publicly on the edict"; see Chantonnay to Philip II, February 23, 1562, *Archivo documental Español*, 3:366.

[143]De Thou, *Histoire universelle*, 2:124–25; *Mémoires de Condé*, 3:82–88.

Dijon faced due to its geographical proximity to Geneva, and its remonstrance was accepted by the royal council. The delegates of the Parlement of Dijon explained in the presence of the king in May that the safety of the city had already been seriously threatened by numerous seditions and conspiracies of Protestants, which were prompted by the issuance of the Edict of January.[144] The king authorized the suspension of the execution of the edict in Dijon and praised the prudent conduct of the Parlement of Dijon.[145] Chancellor L'Hôpital, the author of the edict, sent a letter on June 19 to the Dijonnais parlementaires commending their remonstrance.[146] This incident not only illustrates the resistance that L'Hôpital encountered in implementing the Edict of January in the provinces, but also attests to the danger and uncertainty inherent in the innovative policy of legalizing Protestant worship. The chancellor himself was not completely willing to ignore the risk of the edict and force its execution.

By the spring of 1562, in fact, it seemed that the time had already passed when a legal solution of any kind could be enforced. The massacre of Protestant worshippers at Vassy at the beginning of March triggered an all-out civil war. When the Catholic and Protestant chiefs decided to resolve religious problems by arms, there was really no place for the moderate party, which the chancellor led, to hold out. When the royal council met at the Louvre to decide whether to declare war against the prince of Condé, who had mobilized the Huguenot army, L'Hôpital vehemently opposed commencing hostilities against them. When the constable of Montmorency remarked derisively that a mere "homme de robe" was out of place at a council of war, L'Hôpital retorted that "I and my fellow judges may not know how to fight in a war, but at least we know quite well when to go to war."[147] The chancellor's courageous resistance to war was hopeless, however, and he was temporarily suspended from the royal council. When the court moved to Monceaux, L'Hôpital was left behind in Paris.[148]

[144]M. de la Cuisine, *Le Parlement de Bourgogne*, 2d ed. (Dijon: Rabutot, 1864), 2:47–48.

[145]The king's letter to the Parlement of Dijon, June 16, 1562: "Vous y avez prudemment procédé, qui est la cause que nous louons grandement votre bonne conduite et les effets d'icelle"; Cuisine, *Le Parlement de Bourgogne*, 47.

[146]Letter of June 19, 1562, reads: "Messieurs, j'ai reçu les lettres que vous m'avez envoyées par vos députés et entendu les remonstrances qu'ils ont faites sur l'objet de leur commission, où ils ont très bien accompli leur devoir. Vous saurez par eux ce qui en a été ordonné. Pour le présent, de ma part je vous assure que je vous ferai toujours office de bon ami. Charonne, près Paris, le 19 juin 1562. Signé: Votre bon frère, De Lhospital." Cuisine, *Le Parlement de Bourgogne*, 49.

[147]De Thou, *Histoire universelle*, 2:137.

[148]Santa Croce affirmed on March 15 that the chancellor had sent a person to Monceaux to ask when he should return to court, "only to be told to wait for further orders"; *Archives curieuses*, 6:50–52.

The exclusion of the chancellor from the court bears witness to the dominance of the royal council by the ultra-Catholic members, in particular the Triumvirate, comprising Duke François de Guise, Constable Anne de Montmorency, and Marshal Saint-André.[149] L'Hôpital remained in retirement at his château at Vignay from late May until late June.[150] He briefly returned to court at Talcy on June 26 to assist the queen mother in the negotiations with the prince of Condé and Admiral Coligny.[151] The failure of these negotiations signaled the beginning of the full-fledged civil war, and L'Hôpital went back to Vignay, where he stayed until he was recalled to the court in late July.[152]

L'Hôpital's poems written during his short retirement at Vignay reveal his deep frustration at the worsening political situations.[153] L'Hôpital had been fighting an up-hill battle. His policy of toleration did not seem to please anyone. Catholics abhorred the chancellor's urging of concessions to Protestants. The English envoy Nicholas Throckmorton testified that the staunchly Catholic Parisians' resentment of L'Hôpital's religious policy was so serious that the chancellor could not feel safe in the streets of the capital. In the summer of 1562, some people threatened to attack L'Hôpital's lodging and kill him, so the king had to send his Swiss guards to protect his chancellor.[154] Protestants, on the other hand, were

---

[149]On May 20, while L'Hôpital was still in Vignay, Prince Condé reportedly defended him in the royal council from his accusers, who claimed the chancellor's disgrace: "Michel de L'Hôpital, ministre si distingué qu'il en est peu qui puissent lui être comparés, si l'on considère sa sagesse. sa prudence, son sçavoir et la pureté de se moeurs"; cited in Amphoux, *Michel de L'Hôpital*, 258–59.

[150]L'Hôpital attended the royal council meeting at Louvre on May 13; Paschal, *Journal*, 36.

[151]Paschal, *Journal*, 68–69; Amphoux, *Michel de L'Hôpital*, 265. L'Hôpital wrote to Guy Du Faur, one of the French ambassadors at the Council of Trent, just before he left Vignay: "Here I can freely reflect, read, and write\ … but the clouds are dissipated, the sun is out again, the sea seems calm, and I think about leaving the port, and without any memory of the past danger, I ponder on the means to embark again on the stormy sea"; *Poésies complètes*, 315–20.

[152]The exact date of L'Hôpital's return to court is unknown, but he was back in Paris by the end of July. The English ambassador Throckmorton affirmed on July 23 that L'Hôpital lodged near Vincennes, where the king was staying; Throckmorton to Elizabeth, July 23, 1562, *CSP Foreign*, 5:176. Atkinson, *L'Hospital*, 94, incorrectly argues that L'Hôpital was recalled to the court shortly before the fall of Rouen, which occurred on Oct. 28. L'Hôpital's letter to Pope Pius IV, dated August 3, was written "de la cour"; *Oeuvres complètes*, 2:474–79.

[153]L'Hôpital to Guy du Faur, *Poésies complètes*, 315–20. L'Hôpital still consoled himself: "When I desire, after recreation, to spend time in serious study, I consult Plato or the philosophers inspired by him. I love above all St. Paul's writings, which teach me to know and to worship God." Ibid., 316.

[154]Throckmorton to Elizabeth, July 23, 1562, *CSP Foreign*, 5:176, and August 5, 1562, ibid., 212.

not content with what L'Hôpital offered to them, and they still suspected him as a henchman of the house of Guise.[155] L'Hôpital encountered vehement resistance by the Parlement of Paris to almost every single edict he proposed for pacification. Chantonnay confirmed in June 1562 that L'Hôpital had "no greater enemy than the Parlement of Paris."[156] The memory of friction with the magistrates during his presidency at the Chambre des Comptes remaining all too vivid, chancellor L'Hôpital now had to deal with the Parlement's systematic obstruction to his religious policies. L'Hôpital held back major counterattacks on the Parlement until his position was strengthened by the declarations of the majority and of the king. But conflicts with the Parlement during the first two years of his chancellorship attest to the irreconcilable differences between opinions concerning both the religious and political affairs.

The Parlement opposed L'Hôpital's toleration edicts on grounds that the king had no right to legalize heresy and that the maintenance of true religion was a primary function of government. L'Hôpital denied both contentions. He argued that the king's duty to render justice did not of itself require punishment of religious dissidents, because justice did not demand the chastisement of those who acted according to their consciences. Religious opinion was not criminal, pointed out the chancellor, as long as it did not cause injury to others. L'Hôpital was cautiously expounding his notion of a Christian conscience when he refused to prescribe punishment for those whose heretical opinions derived from a sincere service to God dictated by their own conscience. "Our conscience is such by nature," L'Hôpital told the estates at Orléans, "that it cannot be forced but must be informed."[157] Protestant assemblies were not always seditious, because "those who believe in Jesus Christ and become persecuted for religion have a good doctrine, and therefore are different from seditious people who have bad conscience."[158] L'Hôpital's humanist idealism, in line with that of Erasmus, was compounded by his political pragmatism. In Saint-Germain, L'Hôpital introduced two new principles of far-reaching significance.[159] While the government might be said to have

---

[155]Theodore Beza's comment on the chancellor when he met him at court before the Colloquy of Poissy illustrates Protestant distrust: "The chancellor you know ... wanted to have the honor to introduce me. I had to follow him, but with such a face that he knew well that I did not appreciate it"; Beza to Calvin, August 25, 1562, *Joannis Calvini opera quae supersunt omnia*, ed. Baum, Cunitz, and Reuss (Brunswick: Schwetschke, 1878–1879), vol. 18, col. 630.

[156]Chantonnay to Philip II, June 30, 1562, *Archivo documental Español*, 4:160.

[157]*Oeuvres complètes*, 1:471.          [158]*Oeuvres complètes*, 1:473.

[159]Quentin Skinner, *The Foundations of Modern Political Thought* (Cambridge: Cambridge University Press, 1978), 2:251.

a duty to defend the established religion of the kingdom, it had an even more compelling duty "to maintain the people in peace and tranquility."[160] The king stood above all parties and sects, and his most important business was to care for the interests of all his subjects alike, irrespective of their religious opinions. L'Hôpital was unwilling to accept his opponents' contention that religious innovation was synonymous with the collapse of society. Endowed with a realistic political perspective, L'Hôpital denied that religious changes, such as legalizing worship other than Catholicism, would necessarily bring political and social disorder.

L'Hôpital did not, it should be noted, repudiate the fundamental merit of religious conformity in the kingdom. In his speech in Orléans in December 1560, L'Hôpital pronounced the infinite virtue of "une foi," and viewed with disapproval the continuing proliferation of new religions. L'Hôpital's attitudes towards confessional issues were not divorced from his political conservatism. A royal magistrate by vocation, L'Hôpital, like Jean Bodin, was too impressed by the political advantage of religious uniformity to make religious freedom a fundamental right.[161] Yet, L'Hôpital was also aware that, in the current situation, the legal toleration of Protestants was the only way of escape from prolonged anarchic confusions and crisis. In this sense, L'Hôpital was a true forerunner of the Politiques in the late sixteenth century.[162] For neither L'Hôpital nor the Politiques was political allegiance a matter of religion. None of them contemplated religious liberty as a positive moral value. Their motives were more distinctly social and political; they merely believed in toleration as the only alternative to endemic civil strife.[163] Justifying toleration on account of pure national interest, however, L'Hôpital was even less conservative than the Politiques. The Politiques of the late sixteenth century were still committed to an eventual reunification of France under one faith.[164] For L'Hôpital, on the other hand, the long-term solution of "une foi" no longer held priority in his program. He was convinced that religious unity was not worth preserving at the cost of destroying the kingdom. L'Hôpital did not attempt merely to temporize with Protestants until confessional unifica-

[160]*Oeuvres complètes,* 1:449.

[161]Julian Franklin, *Jean Bodin and the Rise of Absolutist Theory* (Cambridge: Cambridge University Press, 1973), 47.

[162]For historians' appraisal of L'Hôpital's influence on the *Politique* party, see Edmond M. Beame, "The Politiques and the Historians," *Journal of the History of Ideas* 73 (1993): 355–79. For an in-depth study of the *Politiques* during the Wars of Religion, see Mack Holt, *The Duke of Anjou and the Politique Struggle during the Wars of Religion* (Cambridge: Cambridge University Press, 1986).

[163]Skinner, *Foundations of Modern Political Thought,* 2:250.

[164]Jonathan K. Powis, "Gallican Liberties and the Politics of Later Sixteenth-Century France," *Historical Journal* 26 (1983): 515–30.

tion of the kingdom was achieved; he envisioned enduring peaceful coexistence of Catholics and Protestants under one king.

In L'Hôpital's judgment, religious uniformity was not essential to the well-being of France.[165] L'Hôpital's views on this point were crystallized in his treatise written in 1568, shortly after his disgrace.[166] In this discourse, L'Hôpital flatly stated that "le but de la guerre est la paix."[167] It was in this perspective that he placed religious tolerance: "The name of the king, full of love and paternal charity, cannot bear bloody and felonious obstinacy of exterminating such a large party of his subjects; the gist of the well-being of the republic exists in calling them back to their duties and reconciling them together."[168]

L'Hôpital continued in equally remarkable terms:" The solution I find is to make them stop inflicting injuries and violence on each other, to make them drop all the arms, and, under a good law, to bring the depraved to the obedience to their prince, thus putting an end to this bloody and brutal war ... [and thus the king] gives them freedom of conscience, or rather, leaves their conscience in freedom."[169]

Robert Descimon has argued that L'Hôpital only pursued a policy of provisional coexistence, and that the chancellor did not believe in a final solution.[170] But to view L'Hôpital's toleration policy merely as a temporary solution risks underestimating the vitality of his ideals. To be sure, L'Hôpital did not deny the value of religious uniformity. Yet, in his judgment, it was not religious unity but political unity that was essential to the survival of the kingdom, and only toleration of the Huguenots could bring political unity. L'Hôpital maintained that one could live in peace with those of different religious opinions in one kingdom.[171] His vision of peaceful coexistence of Catholics and Protestants was thus more than a temporary expedient. It does not mean, however, that L'Hôpital was a "liberal" in the mode of the nineteenth century. Attributing to L'Hôpital a philosophical doctrine of the liberty of conscience is an anachronistic

[165]R. J. Knecht, *The French Wars of Religion 1559–1598* (London: Longman, 1989), 69.

[166]*Discours des raisons et persuasions de la paix*, BN, Dupuy 472; Dupuy 137, fol. 129v. This discourse is printed in *Oeuvres complètes*, 2:175–214, and Taillandier, *Nouvelles recherches*, 299–322. For a detailed discussion of this discourse, see Vittorio de Caprariis, *Propaganda e pensiero politico in Francia durante le guerre di religione*, vol. 1, *1559–1572* (Naples: Edizioni Scientifiche Italiane, 1959), 407–11; for Caprariis' discussion of L'Hôpital's political thought, see ibid., 167–85.

[167]*Oeuvres complètes*, 2:175. This passage was quoted from Aristotle, *Politics*, 7:15.1; see Descimon, ed. *Discours pour la majorité de Charles IX*, 32.

[168]*Oeuvres complètes*, 2:197.          [169]*Oeuvres complètes*, 2:197–99.

[170]Descimon, ed., *Discours de la majorité de Charles IX*, 25.

[171]Address of January 3, 1562, *Oeuvres complètes*, 2:452.

mistake. His views did not encompass complete religious relativism or freedom of thought.

What distinguishes L'Hôpital from other writers who argued for religious toleration in the sixteenth century can be found in that he was above all a statesman who was actually in charge of directing the religious policy of the government. He doubtless shared the intellectual qualities of the contemporary Christian humanists. As a moderate, L'Hôpital detested religious fanaticism, and thought that institutional reform of church should be the basis for reestablishing religious unity. L'Hôpital did not believe in the use of force in dealing with religious dissidents. As a skeptic, L'Hôpital doubted the soundness of human reason and abhorred doctrinal disputation. But Chancellor L'Hôpital could not remain within the framework of Christian humanism. Confronted with unprecedented religious wars which directly threatened the very existence of the state, he could not entertain the optimism of many other humanists that a reformation of the Catholic Church would bring Protestants back into the old fold. A qualified toleration, even if it looked like an unconscionable novelty contradictory to the tradition of the kingdom, was preferable to the ruin of the commonwealth altogether.

In fact, the seemingly ever-oscillating religious policy of the government appears, on closer inspection, not solely a result of indecisiveness and incoherence in the government's position, as many historians have explained, but also the reflection of the uncertainties which pervaded the political situation in the 1560s. To be sure, the government was constantly swinging between concession and repression towards Protestants. This stance was, however, in part the result of the contradictory attitudes of the Parlement of Paris towards the pacification edicts. The Parlement's intransigent opposition significantly disconcerted the direction of the government. The Parlement of Paris opposed the Edict of Romorantin because, at least in part, the edict diminished its jurisdictional authority by transferring heresy trials to the ecclesiastical courts. The Parlement then nullified the edict of April 1561 because it could not condone the chancellor's disregard of the juridical procedure of registration, the realm which the Parlement cherished as the last bastion of its authority. The Parlement again delayed and attempted to modify the Edict of July, and gave it only a temporary character by "provisional" registration. In 1562, the Parlement resisted the Edict of January on the grounds that it contradicted the past edicts and ordinances, especially the Edict of July. The magistrates apparently did not mind the contradiction in their attitudes, insisting on the legal authority of the July Edict which they themselves had declared only provisional. Obstructed by such resistance from the Parlement, itself incongruous and confounding, on almost every single measure of pacification, the government could not but vacillate and falter in its directions. The reason for the instability of the religious policy in the 1560s therefore needs to be sought in a broader context, not exclusively from the premise that the royal government was indecisive but also from the perspective of constitutional issues.

Some historians viewed the Edict of January as representing an important change in government policy and a significant development of L'Hôpital's position regarding this religious policy. Pointing out that L'Hôpital at the beginning of his chancellorship still thought about the religious divisions in traditional terms, cherishing the precept of "one faith, one law, one king," they argued that L'Hôpital's adjustment from his belief in a single religion to the explicit advocacy of tolerance came after the failure of the Colloquy of Poissy, when he realized the hopelessness for religious uniformity.[172] Joseph Lecler argues that L'Hôpital, after the failure at Poissy, "passed beyond the point of view of Erasmus and the humanists; from being a humanist he has become a *politique.*"[173] Turchetti argued, largely in the same vein, that "Chancellor l'Hospital changed his position radically" after Poissy, sometime between September 1561 and January 1562.[174] L'Hôpital's attitudes towards religious troubles evolved, to be sure, along with the changing circumstances. Yet, to attempt to find the decisive turning point when his position shifted from religious conservatism to tolerance appears to be a somewhat artificial and superfluous effort. L'Hôpital did not deny the unquestioned value of religious agreement. He supported the policy of religious concord, and shared with Catherine de Médicis and the cardinal of Lorraine hopes for religious reunification through a national council. It was after the failure of the Colloquy of Poissy that L'Hôpital was able to implement a turn to a policy of toleration, which culminated in the Edict of January providing for legal coexistence of Catholics and Protestants. But, from the beginning of his chancellorship, L'Hôpital was also aware of the fact that any attempt to enforce uniformity would bring a grave danger to civil peace. He had consciously treated religious division only as a political problem, and toleration as a mere necessity for the maintenance of peace and order in the kingdom. L'Hôpital consistently declined to admit that fundamental dogmatic differences were the cause of the current religious problems. Better

[172]Abraham-Charles Keller, "Michel de L'Hospital and the Edict of Toleration of 1562," *Bibliothèque d'Humanisme et Renaissance* 14 (1952): 301, 308–9; Lecler, *Toleration and the Reformation*, 2:42–43, 65–69, 84–86. Skinner, *Foundations of Modern Political Thought*, 2:251–52, writes in much the same terms, although he does not specify the Colloquy of Poissy as the turning point.

[173]Lecler, *Toleration and the Reformation*, 2:68–69.

[174]Turchetti, "Concorde ou tolérance?" 259, 266.

aware than anyone else of the fatal impact of doctrinal disagreement on national unity, L'Hôpital consciously downplayed the significance of the theological issues in the present circumstances, and showed a striking indifference to the finer points of confessional disputes. He made no appeal to the uncertainties of religious argument and made no pretense of settling religious differences.

In L'Hôpital, the imperative of confessional reunification, an ideal which dictated the sixteenth-century mentality in France did not seem to be absolutely exclusive of the advocacy of religious leniency. L'Hôpital's religious policy indeed represented the middle point of the two seemingly conflicting ideals of concord and toleration. L'Hôpital saw no incompatibility between the ultimate wish for religious reunification and the need to stop persecuting religious dissidents, especially when forced religious uniformity seriously threatened the survival of the kingdom and killing was committed in the name of religion. For him, concord was to be achieved by the will of God, not humans. Meanwhile, tolerance must become the means of concord.

Catherine de Médicis shared her chancellor's indifference to, and impatience with, seemingly endless dogmatic disputes. When the colloquy in February 1562 deadlocked over the issue of religious images, the queen mother expressed her deep frustration. She wrote in a letter: "Having wasted twelve or fifteen days in disputes over a simple issue, the use of images, [the theologians] have only succeeded in remaining stubborn and obstinate to one another, thus fighting in order not to be defeated, instead of debating and conferring over how to comply with truth and reason...."[175]

Chancellor L'Hôpital intervened for the queen mother in the stalemated colloquy, and dismissed the theologians.[176] L'Hôpital was aware that any attempt to enforce uniformity would seriously endanger civil peace, and that there was hence an inherent limit to his desire for forced accord between religious groups. L'Hôpital thus devoted efforts, not to groping for religious reconciliation, but to striking administrative solutions for the question how the kingdom could preserve peace. In his speech at the beginning of the national council, L'Hôpital laid stress on the need for national unity, regardless of the difference in details of dogma. He emphasized that, after all, "it is not necessary to master several books to be able to understand well the words of God."[177] This does not sound like a statement of someone who seriously intended to effect a doctrinal

---

[175]Catherine to the bishop of Rennes, February 16, 1562, *Lettres de Catherine de Médicis,* 1: 276.

[176]Paschal, *Journal,* 3–4.          [177]*Oeuvres complètes,* 1:488.

agreement by means of theological discussion. From Orléans to St.-Germain, L'Hôpital thus continued along the road leading to the innovation of placing the "loi" and the "roi" before the "foi." It was an innovation within the context of the religious mentality of the sixteenth century. It was not a sudden adjustment in his attitudes but a logical evolution of his political outlook.

L'Hôpital justified the policy of toleration from every conceivable point of view, such as religious and social necessity, political expediency, and moral and religious principles. L'Hôpital repeatedly questioned the feasibility of persecution. Protestants were so many and so widely spread throughout the kingdom that it was impossible to exterminate them.[178] They kept strong order and discipline amongst themselves, and the chancellor even admitted that "it is remarkable that they infiltrate the remotest provinces and are still well united."[179] Equally serious, L'Hôpital pointed out, was the fact that many Protestants were noblemen in the service of the king and upon whom royal authority relied. If these nobles were not appeased, they would agitate and challenge the young king. Furthermore, the ruin of the Protestant party would only result in the ruin of France. This warning, uttered more than a century before the revocation of the Edict of Nantes, predicted the deadly impact resulting from the massive emigration of the Huguenots. Their total banishment would result in the "impoverishment of the domain and especially the removal of men of talent, who would be otherwise of great service to the republic."[180] In language anticipatory of Montesquieu in the eighteenth century, L'Hôpital defended tolerance on the grounds that religion could be a promoter of social order. It was not wise for a prince to ban religion, maintained L'Hôpital, because people who were not regulated by religious principles would simply turn to atheism and rise in rebellion.[181] Protestants still obeyed the king, emphasized L'Hôpital, so it was only necessary to encourage their loyalty to the king. If one continued to pressure them, they would inevitably be alienated from the king and rebel against him, as amply shown in the cases of England, Scotland, and the Swiss cantons.[182] For L'Hôpital, to grant Protestants legal rights to worship was to impose upon them the responsibility of conforming to the king's law, thus effectively converting them into loyal citizens.[183]

The humanist call for toleration effected a perfect harmony in L'Hôpital with his pragmatic concern for the public good. L'Hôpital was an inde-

---

[178]*Oeuvres complètes*, 1:474.
[179]*Oeuvres complètes*, 1:474.    [180]*Oeuvres complètes*, 1:476.
[181]*Oeuvres complètes*, 1:477.    [182]*Oeuvres complètes*, 1:477–78.
[183]Hunt, "Religion and Law: The Chancellorship of Michel de L'Hospital," 118–19.

fatigable defender of the French monarchy. It was, indeed, his profound belief in absolutist power of the crown that served as the combining force between his Christian humanism and political pragmatism. In the midst of religious strife, Chancellor L'Hôpital concluded that only unchallenged royal power could negate the seemingly unbridgeable differences between the two religious parties, covering them with the common name of Frenchmen. Protestants did not cease to be the subjects of the king; they were, in his view, entitled to the same rights as Catholics to royal justice, and subject to the same duties to the prince and the kingdom.

Myriam Yardeni has portrayed L'Hôpital as a representative of the sixteenth-century protonationalism.[184] L'Hôpital's cause of toleration was intimately related to the cause of *raison d'Etat*, and was fundamentally based on patriotism. According to Yardeni, L'Hôpital proposed tolerance in the name of the community of the French people, not just Christians, and in particular in the name of their state and their country, France. In this new mentality, toleration became essentially a question upon which the "well-being of the republic" was dependent. Yardeni has thus concluded that L'Hôpital's "tolérance patriotique" foreshadowed the debut of a clear and distinct national conscience.[185]

L'Hôpital's pursuit of peaceful coexistence of Catholics and Protestants in the kingdom, a goal which he tried to achieve by his appeal to patriotism and national interest, had little chance to succeed during his chancellorship. In order to apply the ideal of civil tolerance, the monarchy needed a government headed by a strong king and supported by a powerful moderate party, both of which were lacking in the 1560s. As the twentieth-century historian J.-H. Mariéjol aptly pointed out, "in order to force the intolerant—practically everyone—to become tolerant, it was necessary to devise a government, absolute both in fact and by right."[186] In the nineteenth century, Augustin Thierry called Henry IV "L'Hôpital armé."[187] According to Thierry, Henry IV, with the support from the politiques, accomplished by force what L'Hôpital had attempted by his perennial appeal to reason. Thierry apparently overlooked, however, the fact that Henry IV did not try to separate politics from religion, and that he wished to achieve peace by the Edict of Nantes only until France could be

---

[184]Myriam Yardeni, *La Conscience nationale en France pendant les guerres de religion (1559–1598)* (Paris: Béatrice-Nauwelaerts, 1971), 77–84.

[185]Yardeni, *La Conscience nationale*, 79, 81.

[186]Mariéjol, *Catherine de Médicis*, 93.

[187]Augustin Thierry, *Essai sur l'histoire de la formation et des progrès du tiers état* (Paris, 1868), 152: "Henry IV, c'est l'Hôpital armé; sa victoire fut, après trente-quatre ans d'hésitation publique, de tentatives prématurées et de violents retours en arrière, celle des principes de l'immortel chancelier de Charles IX."

reunited under one faith. On the other hand, L'Hôpital favored coexistence of Catholics and Protestants as long as it maintained the unity of the kingdom under one law and one king.

L'Hôpital was not a naive idealist who failed to perceive the depth of the abyss which separated Catholics and Protestants. Nor was he an indifferent theorizer who was unmindful of the political culture of sixteenth-century Catholic France. The key to understanding L'Hôpital's religious policy therefore seems to lie in the fact that his cause of toleration, born out of the sound and sane judgment of the current situations, could not yet be sympathetically received in the sixteenth century. As Yardeni argued, the principle of toleration which L'Hôpital painstakingly advocated was an ideal pushed to its limit by a person of the sixteenth century.[188] What he pursued was contrary to the basic assumptions of the age and hence could not be accepted. After all, L'Hôpital's ideas were too far ahead of his time. This was precisely the chancellor's misfortune.

[188]Yardeni, *La Conscience nationale*, 84.

# Chapter 4

# The Chancellor's Mass

CARDINAL RICHELIEU, the first minister of Louis XIII in the seventeenth century, carried through his policy of supporting the German Protestants against the Catholic Habsburgs by using his religious credentials to negate the religious element in France's foreign relations. L'Hôpital was less fortunate. When his policy to grant limited toleration to Protestants exposed him to charges of being a "Huguenot," L'Hôpital lacked any warrant of religious orthodoxy, such as Richelieu's red hat, to preempt his adversaries' indictment. L'Hôpital's allegedly dubious religious stance was a constant theme of attacks directed against him during his chancellorship. L'Hôpital's contemporary, the abbé de Brantôme, affirmed that L'Hôpital's Catholic adversaries at court were muttering "Dieu nous garde de la messe du chancelier," accusing him of attending mass only for expediency's sake.[1] The "chancellor's mass" was one of the three so-called wonders of the time, along with the "constable's beads" and the "cardinal of Châtillon's cap." Parisians complained that Chancellor L'Hôpital heard daily mass but was the chief Huguenot in France, that Constable Montmorency was ever mumbling upon his rosary but his head was always occupied with other affairs, and that Châtillon wore a cardinal's hat but defied the pope.[2] The "chancellor's mass" referred to the Catholic service that some adherents of the Reformed churches continued to attend in order to avoid being declared heretics. The phrase was widely circulated and it became in particular a catch phrase in Spain and Rome for those seeking to oust Chancellor L'Hôpital and other French officials who

[1]Pierre de Bourdeille, abbé de Brantôme, *Oeuvres complètes*, ed. L. Lalanne, 11 vols. (Paris, 1864–82), 3:315.
[2]Throckmorton to Elizabeth, December 29, 1563, *CSP Foreign*, 6:645–46.

appeared to compromise Catholic interests.[3] Afraid of the prospect that France might follow Germany's fate, ultra-Catholic leaders specifically focused on L'Hôpital, who was most outspoken in asserting French autonomy in church matters, on the grounds of his supposedly unorthodox belief. Suspicions harbored by L'Hôpital's ultramontane opponents about his religious stance were thus combined with their misgivings about the chancellor's strong assertion of Gallican liberties to engender tenacious hostilities toward him and his policies.

Throughout his chancellorship, L'Hôpital was cordially hated by the Spanish court and Rome, both of which made consistent efforts to diminish his influence at court and have him driven from office. Their attacks against L'Hôpital became particularly vehement after he proposed the toleration edict of January 1562. The "chancellor's mass" provided his adversaries a convenient foil. In March, the Spanish ambassador Chantonnay, in a letter to Philip II, prayed "may the Lord deliver us from the evil chancellor's dissimulation." Chantonnay was optimistic that once the Parlement of Paris completed its investigation into L'Hôpital's dubious religious belief, he would be shipped off or at least deprived of office.[4] The papal nuncio Santa Croce reported that secret conventicles were being held at the chancellor's residence, attended by the prince of Condé, the cardinal of Châtillon, and Jean de Monluc (the bishop of Valence).[5] Santa Croce wrote that suspicion over the chancellor's belief became so serious that there was talk of removing the royal seals from his hands and appointing a garde des sceaux.[6] A month later, Santa Croce complained that L'Hôpital was still in power, but affirmed that the chancellor's opponents were making every effort to disgrace him.[7]

Pope Pius IV also played an important role in this international campaign to secure L'Hôpital's dismissal. In June 1562, the pope offered Catherine de Médicis a subsidy of 200,000 ducats on the condition, among

---

[3]Antoine Varillas, *Histoire de l'Hérésie de Viclef, Iean Hvs, et Jérome de Prague* (Lyon, 1682), 170; Remy, *Eloge de Michel de L'Hôpital*, 64, n.; Pierre Champion, *Catherine de Médicis présente à Charles IX son royaume (1564–1566)* (Paris: B. Grassett, 1937), 29; Paul Van Dyke, *Catherine de Médicis*, 2 vols. (New York: Charles Scribner's Son, 1927), 2:8–9.

[4]Chantonnay to Philip II, March 25, 1562, *Archivo documental Español, Francia, 1559–1566 (Archivo general de Simancas)* (Madrid: Real Academia de Historia, 1950–1954), 3:435.

[5]Santa Croce to Borromeo, March 15, 1562, *Archives curieuses*, 6:50–52. Santa Croce reported again on March 25, *Archives curieuses*, 6:54, that a congregation was meeting at the chancellor's residence "tous les jours," which the queen of Navarre attended.

[6]Santa Croce commented that nothing would be better at that time than to replace L'Hôpital with Christophe de Thou, the president of the Parlement of Paris, "who is a very good Catholic"; Santa Croce to Borromeo, March 15, 1562, *Archives curieuses*, 6:551–52 and March 19, 1562, ibid., 58.

[7]Santa Croce to Borromeo, April 29, 1562, *Archives curieuses*, 6:94.

others, that the chancellor be sent home. This offer did not please the queen mother, who defended her chancellor and protested against the pope's intervention in French internal matters. When some people told Catherine about the bad reputation of the chancellor's faith, she "laughed" and said that "the chancellor was the best man in the world." Ignoring Catherine's complaints, Pius IV repeated his request in July that she dismiss the chancellor.[8] The pope even threatened to summon L'Hôpital to the court in Rome to answer for his heretical belief. This atmosphere kept the French ambassador in Rome busy defending the chancellor.[9]

Yet the pope's own legate, Hippolito d'Este, cardinal of Ferrara, refuted the suspicion about the chancellor's belief as "doubtless very ill-founded." The cardinal wrote to the pope that the chancellor was "regularly seen at mass, at confession, and at communion," and tried to dissuade Pius IV from seeking L'Hôpital's disgrace.[10] Chantonnay's successor, Francès de Alava, grumbled that L'Hôpital had his grandson baptized as Huguenot and then two days later had publicly taken communion, made confession, and heard mass with great devotion.[11]

Catholic accusations that L'Hôpital was hiding his Calvinist belief were eagerly welcomed by Protestants. Protestants, in the hope of enlisting the chancellor in their cause, fueled their opponents' misgivings. But they too were unable to provide any credible proof for the claim that L'Hôpital was a confirmed Calvinist. They asserted, at best, that the chancellor must have held secret sympathies for the Reformed churches because, it was believed, his wife and only daughter were Protestant converts. A century later, Pierre Bayle attempted to prove L'Hôpital's Protestant belief by pointing out that there was no single mention of mass,

---

[8]Chantonnay to Philip II, June 30, 1562, *Archivo documental Español*, 4:159; Chantonnay to Philip II, July 13, 1562, *Archivo documental Español*, 3:184; Chantonnay to Philip II, March 20, 1562, *Archivo documental Español*, 3:418.

[9]See chap. 3, n. 113, above.

[10]Hippolito d'Este, cardinal of Ferrara, to Pius IV, June 14, 1562, in *Négociations, ou lettres d'affaires ecclésiastiques, et politiques: Escrites au pape Pie IV ... par Hyppolite d'Est, cardinal de Ferrare, légat en France au commencement des guerres civiles*, tr. J. Baudoin (Paris 1658), 224–25. The cardinal wrote: "It is not one of the easiest things to alienate from court the chancellor and others as you desire.... If one chased away all those suspects, the court would be no doubt deserted. The new opinions have made such deep impression on the spirit of the courtiers that there are few who have not been, at least a little, tainted ..."; about the chancellor: "One cannot but be convinced that he is Catholic." According to Noël Valois, "Les Essais de conciliation religieuse au début du règne de Charles IX,"*Revue d'Histoire de l'Eglise de France* 31 (1945), 263, Pius IV did not have much trust in the optimistic despatches of the cardinal of Ferrara.

[11]Alava to Philip II, February 4, 1565, *Archivo documental Español*, 7: 121. Alava added: "from this, your Majesty can see how things are going here."

purgatory, or priest in his testament.[12] L'Hôpital wrote in his testament that "as to my funeral, burial, and other things of that sort, which seem silly to Christians, I leave the matter to my wife and my servants."[13] This scandalous statement that Christians do not hold funerals in great respect revealed, argued Bayle, that L'Hôpital's view on funerals was closer to that of Protestants and thus supported his supposed Calvinism.[14] But the absence of a profession of Catholic faith in his will or his entrusting the details of the last rites to his family's care hardly provides anything more than circumstantial evidence.[15]

L'Hôpital's adversaries were not deterred by the fact that the chancellor never publicly professed any religion other than the Catholic faith, and that in fact he vehemently refuted suspicion about his belief. Catholics saw in L'Hôpital simply a thick layer of hypocrisy. Protestants, on the other hand, justified L'Hôpital's foregoing formal conversion on the grounds that he would have lost opportunity to serve the Protestant interest had he revealed his Calvinist belief. According to Bayle, L'Hôpital "was swimming between two waves," in order to remedy the unfortunate situation of France.[16] Bayle repeated in so many words the opinion of Theodore Beza, who deplored the chancellor's having "waited too long to extricate himself from the mud—from which he wanted everyone to get out—because he feared, by taking sides with those of the religion, of being deprived of the means to aid them, and held to the vain hope that the situation would get better." But "when he wanted to drag his feet out of the mud," said Beza regretfully, "it was no longer possible."[17] Calvin stated

---

[12]Bayle, *Dictionnaire historique et critique*, 2:807.

[13]"Funus, sepulturam meam, et caetera ejusmodi quae christianis videntur inania, permitto uxori domesticisque meis... "; Testament, *Oeuvres complètes*, 2:514.

[14]For the refutation of this argument, see P.D.L., *Quelques éclaircissements*, 62–76.

[15]Alain Molinier, "Aux origines de la Réformation cévenole," *Annales: économies, sociétés, civilisations* 39 (1984), 248, argues that testamentary clauses in the sixteenth century that entrusted funerals to "the wishes and discretion" of an heir and opted for rites without pomposity and without a priest indicate that their writer held the Protestant belief. In the case of L'Hôpital, however, his refutation of suspicion about his belief, as evidenced in a letter to the pope below, compels us to take him at his word, i.e., that he was a Catholic. Michel Vovelle, *Piété baroque et déchristianisation en Provence au XVIIIe siècle: Les attitudes devant la mort d'après les clauses des testaments* (Paris: Librairie Plon, 1973), 59, shows that the complete absence of pious formulas in wills was not unknown at the beginning of the eighteenth century, and argues that failure to invoke the saints has no implication about the religious opinion of the deceased.

[16]Bayle, *Dictionnaire historique et critique*, 2:804; ibid. 807: L'Hôpital "nag[eait] entre deux eaux," and "vainly" awaited "the time to get off his dissimulation," to Bayle's regret, which never came.

[17]Theodore de Beza, *Les vrais portraits des hommes illustres en piété et en doctrine ...* (Geneva, 1581; Geneva: Slatkine Reprints, 1986), 143. Beza also stated that L'Hôpital "held the torch to enlighten others but not himself"; quoted in Bayle, *Dictionnaire historique et critique*, 2:807.

that the chancellor, in drawing up toleration edicts, "looked very liberal from our perspective, because deep in his heart he favors us. But the hidden artifices of the queen dodged all the good resolutions made in council."[18] The "chancellor's dissimulation" thesis seemed to be almost unanimously accepted by the Protestant party and by many Catholics; they disagreed only on whether his alleged dissemblance was evil or benign.

L'Hôpital wrote to Pius IV in August 1562 to protest his Catholic faith: "I know all the false accusations against me which my enemies spread throughout Rome, Italy, and Spain."[19] In this letter, he defends himself with such determination that it appears less an apology for himself than a reproach of the pope for having suspected his orthodox faith. L'Hôpital would not have been concerned had the pope merely listened to the calumny against his belief, but "as soon as I learned that you wrote to the queen mother advising her not to listen to my advice and to treat me like a plague, I decided I could no longer defer vindicating myself to you." For L'Hôpital, France's judgment of his actions was more important than the pope's. He would never disclaim his conduct and principles, because he had exerted all his efforts, as "our entire France" witnessed, "to repel the invasion of new doctrines and destroy old abuses." L'Hôpital continued: "The fomenters of disorders cannot put up with me, nor I with them. I would do better, perhaps, to accommodate myself to the circumstances, as so many others who, better advised, made for themselves a republic to satisfy their tastes; but such is my character, such are my manner of being and my nature. And age has made me still more uncompromising and more difficult." L'Hôpital declared that between his accusers and him "it is an eternal war; such is my destiny."

This letter bears witness to L'Hôpital's ample resolution to serve the king and the kingdom before anything else. Indeed Rome's hostility to the chancellor resulted in part from his assertion of complete independence of the crown in affairs of state. L'Hôpital echoed the long-standing tenets of Gallicanism, in particular royal Gallicanism, which was strongly upheld in the sixteenth century by such jurists as Charles Du Moulin. Since the Pragmatic Sanction of Bourges of 1438 redefined the relationship between the crown, the church, and the papacy, Gallican traditions protected the

[18]*Joannis Calvini opera quae supersunt omnia*, vol. 20, col. 133, no. 4007.

[19]L'Hôpital to Pius IV, August 3, 1562, in Dupuy, ed., *Instructions et lettres*, 274–75 ("Sanctiff. D. Domino Nostro Pio IV. Pontif Max"); *Oeuvres complètes*, 2:474–79 (original in Latin and French translation). L'Hôpital had complained to the papal nuncio about the pope's suspicion about his religion, saying all he wanted was to make sure that one lived in the Christian way and to implement a good reform. Santa Croce to Borromeo, June 20, 1562, *Archives curieuses*, 6:106, reports that all this did not seem to the chancellor to be a subject for which His Holiness should have bad opinion about him.

independence of the French crown from Rome but that of the French church as well. Throughout the sixteenth century, however, "ecclesiastical Gallicanism," which granted liberties to French bishops, was gradually overridden by "political" or "royal" Gallicanism, which gave the crown complete authority in clerical administration. The 1516 Concordat of Bologna, in which Francis I and Leo X divided the liberties of the Gallican church between them, marked the height of royal Gallicanism.[20] In the 1550s, Du Moulin renewed the force of royal Gallicanism by emphasizing the prerogatives of the crown at the expense of the papacy. It is possible to presume that Du Moulin's role in the great 1551 crisis with Rome influenced L'Hôpital. In May 1552, Du Moulin found himself charged with heresy by the Sorbonne, after he published a tract attacking the Church of Rome.[21] Among his judges at the Parlement of Paris was L'Hôpital. It is unclear how L'Hôpital would have judged the case because, before his final hearing, the defendant fled to Switzerland.[22] At any rate, L'Hôpital was certainly in line with Du Moulin when he declared at Orléans in 1560 that the king held his authority from God.[23] The immediate implication of this theory of the direct divine authorization of kingship was that the crown, not the pope, held control over all matters pertaining to the organization and discipline of the clergy in France.

From the beginning of his chancellorship, L'Hôpital made consistent efforts to diminish papal authority in church affairs in France. He endeavored to resolve the problems of the French church—which he regarded as the main cause of the current religious troubles—on the national level following its own lines, free from any papal intervention. The Ordinance of Orléans, drawn up by L'Hôpital on the basis of the cahiers of the Estates General in early 1561, was a clear reflection of royal Gallicanism prevalent in the kingdom. It also illustrates how L'Hôpital's independent reform program of ecclesiastical institutions conflicted with the interests of the papacy. The first twenty-nine lines of the ordinance are articles devoted to

[20]Nancy Lyman Roelker, *Queen of Navarre, Jeanne d'Albret, 1528–1572* (Cambridge, Mass.: Harvard University Press, 1968), 121, n. Concerning Gallicanism, consult Victor Martin, *Les origines du gallicanism* (Paris: Bloud & Gay, 1939); Jules Thomas, *Le Concordat de 1516, ses origines, son histoire au XVIe siècle*, 3 vols. (Paris: A. Picard, 1910).

[21]*Commentaire sur l'édit contre les petites dates*, published in 1551. Du Moulin wrote in this tract: "The Pope, the papists, and the Sorbonnists resemble no one so much as that false prophet and antichrist of the East, Mahomet"; cited in Kelley, *Hotman*, 63. Concerning Du Moulin, see the biography by Jean-Louis Thireau, *Charles Du Moulin, 1500–1566* (Geneva: Librairie Droz, 1980).

[22]Donald R. Kelley, "Fides Historiae: Charles Dumoulin and the Gallican View of History," *Traditio* 22 (1966): 399–402.

[23]December 13, 1560, *Discours pour la majorité de Charles IX*, 79; *Oeuvres complètes*, 2:389.

church reforms.[24] Article 1 reestablished the election system of archbishops and bishops, which had been abolished by the Concordat of Bologna in 1516. Electoral commissions would present three candidates to the king, who was to make his choice among them. The ordinance preserved the right of the pope to approve the royal nomination, as prescribed by the concordat. The alteration of the system of episcopal appointment without any consultation with Rome did not please the pope.[25] The more manifest challenge to the papacy was the provision in article 2 that suspended annates entirely. The prohibition of any outflow of money to the Holy See "in the form of annate" was the result of L'Hôpital's effort to reflect the wishes of the estates and stop the draining of the kingdom's resources. This drastic measure was also taken without any consultation with or notice to the pope. The government later sent the president of the Parlement of Paris, Arnauld du Ferrier, to Rome to negotiate the issue, but the parties failed to reach an agreement.[26] Although Charles IX rescinded, within less than a year and at the request of the pope, the prohibition on the annates, the initial action of the government was strikingly audacious. The Venetian ambassador Suriano predicted that the French delegate to the pope would more likely "merely state the causes that moved this government thus to decide," than "ask this as a favor from the pope."[27]

Chantonnay reported on a dispute between the chancellor and the cardinal of Tournon at the Conseil Privé, a few weeks after the conclusion of the Estates General. The cardinal defended papal authority as prescribed in the concordat, whereas the chancellor argued that the pope should not intervene in the church matters of France. The argument became so fierce, reported Chantonnay, that the chancellor accused the cardinal of being too stubborn, to which Tournon replied that he preferred being stubborn to being capricious. When the cardinal criticized L'Hôpital's opposition to the proposed Council of Trent, saying that the chancellor did not understand matters concerning the church council, L'Hôpital retorted that he understood those things better than the cardinal because he had studied and actually attended the council held in Bologna, which

[24]Isambert, *Recueil général*, 14:63–72.
[25]Suriano to the Doge and the Senate, February 17, 1561, *CSP Venice*, 296.
[26]Maugis, *Parlement de Paris*, 1:603; Georges Picot, *Histoire des Etats Généraux*, 2d ed. (Paris: Hachette, 1888), 2:232, n. 1.
[27]Suriano to the Doge, February 17, 1561, *CSP Venice*, 296. Other articles concerning reform of church: in order to maintain the quality of pastoral work, prebend by cathedral chapter was to be limited to a doctor in theology who would teach the Bible three times a week and preach on Sundays and holidays; another prebend would reward a tutor in charge of teaching the children of the town; the minimum lawful age for ordination of priests was set at twenty-five years, and the minimum lawful age for a nun's taking final vows at twenty years.

the cardinal had never done.[28] Rome also had reason to have qualms about the stipulation forbidding clerical absenteeism (article 5). This was a reiteration of the lettres patentes of July 25, 1560, which had commanded all members of the church hierarchy, with the exception of royal councillors and those employed in the diplomatic service, to return to their dioceses by September, on the pain of the confiscation of their temporalities.[29] The threat was not an idle one. Some Italian bishops who were refused permission to leave Rome by the pope, on the grounds that they would soon be required to go to Trent, had their revenues confiscated by the French government.[30]

Almost every provision of the ordinance prescribed, for disciplinary sanctions, the seizure of ecclesiastical revenues. This attests to the fgovernment's acting on the basic assumption that royal power had the right to confiscate ecclesiastical temporalities when clergy violated royal edicts.[31] In February 1561, Suriano remarked that those in the government "tended to diminish the authority of the pope, and it would be the end of all things if hands were put upon church property, as many desired."[32] His forebodings were not ill-grounded. The government, facing the threat of imminent bankruptcy, gave serious consideration to dipping into the church's purse. L'Hôpital had revealed at the Estates General of Orléans that the government deficit amounted to 43 million livres, four times the annual revenue.[33] Describing the desperate situation of royal finance, which he "could not tell the estates, and to which the estates could not listen, without tears and cries," L'Hôpital compared the king to a little orphan, to whom his parents had left a terrible legacy of debts.[34] Pleading with the estates to rescue their sovereign, who was "engagé, endebté, empesché," the chancellor proposed the increase of the taille for six years, and redemption by the clergy of the alienated domains as well as the taille and gabelle.[35] While the secular estates balked at making any financial

[28]Chantonnay to Philip II, February 24, 1561, *Archivo documental Español*, 2:76.

[29]"Lettres patentes du Roy à tous archevesques et évesques et autres prélats ecclésiastiques de résider en la principale ville de leur diocèse," *Actes Royaux*, BN, *Imprimé*, F. 46819 (30).

[30]Evennett, *Cardinal of Lorraine*, 128.

[31]Picot, *Histoire des Etats Généraux*, 2:236–37.

[32]Suriano to the Doge, February 17, 1561, *CSP Venice*, 296.

[33]The chancellor officially confirmed the amount in his address on December 13, 1560.

[34]*Discours pour la majorité de Charles IX*, 89; *Oeuvres complètes*, 1:406.

[35]The chancellor called for an increase in royal taxes on salt, heavier tailles, and higher rates on wine. In return, he promised not to impose another raise in taxes for six years; Cloulas, *Catherine de Médicis*, 157; J. Russell Major, *The Estates General of 1560* (Princeton, N.J.: Princeton University Press, 1561), 103–4; idem, *Representative Government in Early Modern France* (New Haven: Yale University Press, 1980), 106–107, 161–62, also points out that the chancellor, in return for these demands, offered to allow the Estates to oversee the collection of the taxes. If his proposal had been accepted, Major argues, the Estates General, since their

concessions themselves, they were eager to attack the fortune of the church. When the estates met again at Pontoise in August 1561, the deputies of the second and third estates displayed aggressive anticlericalism.[36] They specifically proposed confiscation of church property by the crown to pay royal debts.[37] One bold plan even called for an annual income tax to be imposed on each benefice on a graduated scale: a tax of 20 percent on benefices with a gross income under 500 livres annually, and up to 75 percent for those worth about 12,000 livres annually.[38]

Thoroughly alarmed by these drastic proposals by the lay estates, and aware that the chancellor was determined to wring financial contribution from the ecclesiastics, the clergy offered to make an extraordinary sacrifice. They conceded to pay for six years 1,600,000 livres for the redemption of the royal domains as well as aides and gabelle alienated by the crown. The clergy also agreed that during the following ten years they would amortize the rentes constituted by the king on the Hôtel de Ville de Paris for a capital of 7,650,000 livres.[39] Known as the "Contrat de Poissy," this agreement between the king and the clergy, concluded on October 21, 1561, established a new principle of the annual subsidy of the clergy. The church itself imposed dues on the benefice holders and collected it through the network of diocesan and provincial collectors, which was more efficient than the tax collection system of the monarchy.[40] The church was allowed, in return, to handle its own payments to the treasury with-

---

right to participate in the tax collection was conceded by the crown, would almost certainly have been reborn.

[36]Noël Valois, "Les Etats de Pontoise," *Revue d'histoire de l'église de France* 29 (1943), 237–56.

[37]Its sale was expected to bring at least 120 million livres: 42 million to reimburse royal creditors; 48 million, with interest at 8.33 percent (denier douze) to assure the clergy an annual revenue of 4 million, the amount that the church claimed to gather each year from its property; the remaining 30 million would be available for loan to individuals to promote commerce and trade. The king would collect from it an annual revenue of 500,000 livres, which would be used for fortification of frontier towns and maintenance of the troops; they justified this measure by arguing that church revenue was national property, and since it derived from foundations once established by the consent of the people, it could be appropriated for the needs of the realm; see Cloulas, *Catherine de Médicis*, 163.

[38]Wolfe, *Fiscal System of Renaissance France*, 42.

[39]Ibid., 121–23.

[40]Claude Michaud, "Finances et guerres de religion en France," *Bulletin de la Société d'Histoire Moderne* 2 (1979): 4; Frederic J. Baumgartner, *Change and Continuity in the French Episcopate: The Bishops and the Wars of Religion, 1547–1610* (Durham: Duke University Press, 1986), 74–75. For the clause of the Contrat de Poissy, see Louis Serbat, *Les Assemblées du clergé de France, origines, organisation, développement 1561–1615* (Paris: Champion, 1906), 36–37.

out interference from royal officials, preserving the fiction of "free gifts."[41] The Contrat de Poissy was the result of L'Hôpital's fiscal skill, which caused even the papal nuncio to acknowledge that in financial matters the chancellor was "the most skillful minister that has ever been in this kingdom."[42] Under L'Hôpital, the government successfully induced the first estate of the kingdom to contribute to the public expenses.

Pius IV expressed his strong displeasure at these outright attacks on such papal revenues as the annates and the temporalities of the church. Above all, these measures contributed to augmenting the pope's dislike of L'Hôpital, who had already been accruing Rome's resentment for his tolerant attitudes towards Protestants. The pope reportedly considered France "lost and abandoned," and blamed the "unorthodox" chancellor.[43] When the papal nuncio delivered the pope's complaint about the prohibition of the annates, L'Hôpital replied that the measure was necessary in order to satisfy people, and that French people "wished to show their confidence in His Holiness, convinced that [the pope], in his goodness, would not regard with disfavor this small reduction in his revenues."[44] Notified of the Contrat de Poissy, Rome had no choice but to insist belatedly that church property be used only for the suppression of heresy, a demand which was not taken very seriously by the government.[45] The pope's reaction to these visible signs of defiance to his authority was to send the cardinal of Ferrara as legate to France in September, on a mission to contain as much as possible the impact of growing Gallican sentiment. When the royal council decided to award this visiting cardinal the "faculties," privileges reserved to the papal envoys, L'Hôpital refused to affix the royal seal

---

[41]This measure reserved to the clergy the right to determine the form of its subsidy to the king; see Doucet, 2:838. More importantly, the clergy were to hold regular meetings (a practice that continued until the Revolution). Major, *Representative Government,* 57, 106–7, argues that whereas the regular clergy made it an integral part of the government, fulfilling a significant administrative function, the secular orders, by refusing to make financial concessions to the crown, failed to obtain similar privileges. L'Hôpital was willing to let the secular estates at the Estates of Pontoise decide the best means by which to raise money and supervise the collection, if they agreed to pay. The government, in short, was anxious to rule in conjunction with the estates in return for additional revenue. Without their cooperation, the crown imposed on them a wine tax anyway in September 1561.

[42]Quoted in Van Dyke, *Catherine de Médicis,* 2:8.

[43]Nugent, *Colloquy of Poissy,* 62.

[44]Suriano to the Doge, September 11, 1561, *Despatches of Suriano,* 43.

[45]Some historians argue that the duc de Guise and Montmorency tried to raise funds from the church, not so much to pay off the king's debts but to finance an army to be used under their leadership to exterminate the Huguenots; see, e.g., James Westfall Thompson, *The Wars of Religion in France, 1559–1576* (Chicago: University of Chicago Press, 1909), 98–101; Wolfe, *Fiscal System of Renaissance France,* 121–22. But such an assertion misreads the financial crisis of the government and its religious policy in 1561.

to the document. The chancellor argued that this grant of "faculties" to the legate was in contradiction to the Ordinance of Orléans, which deprived the papacy of its right to subsidies and other prerogatives. According to contemporary observers, L'Hôpital protested in the king's council that the grant was not valid because it was opposed to the decrees emanating from the Estates General of the kingdom.[46] L'Hôpital eventually fixed the royal seal at the order of the king, but made his objection explicit by adding under the seal "me non consentiente."[47] L'Hôpital later confirmed to the Parlement of Paris that the grant was awarded against his will.[48]

The Contrat de Poissy soon proved inadequate to satisfy the monarchy's need of funds. The government thus began seriously to consider alienating church property, an idea that the anticlerical forces had consistently suggested since the meeting of the Estates General. Philip II of Spain tried to dissuade Catherine from the project, a move that she protested was an intervention in internal matters.[49] As the French legal historian Marguerite Boulet-Sautel points out, the Contrat de Poissy maintained the form of voluntary accord concluded between the crown and the clergy. Passed as a lettre de juridiction, which had itself an executory force, and not as a royal decision of lettres patentes registered at the Parlement, the contract preserved the form of negotiation between the two parties. The government's discretion—not giving the impression that it forcefully compelled the clergy to pay subsidies—did not last long. By the edict of May 1563, issued at St.-Germain-en-Laye, the king ordered the forced alienation of church property.[50] The scale of alienation was indicated not in the amount of principal but in the value of rentes: The king ordered the sale of church land to create rentes worth 100,000 écus yearly,

[46]Suriano to the Doge, November 3, 1561, *Despatches of Suriano*, 48; *Histoire ecclésiastique*, 1:615–16.

[47]BN, MS Fr. 23110, fol. 101. Concerning this incident, see Bernard Barbiche and Ségolène de Dainville-Barbiche, "Les légats *a latere* en France et leurs facultés aux XVIe et XVIIe siècles," *Archivum Historiae Pontificiae* 23 (1985), 127.

[48]Chantonnay to Philip II, November 4, 1561, *Archivo documental Español*, 3:77. According to the English ambassador Throckmorton to Elizabeth, November 14, 1561, *CSP Foreign*, 4:402, this incident testified that the chancellor was "a sincere minister and a promotor of the true religion."

[49]Catherine to Sébastien de L'Aubespine, bishop of Limoges, August 1, 1561, *Lettres de Catherine de Médicis*, 1:222.

[50]Isambert, *Recueil général*, 14:140. Suriano to the Doge, February 17, 1561, *CSP Venice*, 7: 296, reported hat those at court tended to diminish papal authority, and predicted that "it would be quite at an end were they to lay hands on the church property, as desired by many persons."

at the standard interest of douze deniers, or 8.33 percent.[51] The edict was of extraordinary significance, not only for its material consequences but also for its constitutional implications. It was an express negation of the principle of the inalienability of ecclesiastical patrimony, which the clergy had claimed as indisputable. In order to sell church property legally, the royal act at least needed the preliminary authorization of the pope and of the clergy of France. But the need to meet these preconditions was simply ignored. The government did not bother to seek permission of the papacy before making its decision. L'Hôpital declared that the alienation of church land could be done "through the sole authority of the king." After the issuance of the edict, L'Hôpital simply said, "I do not know how the pope will take it ... but hope that he does not take too much time in responding."[52]

The implementation of the edict encountered serious resistance, not just from the clergy but, more importantly, from the Parlement of Paris. The Parlement, reasserting its role as the guardian of law and the defender of the property rights of individuals against arbitrary royal power, refused to register the edict.[53] At the consequent Lit de Justice on May 17, L'Hôpital spoke for the king to justify the legality of the measure.[54] In a situation where taxes were already heavy and royal domains alienated, maintained the chancellor, the sale of church property was of all possible measures "the most prompt and the least harmful."[55] The king and the royal council had only regretfully reached the decision, convinced that "public necessity is the most strong and dominant consideration," before which all others must yield. L'Hôpital reminded the parlementaires that even royal

---

[51]Claude Michaud, "Les Aliénations du temporel ecclésiastique dans la seconde moitié du XVIe siècle: Quelques problèmes de méthode," *Revue d'histoire de l'église de France* 67 (1981): 62, n. One écu was equivalent to 2 livres 10 sous tournois.

[52]*Oeuvres complètes*, 2:40.

[53]At the king's request for prompt registration of the edict, the Parlement replied that it "could not and ought not to do it"; J. Laferrière, *Le Contrat de Poissy, 1561* (Paris: J.-B. Sirey, 1905), 239.

[54]*Oeuvres complètes*, 2:27–42; also in *Mémoires de Condé*, 3:352–53. About the alienation of church land, see Laferrière, *Contrat de Poissy*, 232–74; Baumgartner, *Change and Continuity*, 76–77.

[55]*Oeuvres complètes*, 2:33. L'Hôpital enumerated specific numbers in order to precisely disclose "the poverty of the king to his loyal councillors, who, I hope, would not tell foreigners." The king had about 50 million livres in debts, of which 5 million were immediately needed to pay troops, in particular to expel the English installed at Havre: 1,660,000 livres were needed for gendarmerie, 353,000 livres for the troops in Picardy and Champagne, 230,000 livres for reîtres of the king, 75,000 livres for the Italian mercenaries, 600,000 livres for the German soldiers, and 1,030,000 livres for the Swiss. The previous year's revenues amounted to 8,460,000 livres and the expenses 18 million livres; thus one year's deficit alone totaled 10 million livres; see ibid., 34–36.

domain, despite *loi fondamentale*, had been sold in times of war. Since the inviolability of royal domains was "more ancient than that of the church," the chancellor reasoned, the sale of church land should not be found so unfeasible.[56] L'Hôpital had earlier declared at Orléans that the ecclesiastics were simple administrators of church property.[57] In times of pressing necessity of the kingdom, therefore, the clergy ought to relinquish its financial privileges. Above all, L'Hôpital tried to convince the Parlement that the edict was not a result of royal caprice but a measure imposed by public necessity, and that it was therefore not a breach of property rights. He argued that the alienation of church land was proposed for the preservation of the church itself, because "it would be unreasonable to think that the church could still survive when the kingdom, of which church exists as a part and a member, was lost and ruined."[58]

L'Hôpital's address at the Parlement was indeed a strikingly precise and powerful exposition of the theory of secular authority over the church. The chancellor did not simply intend to persuade the parlementaires to register the edict. He attempted to have it confirmed that the sovereign had indisputable rights over ecclesiastical property in his state. The king was employing his legitimate rights, inherent in the crown, for the common interest. L'Hôpital asserted that the king could impose taxes on the clergy without the consent of its assembly, because the Gallican church, once assembled, could not possibly have been of opinion different than the king. The chancellor thus maintained that the alienation decided upon the king's own authority was a strictly legitimate measure in accordance with the laws of the kingdom. The Parlement, the traditional defender of Gallican liberties, could not object to the chancellor's brilliant justification of the edict, carefully exposed under the banner of Gallicanism. The law court still upheld the principle of the inalienability of church property, but proclaimed that "seeing the urgent necessity which the kingdom faces ... we can and ought to confirm openly that all law and constitution are subject to limitations for the safety of the people and the republic."[59] The Parlement expressed, it is important to note, its concerns about the measure's having neither the consent of the pope nor that of the clergy, but declared that the tribunal "believed it sufficient that alienation can be pronounced by the authority of the king." By invoking royal sovereignty and by appealing to preponderant Gallican sentiment, L'Hôpital

---

[56]*Oeuvres complètes*, 2:39.

[57]Ivan Cloulas, "Les Aliénations du temporel ecclésiastique ordonnées par les rois Charles IX et Henri III de 1563 à 1588," *Positions des thèses de l'Ecole Nationale des Chartes* (1957): 37.

[58]*Oeuvres complètes*, 2:41.

[59]Laferrière, *Contrat de Poissy*, 245–46.

thus succeeded in bringing the obdurate parlementaires into an alliance with the king against the papacy. Confronted with this concerted affirmation of royal prerogatives and Gallican liberties, the pope found himself deprived of any other choice but to confirm solemnly the measure in October 1564, solacing himself by pretending that the alienation acquired juridical effect only after the ratification by the papacy.[60] Charles IX's instruction to his ambassadors at the Council of Trent in September 1562 strictly enjoined them to oppose any measures that would compromise the king's rights to make the ecclesiastics contribute to the needs of the kingdom.[61] When the council affirmed in August 1563 the sacrosanct principle of the fiscal immunity of the clergy and prohibited any imposition of taxes on ecclesiastics, Charles IX sent orders to his delegates to protest against the measure, which "would trim the nails of the kings and extend those of the pope in a way that I do not know how to endure."[62] The French ambassadors duly left the floor in protest.

L'Hôpital had consistently expressed his skepticism about the Council of Trent. The French government's reception of the papal bull of November 1560 to reconvene the general council had been far from enthusiastic. France was opposed to the resumption of the Council at Trent, because the continuation of the two earlier councils would destroy the hard-won settlement with the Huguenot faction.[63] The Spanish ambassador and the papal nuncios testified that the envisaged council had no more bitter enemy in France than the chancellor. Chantonnay wrote to Philip II in April 1561 that L'Hôpital scoffed at the council saying that it would be superfluous without the participation of Protestants.[64] L'Hôpital asked, according to Chantonnay, "for what purpose we should send delegates to the council," where "this kingdom runs risk of being declared heretic, from which would follow a number of inconveniences?"[65] The chancellor's skepticism about the council was confirmed by the papal

[60]Laferrière, *Contrat de Poissy,* 271.

[61]"Mémoire envoyé par le Roy à ses ambassadeurs au Concile à Trente," September 6, 1562, in Dupuy, *Instructions et lettres,* 284–88; Laferrière, *Contrat de Poissy,* 271.

[62]Laferrière, *Contrat de Poissy,* 272.

[63]As early as March 1560, Francis II had made known his project to assemble within a six-month period a council of all the bishops of the kingdom to formulate a plan of religious reform; Claude Devic and Joseph Vaissète, *Histoire générale de Languedoc,* 15 vols. (Toulouse: E. Privat, 1872–92), 12:566; Alfonso Tornabuoni to Cosimo I, March 25, 1560, *Négociations avec la Toscane,* 3:411–12. The cardinal of Lorraine to Pope Pius IV, March 22, 1560, printed in Evennett, *Cardinal of Lorraine,* appendix 1:471–72.

[64]Chantonnay to Philip II, April 11, 1561, *Archivo documental Español,* 2:166; January 8, 1562, 3:256.

[65]Chantonnay to Philip II, January 8, 1562, *Archivo documental Español,* 3:256.

nuncio Gualterio.[66] Santa Croce reported that L'Hôpital told him that "all the problems in this kingdom come from the French themselves and are caused by the corrupt lives of the ecclesiastics," and that the problems needed to be tackled by national solutions and not by those at the Council of Trent.[67] The council would be dominated, the chancellor asserted, by "men who are mostly foreigners, ignorant of our affairs."[68]

The French ambassadors, arriving at Trent in June 1562, betrayed as much enthusiasm for the council as the chancellor. One of the French delegates, Guy du Faur, seigneur de Pibrac, wrote to L'Hôpital: "If you ask me what is going on here, I can answer in a word: rien...."[69] L'Hôpital himself wrote in October to the cardinal of Lorraine, who was then about to leave for Trent, and urged him not to waste time at the council unless "the pope is well disposed, unlike his predecessors, and willing to listen to foreign princes." "If you see everything is false and a lie, if it is impossible to reach the expected results," wrote L'Hôpital, "come back immediately and do not await the end of the conference."[70] The French ambassadors were strictly instructed to assert the traditional rights of Gallican church.[71] L'Hôpital drew up thirty-four articles of remonstrance to be submitted to the council.[72] Among the articles detailing reforms of the clergy, L'Hôpital stressed in particular issues safeguarding Gallican liberties and limiting pontifical influence. Article 17 specified that prayers in the mass should be said in the vernacular; article 18 demanded communion under both kinds; article 19 demanded that sacraments be explained in the vulgar language before their administration; and article 22 prescribed that resignations of

---

[66]Gualterio to Cipriano, September 8, 1561, *Acta Nuntiaturae Gallicae, Correspondance des nonces en France: Lenzi et Gualterio, légation du Cardinal Tribultio (1557–1561)*, vol. 14, ed. J. Lestocquoy (Rome: Université Pontificale Grégorienne, 1977), 377; *Die Römische curie und das Concil von Trient unter Pius IV: Actenstücke zur geschichte des Concils von Trient*, ed. Josef Susta, 4 vols. (Vienna: A. Hölder, 1904–1914), 1:253–54. Also Gualterio to Borromeo, April 15, 1561, *Acta Nuntiaturae Gallicae*, 14:336; *Die Romische curie*, 1:181, 184. See Dupuy, *Instructions et lettres*, 74; Nugent, *Colloquy of Poissy*, 61, n.

[67]Santa Croce to Borromeo, March 29, 1563, *Archives curieuses*, 6:138–39.

[68]*Oeuvres complètes*, 2:476.

[69]Guy du Faur de Pibrac to L'Hôpital, June 4, 1562, BN, Dupuy 357, fol. 140; Dupuy, *Instructions et lettres*, 251–53; *Oeuvres complètes*, 2:486.

[70]L'Hôpital to the cardinal of Lorraine, *Poésies complètes*, 291. The cardinal of Lorraine notified Pius IV of his departure for Trent by a letter signed on September 19, 1562; Daniel Cuisiat, *Lettres de Charles de Lorraine (1525–1574)* (Nancy, 1971), 2:363, cited from Michel Pernot, "Le rôle du cardinal Charles de Lorraine dans la vie politique et religieuse de la France au troisième quart du XVIe siècle," *Les Cahiers Haut-Marnais* 188–89 (1992): 37.

[71]The royal instruction of September 6, 1562, in Dupuy, *Instructions et lettres*, 284–88.

[72]BN, Dupuy 358, fols. 48–50v, a draft handwritten by L'Hôpital, titled *C'est ce qui sera remonstré par les ambassadeurs du Roy nostre sire à messieurs les légats et aultres prélats estans au concile*; the final draft is printed in De Thou, *Histoire universelle*, 3:430–34; Amphoux, *Michel de l'Hôpital*, 293–97.

episcopal offices *in favorem* be received by the court of Rome. He had the list signed by the king and the queen mother before it was presented to the legates at Trent on January 3, 1563.[73] L'Hôpital told Santa Croce that this French petition should not irritate His Holiness but rather please him.[74]

The publication of canons and decrees of the Council of Trent, which adjourned on December 4, 1563, was one of the thorniest issues between the papacy and France. Upon his return to France in February 1564, the cardinal of Lorraine attempted to arrange the immediate publication of the council's decrees in France. L'Hôpital was, however, more cautious about accepting the Tridentine decrees in France. In an enlarged royal council summoned in late February 1564 to discuss the matter, L'Hôpital cogently argued that it would be heedless to take any resolutions about the council's decrees since, although the king was well informed of the council by the cardinal of Lorraine, France had not yet been officially notified of the decisions of the council and it was not yet known whether or not the pope would ratify them in their entirety. The chancellor thus advised that the government wait until the pope announced the council's decisions in a papal bull in forma probanti.[75] L'Hôpital's opposition to the cardinal of Lorraine's request for the immediate acceptance of the Tridentine decrees was not, however, prompted merely by his concerns about due procedure. L'Hôpital saw no reason, in the first place, for obliging France to follow formulas that might diminish her prerogatives or infringe on Gallican liberties.

More important for Chancellor L'Hôpital was the realistic consideration that to accept the decisions of the Council of Trent was to negate the terms of the Edict of Amboise, which had been issued on March 19, suspending the first religious war.[76] The Edict of Amboise granted to all "noblemen holding full fief" the right to exercise the "so-called religion" with their families and subjects; it granted to "noblemen holding simple fief" the same right, but for themselves and their families only. In each bailliage, Paris excepted, one town (as well as in all cities in the hands of Protestants on March 7) was set aside in which the exercise of Protestant religion would be permitted. The edict prescribed that "each one live and reside in his house freely, without being searched or molested, forced or constrained due to his conscience."[77] It was thus feared that the text of the

---

[73]Jedin, *History of the Church*, 5:494.

[74]Santa Croce to Borromeo, September 28, 1562, *Archives curieuses*, 6:110.

[75]Alava to the duke of Alburquerque, February 23, 1564, *Archivo documental Español*, 5:126; Santa Croce to Borromeo, February 25, 1562, *Archives curieuses*, 6:155; Smith to Cecil, March 9, 1564, *CSP Foreign*, 7: 39–40.

[76]Isambert, *Recueil général*, 14:135–40.

[77]Article 4, Isambert, *Recueil général*, 14:137.

decrees of the Council of Trent, whose legitimacy Protestants denied, would mark the expiration of the hard-won peace. The majority opinion in the Conseil Privé was that the publication of the Tridentine decrees would indeed call into question the liberties conceded to Protestants. Convinced that the reception of the council's decrees would provoke a Protestant revolt, the queen mother and the chancellor were determined not to publish them. Catherine remarked that "the experience of perils and calamities convinces us not to change at all the edict of pacification."[78]

The publication of the Tridentine decrees ran into opposition from various quarters. Du Moulin argued that one could not accept the Council of Trent without subjecting the kingdom to "the obedience to the pope."[79] He adopted so strong a royalist stance that it gave the crown complete authority in clerical administration. The staunchly Gallican-minded Parlement of Paris also objected to accepting the Council's decrees, because the enforcement of them under the papal leadership would encroach upon royal prerogatives.[80] The parlementaires flatly concluded that recognizing the Tridentine decrees would be nothing other than "lowering the authority of the king and his edicts, annulling his laws and those of the estates of France, depriving them of ancient liberties of the church in order to support papal abuse, and by the same means rekindling troubles and divisions, not only between the subjects of the king, but throughout Christendom, which each good subject of the king should avoid with all his power."[81] Aided by this widespread Gallican sentiment, especially that of the sovereign court, L'Hôpital succeeded in preventing the decrees of the Council of Trent from being accepted in the royal council of the roi très Chrestien.

By the end of the first religious war in March, the situation in the Conseil Privé had become more favorable than ever for the moderate forces led by L'Hôpital. Catholic leaders had suffered heavy losses during the war: the marshal of St. André was killed and the constable of Montmorency was taken prisoner at the battle at Dreux in December; the king of Navarre had earlier died on November 19; and the duke of Guise, the

---

[78]Catherine to Bochetel, February 28, 1564, *Lettres de Catherine de Médicis*, 3:153.

[79]Charles Du Moulin, *Conseil sur le faict du concile de Trente, par Charles du Molin, docteur ès droit, jurisconsulte françois, maistre des requestes de l'Hostel de la Royne de Navarre* (1564). Victor Martin, *Le Gallicanisme et la Réforme Catholique* (Paris: Picard, 1919), 70–72; Robert M. Kingdon, "Some French Reactions to the Council of Trent," *Church History* 33 (1964): 149–56.

[80]BN, Dupuy 689, fol. 137; 358, fol. 88v. Discussions of the parlementery session at Fontainebleau were recorded in the memoir of avocat Baptiste du Mesnil in his *Advertissement sur le faict du concile de Trente, faict en 1564* (Lyon); see Martin, *Gallicanisme*, 49–53.

[81]Martin, *Gallicanisme*, 53. This was the consistent position of the Parlement throughout the sixteenth and the seventeenth centuries.

only surviving member of the triumvirate, was assassinated on February 18 by a Huguenot seigneur, Poltrot de Méré. Catholic forces were thus abruptly weakened in the Conseil Privé, and L'Hôpital and other royal councillors who favored moderate solutions for religious problems had a relatively free hand in controlling the government affairs. The Venetian ambassador Suriano observed in April that "the queen consulted in most things the chancellor, who, for the time being, held the first place with her."[82] Suriano doubtless had the cardinal of Lorraine on his mind, who was then at Trent, when he said that L'Hôpital held control at court "for the time being." The absence of the cardinal of Lorraine at court had significantly changed the balance of power in the royal council in favor of the moderates and Protestants. The papal nuncio Santa Croce contended that the queen mother had decided to send the cardinal to the Council of Trent, mainly in order to "get rid of [the cardinal] before her eyes."[83] Santa Croce further maintained that the chancellor, "who has affection for [the cardinal], yet does not want to have him in the kingdom."[84] It thus seemed almost inevitable that there would be friction over the publication of the Tridentine decrees between the cardinal of Lorraine and L'Hôpital, who led the objections to them in the Conseil Privé.

Apart from its political and public ramifications, the controversy surrounding recognition of the Tridentine decrees contributed to the definite tarnishing of L'Hôpital's relations with his patron the cardinal of Lorraine. At the Council of Trent, Lorraine was the unquestionable leader of the opposition against the pope in regard to the authority of the council itself. The cardinal had proclaimed, as late as in February 1563:, "I cannot deny that I am a Frenchman who was nourished at the University of Paris, where the authority of a council overrides that of the pope and where those who think otherwise are censured as heretics."[85] Seeing the threat of the schism of Catholic forces, however, Lorraine accepted a compromise which provided that the Council limit itself to rejecting the Protestant teaching on the episcopal office while avoiding a definition of papal primacy.[86] The cardinal decided that the Council of Trent (where he at first had persisted in his Gallican stance) was the last resort to procure Catholic unity against Protestants. The strong Gallican sentiment of the cardinal of Lorraine gradually dissipated, and by the final session of the Council of Trent, the cardinal was transformed into a staunch supporter of Ultramon-

---

[82]Suriano to the Doge, April 30, 1563, *Despatches of Suriano*, 91.

[83]Santa Croce to Borromeo, June 27, 1563, *Archives curieuses*, 6:145–46.

[84]Ibid.

[85]Cuisiat, *Lettres du Cardinal Charles de Lorraine*, 1:7, cited from Pernot, "Le rôle du Cardinal Charles de Lorraine," 25.

[86]Jedin, *History of the Church*, 5:493–94.

tanism.[87] Upon his return to France, the cardinal asserted that publication of its decrees was very necessary for the repose of the kingdom.[88] L'Hôpital's advice to the king to wait until the official papal bull was a subtle defiance of the cardinal who had presented to the king the decisions of the Council. The cardinal was thus sharply pitted against the chancellor in the Conseil Privé over acceptance of the Tridentine decrees; their rapidly deteriorating relationship soon evolved into estrangement. At the royal council's meeting of February 22 at Melun, the cardinal reproached L'Hôpital for always opposing any proposition for the good of France. Faced with the chancellor's contention that recognition of the Tridentine decrees was contrary to the privileges of the Gallican church, the cardinal, in exasperation, shouted that he did not know of what religion the chancellor was. The argument between the two became so fierce that Lorraine called L'Hôpital an "ingrat," who was only trying to harm the cardinal and his family in spite of all the debts he owed to them. L'Hôpital calmly replied that he had always been loyal to his office and that the cardinal must know who had trampled on the Edict of January in Vassy, a violation which had caused so many troubles to the kingdom. As to his indebtedness to the Guises, he always remained grateful and would risk his life to repay them, but, the chancellor declared, he would never desire to pay his debts at the expense of the honor and profit of the king.[89]

This breach between L'Hôpital and the cardinal of Lorraine irreparably contaminated their friendship. Contrary to what has been said by many historians, L'Hôpital had kept a close relationship with the cardinal even after the failure of the Colloquy of Poissy. L'Hôpital had written to him in affectionate terms to console him on the death of his brother, François de Guise, who was killed in February 1563. He also expressed a sincere wish, before the cardinal's departure to Trent, that the cardinal might find means of restoring the church to its ancient unity. Their estrangement was, to be sure, more than the mere result of a momentary outburst of hostility at the royal council. L'Hôpital's religious policy and

---

[87]Pernot, "Le rôle du cardinal Charles de Lorraine," 37.

[88]Smith to Cecil, March 9, 1564, *CSP Foreign*, 7: 39–40.

[89]BN, Dupuy 689, fol. 137. The description of this altercation is also found in Santa Croce to Borromeo, February 25, 1564, *Archives curieuses*, 6:156; Smith to Cecil, March 9, 1564, *CSP Foreign*, 7: 39–40; Brantôme, *Oeuvres complètes*, 3:312–13; Theodore Beza to Henry Bullinger, March 6, 1564, *Correspondance de Théodore de Bèze*, 14 vols. (Geneva: Droz, 1960–1990), 5:37; "Deux Altercations entre le Cardinal de Lorraine et le Chancelier L'Hôpital," *Bulletin de la Société de l'histoire du protestantisme français* 10 (1975): 409–15; *Lettres de Catherine de Médicis*, 2:xxxv; Martin, *Gallicanisme*, 46–47. The *Mémoires de Condé* provides a description of the disputes between the two, which allegedly happened on February 24, 1564, but it is rather a description of the incident that occurred on March 16, 1566, at Moulins, not in February 1564 at Melun. For the 1566 incident, see chap. 5, pp. 144–45, below.

ideals had been much the same as those of the cardinal, at least until the latter's return from Trent, where his opinion had changed completely. The cardinal of Lorraine had taken a decidedly Gallican approach to the issues of church property and discipline, and had endeavored, in collaboration with the chancellor, to secure a national religious settlement in France.[90] He had pursued on behalf of the French government the convocation of a new general council free from the commitments of Trent, which Protestants refused to recognize as an ecumenical synod.[91]

Evidence shows that the cardinal of Lorraine was committed to a policy of concord at least until early 1563. The cardinal was willing to negotiate with the Huguenots toward compromise at Poissy and, following the failure of the Colloquy of Poissy, attempted theological rapprochement with the German Lutherans. The cardinal suggested a turn to Lutheran doctrines, less alienated from Catholic doctrines than Calvinist doctrines, as a theological middle way that would make reunification of all Christians possible. A meeting between the cardinal and Duke Christopher of Württemberg took place in Saverne from February 14 to 18, 1562.[92] In the course of discussions with the Lutheran leaders and theologians, the cardinal of Lorraine appeared to be willing to make significant concessions, even declaring himself a supporter of the Augsburg Confession. Many historians have argued that the cardinal simply wanted to divide the Protestant camp by depriving the French Calvinists of support from the German Lutherans, and that the Saverne conference was nothing but a cynical anti-Calvinist maneuvering on the part of the Guises. But others have raised the question whether the cardinal of Lorraine sincerely envisioned the end of religious quarrels and a reunion of Christianity through negotiations on the basis of Lutheran theological creeds. According to Henry Outram Evennett, the cardinal hoped for a colloquy with moderate Lutherans which, through accord between Catholic and Lutheran theologians, would open the path to religious reunifications, rendering the general council unnecessary. The cardinal was not yet the intransigent

[90]Traditional interpretations suggest that the cardinal of Lorraine opposed the proposal for a national council, but more recent studies show that the cardinal was the main advocate of a national council and took the initiative in its convocation. For the revisionist interpretation, see Evennett, *Cardinal of Lorraine*, 463; idem, "The Cardinal of Lorraine and the Colloquy of Poissy," *Cambridge Historical Journal* 2 (1927): 133–50; Nugent, *Colloquy of Poissy*, 204–207. This interpretation is confirmed by the papal nuncio: "Il cancelliere et Lorena si opponevano alla bolla [the convocation of the Council of Trent], la quale dicevano che il Papa non l'haveva fatto per altro che per rompere il Nationale," Gualterio to Borromeo, January 20, 1561, *Acta Nuntiaturae Gallicae*, 14:308.

[91]Before the Council of Trent, the pope criticized Lorraine and declared that the cardinal of Tournon was "the only good Catholic in France"; Nugent, *Colloquy of Poissy*, 50, 60.

[92]For the Conference of Saverne, see Evennett, *The Cardinal of Lorraine*, 415–21, 429–40.

champion of the orthodoxy that he would later become. The hopes for religious rapprochement quickly evaporated, however, at the news of the Massacre of Vassy on March 1, 1562. Jean-Marie Constant assertes that the death of François de Guise in February 1563 was a turning point in the cardinal's attitudes. After the assassination of his brother by a Huguenot, argued Constant, the disillusioned cardinal discarded his reforming and conciliatory ardor and, becoming increasingly intransigent towards Protestants, attempted rapprochement with the pope.[93]

L'Hôpital, on the other hand, while supporting the policy of concord of the court through the Colloquy of Poissy, consistently upheld his belief that toleration of Protestants was the only alternative to endemic civil wars; at the same time he steadfastly pursued his Gallican stance. L'Hôpital conceived the policy of tolerance as an instrument for the termination of the civil war, but the exigencies of the religious wars inevitably drove him into conflict with his old patron. Thus his estrangement from the cardinal of Lorraine appears to have been a consequence, not so much of his personal opposition to the cardinal, as of his fundamental political considerations, which always took precedence over his religious commitments. Mario Turchetti's interpretation that the cardinal of Lorraine and Chancellor L'Hôpital shared the ideal of "concord" at the Colloquy of Poissy confirms the fact there was no need for L'Hôpital's being "ungrateful" to his patron.[94] But L'Hôpital was above all a politician whose devotion to the interests of the state dictated his politics, religious policies, and even friendships. As the papal nuncio Santa Croce observed, L'Hôpital had deep affection for the cardinal, yet he did not want to let Lorraine stand in his way of pursuing religious policy.[95] L'Hôpital himself confided his thoughts to the cardinal at Trent in a touching letter in 1563, which proves to be the last extant epistle dedicated to him:

> It is folly to imagine that one can destroy by force the division that exists in spirit…. I do not condemn anyone for the beginning of the war. I do not accuse anyone of foolishness, ill will, cruelty, or hatred. There is no point today in recrimination…. I only want to prove that the remedies that we have hitherto applied to our calamities do not have any chance to succeed.

L'Hôpital continued: "I do not want to impose on your wisdom my naive reasoning … [but] you ought to cede to what your friends and your ministers say, and to sacrifice your greatness before the exigencies of the situ-

[93]Jean-Marie Constant, *Les Guises* (Paris: Hachette, 1984), 58.
[94]See chap. 3, pp. 73–74, above.
[95]Santa Croce to Borromeo, June 27, 1563, *Archives curieuses*, 6:145–46.

ation. It is the misfortune of all civil wars."[96] It was at this point that L'Hôpital inevitably broke away from his old patron.

L'Hôpital's estrangement from the cardinal of Lorraine seems to have been an inevitable consequence of his profound concern for royal interests. For L'Hôpital, the kingdom, on the verge of disintegration as a result of the prolonged religious conflicts, could only be salvaged by recognition of the Huguenots, a solution which the cardinal of Lorraine did not contemplate. When L'Hôpital judged that the interests of the crown and those of the Guises no longer converged, he was compelled to compromise his friendship with the cardinal of Lorraine. Catherine de Médicis was certainly aware of her chancellor's efforts to promote royal interests, and closely followed his initiatives in support of government policies. A letter of Catherine attests to her trust in the chancellor's religious policy. She wrote that the experience of twenty or thirty years had shown that the use of force "only serves to multiply the evil" and rigorous persecution only to confirm the heretics in their errors, and "many men of judgment consider that there is nothing so fatal to the prospect of extirpating these new opinions as the public execution of those who hold them." Accordingly, Catherine concluded, a policy of toleration ought to be tried.[97] It is not easy to determine precisely to what extent the queen mother was responsible for the religious policies of the government headed by L'Hôpital. What is certain, at least, is that Catherine and L'Hôpital were in fundamental agreement that religious reconciliation was not an end in itself, but a means to a higher end. Catherine made it explicit that the Edict of Amboise was intended to be a temporary response to religious conflict. She wrote: "... the intention of the king my son and mine are not to allow to be established, by means of the said pacification, a new form and exercise of religion in this kingdom, but to reach with the least contradiction and difficulty the reunion of all our people in the one holy and Catholic religion."[98]

Both Catherine and L'Hôpital believed that royal authority, above all else, must be defended and preserved in the midst of devastating religious conflicts. Catherine sincerely acknowledged her chancellor's struggle to preserve royal power: "My servant [L'Hôpital] is a man better than those who talk about him ... , but because he does not serve anyone other than

[96]L'Hôpital to the cardinal of Lorraine, *Poésies complètes*, 287, 298.

[97]Catherine to L'Aubespine, bishop of Limoges, January 31, 1561, *Lettres de Catherine de Médicis*, 1:577. The Venetian ambassador Suriano reported in April 1563 that in most things the queen consulted the chancellor, who held the first place with her; Suriano to the Doge, April 30, 1563, *Despatches of Suriano*, 91.

[98]Catherine to the bishop of Rennes, the ambassador to the emperor, April 20, 1563, *Lettres de Catherine de Médicis*, 2:19; Turchetti, *Concordia o Tolleranza?* 443, n. 117.

me and does not depend on anyone, they hate him, but that is why I like him."[99] L'Hôpital confirmed his devotion to the queen mother in his testament: "The queen often complained to me about the circumstance that she was almost excluded from the administration of the kingdom. I had nothing to tell her but to reassert the authority of Her Majesty; if she could do it wisely, she could easily counterattack and weaken the ambition and stupidity of her adversaries...."[100]

L'Hôpital wanted above all to achieve the more complete independence of the French king in the governing of his state. Apart from his theoretical defense of Gallican liberties against pontifical influence, L'Hôpital believed that religious problems in France should be resolved by national settlement, flexible and compatible with the peculiar circumstances in France. In one such illustration, L'Hôpital expresses his concern about a decree of the Council of Trent that decided that abbeys and monasteries not be conferred on anyone other than the regular clergy, and which also abrogated pensions to laymen in consistorial benefices. The latter was a hard blow to a number of royal officials, especially the parlementaires.[101] The right of the king to assign pensions in benefices to individuals, even to laymen, was one of the most useful ways that he had to reward or buy service and loyalty. Consequently, though admitting that these pensions were sources of abuses, L'Hôpital cautiously pointed out the difficulties that would result from their abolition. When the cardinal of Lorraine refuted the chancellor's assertion in this regard, insisting that they were important sources of corruption, L'Hôpital, somewhat impatient, sarcastically remarked that "it is easy to make others fast, while one has his own stomach well filled."[102] L'Hôpital had already told the papal nuncio that "the first chapter of reform should be to cut down the number of abbeys His Eminence of Lorraine and Monsieur the legate possessed."[103] The entire policies of L'Hôpital were indeed those of an administrator armed with striking pragmatism. L'Hôpital drew up an edict in March 1565 to prohibit eating meat during the Lent. In this edict, L'Hôpital cited the shortage of the cattle in the kingdom, before he quoted religious reasons. Appalled by the chancellor's alleged impiety, the papal nuncio Santa Croce made fierce remonstrances to the queen mother.[104]

[99]Catherine to her daughter Elizabeth, Queen of Spain, February 1562 [no date], *Lettres de Catherine de Médicis*, 1:614.

[100]Testament, *Oeuvres complètes*, 2:520.

[101]The council strictly abrogated secular *commendes*, or trusts, and all *indultes*; Martin, *Gallicanisme*, 63.

[102]Santa Croce to Borromeo, March 3, 1564, quoted in Martin, *Gallicanisme*, 63–64.

[103]Santa Croce to Borromeo, September 28, 1562, *Archives curieuses*, 6:110.

[104]Santa Croce to Borromeo, March 16, 1565, quoted in Martin, *Gallicanisme*, 45.

Having witnessed L'Hôpital's bold assertion of independence from the Gallican church, the ultra-Catholic leaders were all the more eager to procure the removal of this troublesome chancellor. L'Hôpital's treatment of Protestant rebels in Toulouse and in Rouen deepened his enemies' misgivings that the chancellor was "overly favorable" towards Protestants.[105] In Toulouse in October 1562, over two hundred Protestants were publicly executed, and twenty-two conseillers were expelled from the Parlement of Toulouse on suspicion of being Protestant. Jean de Coras and Arnaud de Cavagnes, two suspended conseillers, personally petitioned L'Hôpital, who procured them a declaration of the king allowing both public and private assemblies of Protestants, as permitted by the Edict of January.[106] The royal edict also pardoned the participants in the sedition on account of religion, and reinstated those parlementaires who had been expelled.[107] The Parlement of Toulouse refused, however, to register these lettres patentes, despite repeated orders from the king. Finally, the king sent the declaration to the sénéchal of the city, and not to the Parlement, for its prompt enforcement.[108] In a similar situation in Rouen, where Protestant uprisings were put down in late October, the chancellor persuaded the king to issue another edict to pardon rebels.[109]

In June 1562, the Parlement of Paris required every member of the court to make a profession of faith, and decided not to allow any nonjuror to return to his seat in the Parlement. The Parlement also asked Chancellor L'Hôpital to order the secretaries of state to take the oath, a request flatly refused by the chancellor.[110] L'Hôpital was, furthermore, far from willing to condone the Parlement's mandatory profession of faith. The Spanish ambassador predicted that L'Hôpital would not be admitted into the Parlement until he made profession of faith in writing and that because of this he would avoid as long as possible the occasion of coming to the Parlement.[111] Appearing at the Parlement of Paris on May 9, 1563, however, the

[105]Chantonnay to Philip II, November 4, 1562, *Archivo documental Español*, 5:368.

[106]Jean de Coras was the *juge d'instruction* of the famous case of Martin Guerre, responsible for preparing a report to the court. See Natalie Zemon Davis, *The Return of Martin Guerre* (Cambridge, Mass.: Harvard University Press, 1983), chapter 10.

[107]De Thou, *Histoire universelle*, 3:294.          [108]Ibid., 295.

[109]*Mémoires de Condé*, 2:104, 123; De Thou, *Histoire universelle*, 3:334.

[110]Chantonnay, July 26, 1562, *Archivo documental Español*, 4:203. The Parlement of Paris required its entire membership to profess Catholic faith through June and July. In the list of those who took the oath on June 6 is the name of avocat Jehan Bodin; see Delachenal, *Histoire des avocats*, 405.

[111]It was not the chancellor but Artus de Cossé, sieur de Gonnor, *surintendant des finances*, who went to the Parlement on March 22, 1563, to register the Edict of Amboise. Gonnor told the parlementaires, "I am speaking without passion; I am not Huguenot and I beg the court not to defer the registration of the edict"; *Lettres de Catherine de Médicis*, 2:iii-iv.

chancellor sharply rebuked the Parlement, because its ruling not to readmit to the court members who had not made profession of faith was clearly prejudicial to the pacification edict. Admonishing the court for its defiance of royal authority, L'Hôpital ordered that any conseiller who wished to return be allowed to do so and not be pressed to take the oath.[112]

These incidents seemed enough to confirm the Spanish ambassador in his suspicion of the chancellor's orthodoxy. Clinging to the accusation of L'Hôpital's alleged Calvinism, the Spanish court and the papacy did not lessen their indefatigable effort to procure the chancellor's dismissal. Chantonnay confirmed in March 1563 that the French ambassador in Spain, L'Aubespine, the bishop of Limoges, was working hard to remove L'Hôpital from his office.[113] In 1565, at the Franco-Spanish conference at Bayonne, the Spanish envoy, the duke of Alba, told Catherine de Médicis that she was the only person who did not believe that her chancellor was a Huguenot, and warned that as long as she listened to L'Hôpital she would hardly be able to do justice.[114] Having consistently defended her chancellor, Catherine once again guaranteed L'Hôpital's orthodoxy. When the duke repeatedly denied L'Hôpital's Catholic belief, the queen mother retorted that "it is your malicious wish that makes you say so," and that her chancellor "is not as bad as you think."[115] Yet it is possible to presume that the instigation of Alba and the persuasions of the Spanish Queen Elizabeth, Catherine's own daughter, at the Bayonne meeting made a considerable impression on her. Elizabeth claimed that L'Hôpital had already been regarded as a Protestant during the reign of her father, Henry II.[116] The Spanish ambassador Alava boasted after the meeting that the queen mother would soon get rid of L'Hôpital.[117]

L'Hôpital's efforts to legalize Protestant worship in France and to implement reforms in the church in France without intervention from Rome inevitably caused him to be called an "enemy of the Roman church and the pope." L'Hôpital found himself accused of hypocritically hiding

---

[112]Taber, "Royal Policy and Religious Dissent," 348–51. Only a few weeks later, however, on May 22, the Parlement of Paris stubbornly protested to the king that all royal councillors should be required to take the oath of faith; AN, X 1a /1605, fol. 217.

[113]Chantonnay and Alava to Philip II, March 11 and 15, 1563, *Archivo documental Español*, 5:114–15.

[114]Alba had been speciffically instructed to have L'Hôpital expelled from his office; *Lettres de Catherine de Médicis*, 2:lxxviii, lxiv.

[115]*Lettres de Catherine de Médicis*, 2:lxxviii.      [116]Ibid.

[117]Alava to Philip II, March 2, 1565, *Archivo documental Español*, 3:163. Alava had complained earlier that "even if the queen mother would restore the Catholic religion in France as a result of the Bayonne meeting, the chancellor would easily make her change her mind"; *Lettres de Catherine de Médicis*, 2:lxiv.

his Calvinist belief.[118] The efforts of L'Hôpital's opponents to remove the tolerant chancellor from the scene were not in vain. Suspicion about L'Hôpital's religion, however ill-founded, eventually helped bring about the chancellor's fall in 1568.

Controversy over L'Hôpital's religion was, after all, a concomitant of the polemics of the French religious wars. It has created, however, unwanted ambiguity about L'Hôpital, which has significantly affected historians' interpretation of the chancellor. L'Hôpital's policies have often been viewed as being tainted by his religious stance. Those who are much impressed by the "L'Hôpital's dissemblance" thesis, have groped for his ulterior motives in his political actions, and L'Hôpital has been viewed as a highly crafty, almost double-dealing, politician who hid his true colors in order to achieve his goals against stiff opposition. The twentieth-century historian Jean H. Mariéjol has stated that L'Hôpital "behaved with such prudence that he dissimulated his intentions to the other ministers."[119] For those in quest of a veritable portrait of the chancellor behind his presumed facade, L'Hôpital's early rapport with the cardinal of Lorraine seemed to offer a fine illustration of his dissimulation. If he had openly opposed the policies of the cardinal as he wished, they argued, he would not have been appointed chancellor and thus would have been deprived of the opportunities to improve Protestants' lot.[120] To historians who found it almost embarrassing that the chancellor was a self-declared client of the Guises, the theory of L'Hôpital's duplicity provided a ready answer.

Likewise, L'Hôpital's repeated plea that the government had to pursue the policy of Protestant toleration simply because it was the lesser evil and the only alternative to endemic religious strife has not been taken at face value. The chancellor's straightforwardly political solution to the civil war has instead been seen as the manifesto of his Erasmian evangelism, or the enlightened ideal of freedom of conscience. Albert Buisson argued that L'Hôpital's Christianity "inspired his reforms and his everyday action as a statesman."[121] Chancellor L'Hôpital could not, however, afford the naive idealism of contemporary humanists. L'Hôpital had no pretension to lofty evangelism. He should be credited with sincerity when

---

[118]Suriano to the Doge, *Relations des ambassadeurs vénitiens*, Tomasseo, 1:553.

[119]J.-H. Mariéjol, *La Réforme et la Ligue, L'Edit de Nantes*, vol. 7 of *Histoire de France*, ed. E. Lavisse (Paris: Hachette, 1904), 20–21.

[120]La Planche commented, "Il luy faloit user de merveilleux stratagêmes pour contenir les Lorraines en leurs bornes"; see Louis Regnier de La Planche, *Histoire de l'Estat de France, tant de la république que de la religion, sous le règne de François II*, ed. Mennechet, 2 vols. (Paris: Techener, 1836), 1:256.

[121]Buisson, *L'Hospital*, 12.

he professed his true intentions. Just as L'Hôpital needs to be rescued from his hackneyed reputation as a lonely apostle of toleration, so he ought to be freed from the old reproaches surrounding his religion and politics. L'Hôpital has too long remained a victim to the polemics of religious war. It is now time that he be freed from the spell of the "chancellor's mass."

# Chapter 5

# The Chancellor versus the Judges

I N HIS FINANCIAL AND LEGAL CONFLICTS with the papacy, L'Hôpital sought and found an ally in the Parlement of Paris, the undisputed champion of Gallican liberties. The truce with the magistrates was rather ephemeral, however. When France was faced with the overwhelming threats of both internal conflict over religion and intervention from Rome, L'Hôpital concluded that only the prince could preserve the unity of the kingdom and protect the Gallican liberties of the French church. L'Hôpital's eight years as chancellor were thus unreservedly devoted to defending and promoting the authority of the crown. But the parlement that defended the crown's complete control over church matters in France was not willing to concede the same assertion of royal authority over constitutional matters. When L'Hôpital began to concern himself with questions of judicial reform, the Parlement proved more intransigent than ever in its opposition to the chancellor's program. The magistracy had sought to reassert its constitutional authority and privileges during the period of royal minority and the regency of a foreign queen. L'Hôpital had deferred direct confrontation with the Parisian Parlement as well as its provincial counterparts until the king attained his majority. When Charles IX turned fourteen years of age in July 1563, L'Hôpital was no longer willing to condone the parlements' defiance of royal authority. The Majority lit de justice, held at the Parlement of Rouen in August 1563, signaled the beginning of the chancellor's offensive against the obdurate judges.

The French historian Jean-Louis Bourgeon provides a curious perspective for understanding the French religious wars by proposing the concept of "the parlementary Fronde" for the years prior to the massacre of St. Bartholomew's Day.[1] According to Bourgeon, the twelve years from 1560 to 1572 witnessed the growing agitation of the Parlement of Paris that led directly to the massacre. The Parlement hoped to become the preponderant political element in the kingdom, and its increasingly adamant constitutional pretensions had dangerously threatened royal authority. The Parlement of Paris in the 1560s was concerned, argued Bourgeon, "less with defending the Catholic religion (albeit it was the pretext so invoked) than with undermining and holding, by whatever means, royal power in check," and the law court "profited from the 'troubles of religion' to promote its interests and claim its 'liberty' vis-à-vis the sovereign and his Conseil Privé." The massacre of 1572 broke out, Bourgeon thus claims, "only at the end" of this long struggle "between the crown and this *nouvelle féodalité*."[2] Bourgeon's arguments of the Parlement's position in the 1560s are the subject of dispute among historians. In particular, his claim that the Parlement of Paris, not Charles IX or Catherine de Médicis, was responsible for the St. Bartholomew's Day massacre has been widely repudiated by scholars. To characterize the Parlement in the 1560s as *frondeur* is indeed an oversimplification, if not a distortion, of the constitutional tension between the crown and the Parlement. Controversial as it is, nevertheless, Bourgeon's discussion of the Parlement is of peculiar interest, because Chancellor L'Hôpital was the main opponent of the judges in this escalating contest for power between the crown and the law court.

L'Hôpital relentlessly fought against the Parlement's claim to be a key political power, and he often harshly admonished the magistrates for their disobedience to the royal will. To be sure, the Parlement's resistance to royal authority was hardly new in the 1560s. L'Hôpital's predecessor, Antoine Duprat, the chancellor of Francis I, had already vehemently confronted the Parlement's pretensions on many occasions. L'Hôpital's clashes with the Parlement can indeed be seen in the broader pattern of conflict between a royalist minister and the king's chief law court in early modern France. What was significant, and conspicuously unpropitious for L'Hôpital, was that the magistracy's challenge to the crown's authority coincided with the devastating religious conflict in the kingdom. It was in this markedly unfavorable climate, against the backdrop of civil war, that L'Hôpital found himself defending royal authority and, inevitably, increasingly at odds with the magistrates. It has been argued, with certain justification, that L'Hôpital's policy of religious toleration was rendered

---

[1]Jean-Louis Bourgeon, "La Fronde parlementaire à la veille de la Saint-Barthélemy," *Bibliothèque de l'Ecole des Chartes* 148 (1990): 17–89.

[2]Bourgeon, "La Fronde parlementaire," 29, 35, 86. Henri Hauser, *Les Sources de l'histoire de France: XVIe siècle (1494–1610)* (Paris: Picard, 1912; reprinted Nendeln, Liechtenstein: Kraus Reprint, 1967), 4, views the French religious wars as a period of "réaction féodale."

unsuccessful because it was incompatible with the orthodox mentality of the Parlement. Committed to the maintenance of religious order, and assuming the role as the champion of Catholicism, the parlementaires opposed almost every single initiative of L'Hôpital to grant limited freedom of worship to Protestants.[3] More unfortunate for L'Hôpital, his religious policy exposed him to charges of being a "Huguenot," and this persistent suspicion of the chancellor's own religious stance, however ill-grounded, further alienated the Catholic parlementaires from him.[4] In fact, the adversarial relationship between the magistracy and L'Hôpital dates back to the 1550s. L'Hôpital had already incurred the deep hostilitiy of the judges before he became chancellor. During his presidency at the Chambre des Comptes from 1555 to 1560, L'Hôpital attempted to promote the authority of the Chambre at the expense of the Parlement, an action that seriously aggrieved the parlementaires. It is difficult to estimate precisely to what extent L'Hôpital's earlier friction with the magistrates affected their relationship during his chancellorship. At the least, it is safe to presume that it did not help L'Hôpital much in office.

After his elevation to the chancellorship, the court's repeated cavilling over the registration of pacification edicts convinced L'Hôpital that its constitutional pretensions not only compromised royal authority but posed the main obstacle to preserving peace during the civil wars. Historians differ over whether the repeated clashes between the Parlement of Paris and the royal government during the 1560s were mainly over religious issues or constitutional issues. Many emphasize the importance of the religious problems that led the Parlement of Paris to try to exaggerate its own role in the legislative process.[5] Yet others argue that the Parlement of Paris was concerned less with defending the Catholic religion than with undermining royal power and that the law court used the religous disputes to assert its liberty from the crown. These differing opinions underscore the need to examine L'Hôpital's relationship with the Parlement from various perspectives, not just from the religious angle but also from the viewpoint of conflicting constitutional pretensions as well as political outlook.

---

[3]The parlements' profound assumption that maintaining social order was inseparable from upholding Catholicism as the only religion in France is discussed by many; see, inter alia, Jonathan K. Powis, "Order, Religion, and the Magistrates of a Provincial Parlement in Sixteenth-Century France," *Archiv für Reformationsgeschichte* 71 (1980): 180–97; idem, "Gallican Liberties and the Politics of Later Sixteenth-Century France," *Historical Journal* 26 (1983): 515–30; Mack P. Holt, "The King in Parlement: The Problem of the *Lit de Justice* in Sixteenth-Century France," *Historical Journal* 31(1988): 507–23.

[4]See chap. 4 above.

[5]Holt, "The King in Parlement," 515, 520–21.

   In this chapter, L'Hôpital's clashes during the 1560s with the Parlement of Paris over major constitutional issues will be examined. The two
principal constitutional issues in contention were the Parlement's right of
remonstrance, and *inamovibilité,* or irremovability, of magistrates. The Parlement contended that neither its right to register and verify royal edicts
nor the inviolability of its members' permanent tenure ought to be
encroached upon by royal power.[6] Chancellor L'Hôpital repudiated the
Parlement's arguments forcefully and articulately. He knew that unrestrained remonstrance would constitute a serious judicial check upon
royal authority; he was also aware of the disastrous effects of irremovability of royal officials on the administration of justice. The chancellor's refutation and attacks against these traditional rights of the Parlement
illustrate best his constitutional stance. In their attacks against the nineteenth-century version of L'Hôpital that wistfully represented the chancellor as an advocate of "political moderation," historians have emphasized
his authoritarian stance.[7] Yet scholars are not in consensus over the sincerity of L'Hôpital's belief in absolutist authority of the crown, and some propose that his absolutist statements were largely a response to the crises of
the times, which was compelled and exaggerated by opposition from the
Parlement of Paris over religious issues. This problem is directly linked to
the question of where to place L'Hôpital in the sixteenth-century debate of
constitutional ideas. A close examination of what the chancellor actually
said and did will offer some clarification. After all, L'Hôpital was a statesman and not an abstract theorist, and hence it is not so much his political
thought as his political action that really counts.
   L'Hôpital's constitutional views were first expounded in his address
to the Estates General at Orléans in 1560. In that speech he emphasized the
all-powerful character of the crown, and he declared that the king "does
not derive the throne from us, but from God, and from the ancient law of
the kingdom."[8] No human power could compel the monarch, because he
was responsible to God alone. According to L'Hôpital, the various assemblies of subjects, such as the Estates General and the Parlement of Paris,
were only consultative institutions. He defined the functions of the two
bodies, referring to historical customs:

   The holding of the estates means simply that the king communi-
   cates with his subjects concerning his most important affairs in

---

   [6]The Parlement's advocates maintained that these rights amounted to little less than *lois
fondamentales;* Doucet, *Les Institutions de la France,* 1:66–67.
   [7]The nineteenth-century portrait of L'Hôpital was effectively refuted in Neely, "Misattribution." See Introduction, n. 9, above.
   [8]December 13, 1560, *Discours pour la majorité de Charles IX,* 79; *Oeuvres complètes,* 1:389.

order to take their advice and counsel.... This was in early times called a parlement, and it has kept this name in England and Scotland. But because French kings had cognizance over general grievances by the same means as they did over particular ones, the name parlement remained concerned with the private and particular audiences which were held by judges appointed by the king, while the public and general audiences were reserved for the king and called Estates.[9]

L'Hôpital attempted to draw a clear line between legislative and judicial functions: legislative power belonged to the king, who was an overseer of the public good; the parlementaires were judges, who administered royal justice to the king's subjects. Since legislation was a royal prerogative and the Parlement's power was limited to judicial functions, L'Hôpital maintained, the court ought not to interfere with legislation by refusing to register royal edicts.

L'Hôpital appeared at the Parlement of Paris on June 18, 1561, in order to discuss a new pacification edict. He told the parlementaires that the king sent him to the court in order to obtain their advice, because the magistrates were for the king "councillors not only in judging cases, but also in the most important affairs of the state, when it pleases him to request it." Noting the unusually conciliatory tone of the chancellor, Roger Doucet viewed this particular statement as opposed to what L'Hôpital had frequently affirmed, that is, his intention to confine the Parlement to its judicial attributions.[10] But Doucet apparently did not observe that even on this occasion L'Hôpital left the king with complete authority, because he made it clear that the magistrates were summoned to furnish counsel to the king only "quand il luy plaist les en requérir." L'Hôpital was setting forth his views of the Parlement's authority and at the same time its limits: The Parlement could give advice on all the issues regarding the state, but only on the condition that such advice was requested by the king. "It is a good thing that the king does all things through counsel, but," he maintained, the king "is not constrained and required" to take counsel. The supreme decision whether or not to consult the Parlement belonged to the king. The chancellor's message could not be mistaken: The magistrates, as councillors to the king, could help him decide state policies through their advice; but the king never shared with them authority to make laws.

The first major confrontation between L'Hôpital and the Parlement of Paris over legislative authority was occasioned by the problem of registering the Ordinance of Orléans. The ordinance had been drawn up follow-

[9]*Discours pour la majorité de Charles IX*, 72–73; *Oeuvres complètes*, 378–79.
[10]Doucet, *Les Institutions de la France*, 1:133–34.

ing the meeting of the Estates General in January 1561, mainly on the basis of the estates' cahiers. When the Estates General met again on August 1 at Pontoise, the deputies pointed out that the ordinance had not yet been registered, and they threatened to withhold their consent to a subsidy requested by the king until the ordinance was published.[11] The next day the ordinance was brought to the Parlement to be verified, and the king ordered its immediate registration without any modifications. The Parlement evidently saw this as an opportunity to assert openly its right to remonstrate against royal edicts and began to deliberate on the ordinance article by article. When the king repeatedly pressed the court to expedite the registration process, Gilles Le Maistre, the premier président, responded that if the king wanted the prompt registration of the Ordinance, he should have sent it to the court in January when it was drawn up, not in August. The parlementaires complained that the king deliberately "waited until the last moment to surprise the Parlement," when it was approaching its last sessions before vacation.[12]

Confronted with the obdurate attitudes of the parlementaires, the royal government could hardly conceal its dilemma. The king desperately needed the subsidies from the Estates General, which threatened not to grant any until the publication of the ordinance. The Estates complained that the Parlement had no right to scrutinize the ordinance, made on the cahiers of the king's subjects.[13] On the other hand, the king wanted as soon as possible to implement the judicial and ecclesiastical reforms prescribed in the ordinance, and hence needed the Parlement's cooperation. The parlementaires persisted and resisted. They denied the theory that the Parlement was a part of the Estates General and contended that the ordinance needed careful scrutiny by the Parlement, because the court had not been invited to participate in any preliminary discussions of the edict. Caught between these contending claims of the two assemblies, the king was faced with the difficult task of satisfying them both. The situation was complicated because it was the first time, since the Parlement's right to register laws was firmly established in the mid-fifteenth century, that an ordinance was made at the behest of the Estates.[14]

---

[11]Picot, *Histoire des Etats Généraux*, 2:206.

[12]To this complaint the chancellor responded that the government needed time to negotiate with the pope concerning important issues in the ordinance that affected the papacy, and that the king's delegate had returned from Rome only a few days earlier; AN, X1a, 1598, fol. 213v, August 12, 1561; Maugis, *Parlement de Paris*, 1:667; Picot, *Histoire des Etats Généraux*, 2:232, n. 1.

[13]Picot, *Histoire des Etats Généraux*, 2:206.

[14]Denault, "Legitimation of the Parlement," 263–64.

L'Hôpital attempted to resolve this problem by carefully outlining the separate roles of the Estates General and the Parlement. In his response to the Parlement's delegates on August 11, the chancellor rejected the argument that the ordinance needed the Parlement's deliberation: "There was no need to send the ordinance, which the king had made at the request of his estates and which had gone through long discussion at the Conseil Privé, to the court to be verified, since this was not done in the estates of preceding kings." He maintained that the Parlement, limited to judicial business, should not oppose the decisions of the Estates General. Having repudiated the very ground of the parlementaires' contention, L'Hôpital then emphasized that the king still sent the edict to the court because he "wanted to honor the company by seeking its authority and counsel." The king was always of the opinion that the Parlement should deliberate on his edicts, because the Parlement was the judge of his laws. The king would always take its remonstrances in good faith. But, warned the chancellor, "the Parlement must not abuse this honor by being curious and excessively long [in its deliberation]."[15]

L'Hôpital's response to the Parlement was indeed strikingly diplomatic and adept. He acknowledged the prerogative of the Estates General and recognized that body as instigator of the reforms in the ordinance, while he confirmed the Parlement's juridical authority over those reforms and respected its right, however limited, to go through the formalities of registration. But L'Hôpital was not simply trying to appease them both. He was, in fact, consciously pitting the two assemblies against each other by carefully underscoring their rival pretensions. He was well aware of the immense danger the crown would face in case of an alliance between the two bodies: the Estates General could refuse to vote any subsidy, while the Parlement could refuse to register the ordinance. Inevitably the result would be encirclement of royal power by two opposing forces. By highlighting their conflicting constitutional claims, therefore, L'Hôpital shifted the burden of conflict away from the king to the assemblies themselves and thus checked their tendency to become less dependent on royal authority.

While attempting to divide the Estates and Parlement in order to free the royal government to do as it wished, L'Hôpital also used tactics of intimidation. When the Parlement, headed by the recalcitrant Premier Président Le Maistre, persistently ignored the king's request for a summary registration of the ordinance, the government turned to an unusually drastic measure. The king of Navarre, who had been sent to the Parlement on August 9 to expedite the registration procedure, reported to

---

[15]Maugis, *Parlement de Paris*, 1:667; Denault, "Legitimation of the Parlement," 187.

the queen mother that the Parlement was willing to obey the king, but that the premier président was inciting opposition to the ordinance. Navarre also complained that Le Maistre, "trop licencieux," made statements disrespectful of the king. On the basis of Navarre's report, the king suspended Le Maistre from office on August 18 on the rather questionable charge of offending the throne.[16] When the Parlement's delegates protested that their president had not made any remarks against His Majesty, the chancellor curtly retorted, "au reste, nous sçavons ce que vous faites en vostre cour."[17] The nineteenth-century historian Antoine de Ruble expressed regret that L'Hôpital was an accomplice of this injustice to Le Maistre, from apparently blatant political motives since Le Maistre was an open adversary of the chancellor.[18] It is likely, though not easy to prove, that personal antipathy between L'Hôpital and Le Maistre tainted the development of this incident. But it does demonstrate that the chancellor was willing to adopt high-handed methods in dealing with the magistrates. The Parlement finally capitulated to the king. The Ordinance of Orléans was registered on September 12.

Two months later, at the annual opening of the Parlement of Paris on November 12, L'Hôpital came back to the theme of the separation of legislative and judicial functions. This time he focused on the respective roles of the Parlement and the royal council. L'Hôpital maintained that there were two principal parties in a kingdom: one preserved the state with arms and forces; the other with advice and counsel. The latter function was carried out by two bodies: one managed affairs of state; the other judged the differences between the subjects. The royal council thus made laws concerning the general public good, while the Parlement administered justice to the individuals in particular cases at particular times. L'Hôpital stressed that "aultre prudence est nécessaire à faire les loyx, que à juger les différentz." Those who judged private cases ought not, therefore, to regard themselves as legislators. Following this division of duties, the chancellor addressed the thorny problem of remonstrance. The king

---

[16]Throckmorton to the Queen, *CSP Foreign*, August 30, 1561, 4:281–82.

[17]The government based its accusation of Le Maistre on an anonymous "Mémoire sur les propos tenus en la cour de parlement par le roy de Navarre" in which the premier président reportedly said, "s'il plaist au roy les faire publier de par luy, face ce qu'il luy plaîra, mais pour les faire de par la cour; fault avoir patience que chacun en ait délibéré"; cited in Maugis, *Parlement de Paris*, 1:668. This particular statement is not included in the register of the Parlement, but the government claimed that the court's register was "déguisé," and that the premier président had denied what was reported by princes, who could not be accused of lying; see A. de Ruble, *Antoine de Bourbon et Jeanne d'Albret* (Paris: Adolphe Labitte, 1881–86), 3:151–52. This incident is described in detail in Maugis, *Parlement de Paris*, 1:666–70. Le Maistre was not reinstated in his office until December 9, 1561.

[18]Ruble, *Antoine de Bourbon*, 3:148, 151.

and the royal council drew up edicts and sent them to the court because the king wanted the magistrates to give him advice through remonstrances when they found something to appeal. Remonstrances were always well received by the king and his council. But, L'Hôpital pointed out, "sometimes one goes far beyond the duties of judge." This court—he reminded the magistrates of their recent resistance to the Ordinance of Orléans—"in deliberating over edicts exceeded its function completely or partly, and having made remonstrances and learned the wishes of the king, did the contrary." Some thought, like the chancellor himself, that this was done out of well-intentioned zeal; others thought that the court had transgressed its power. The higher status of the king's council required that the Parlement accept the council's legislation after remonstrances had been made. L'Hôpital gravely admonished the Parlement that it should "know its station vis-à-vis its superiors."[19]

Throughout his chancellorship, L'Hôpital maintained that the king made laws and the Parlement executed them. But this theory of legislative kingship was seriously weakened in practice because of the young age of Charles IX. The Parlement frequently alluded to the legislative incapacity of a minor king. Although he was determined to subjugate the Parlement to royal will, L'Hôpital thus preferred to avoid an open conflict, biding his time until the king attained his majority. In July 1563, France won the campaign to recapture Le Havre from England. This victory was particularly meaningful, because Catholics and Protestants had fought together against the foreign enemy, not long after the Peace of Amboise, and they temporarily overlooked their differences. As much as L'Hôpital hated civil war, he was fully aware that a defensive foreign war provided the best chance to reunite a divided kingdom. When the victory significantly boosted royal prestige and popularity, the king propitiously entered his fourteenth year the very same month, thereby legally achieving his impatiently awaited "majority." At this strategic moment, L'Hôpital saw an opportunity to assert dramatically royal authority. The chancellor, probably in concert with the queen mother, persuaded the king to go to

---

[19]November 12, 1561, *Oeuvres complètes*, 2:12–13. The responses of President François de Saint-André to the chancellor's harangue touched the very heart of the disagreement about the Parlement's legislative power. The president insisted that deliberations and remonstrances, if they were to be useful and effective in promoting the virtue of laws, should be more than written documents; Maugis, *Parlement de Paris*, 1:606; Sarah Hanley, *The Lit de Justice of the Kings of France: Constitutional Ideology in Legend, Ritual, and Discourse* (Princeton, N.J.: Princeton University Press, 1983), 151. The Parlement contended that its role was not simply advisory but strictly consensual, because its approval to royal edicts constituted an essential part of legislation.

Le Havre to celebrate the victory and to declare his majority at a lit de justice ceremony at the Parlement of Rouen.[20]

Rouen's geographical proximity to Le Havre seemingly justified the royal decision to hold a lit de justice at the Parlement of Normandy. More important, however, were the political reasons. Lit de justice ceremonies had until then been held only at the Parlement of Paris. Sarah Hanley, in her study of the lit de justice in early modern France, convincingly argues that it was the Parlement of Paris that introduced the notion that lit de justice assemblies belonged exclusively to the grand' chambre of the Parisian court, and that it was the king and royal council who ignored that notion.[21] The choice of a provincial Parlement as the site for the lit de justice to declare royal majority was therefore a result of important political considerations—specifically, to undermine the political pretensions of the Parlement of Paris.[22] According to Hanley, L'Hôpital had already in 1560 considered holding a lit de justice outside Paris. She points out that an anonymous memorandum on lit de justice, which she believes to have been commissioned by the chancellor, suggested that a lit de justice ceremony could be held outside of the Grand Chambre of the Parlement of Paris.[23] L'Hôpital's decision to convoke the majority lit de justice at the Parlement of Rouen, and not at the Parlement of Paris, was thus an open blow against the Parisian court's claim to preeminence among parlements in France. The Spanish ambassador Chantonnay rather bluntly, but trenchantly, asserted that the motive for declaring royal majority at a provincial parlement was"to frustrate the Parlement of Paris and reduce its authority and preeminence, because ... neither the chancellor nor the queen liked the said Parlement, nor the city, for [Paris] did not find their actions desirable, and people say that [the Parisian magistrates] are rebellious and oppose every single ordinance of the king."[24] Chantonnay's comment indicates that the decision to hold the majority lit de justice

---

[20]As in many other cases of royal policy during L'Hôpital's chancellorship, it is hard to decide precisely whether it was L'Hôpital or Catherine de Médicis who was mainly responsible for the idea of holding the Majority lit de justice at Rouen. No matter whose initiative it was, it seems certain that there was hardly any disagreement between the two over royal policies, at least during this period.

[21]Hanley, *Lit de Justice*, 201–3, thus repudiated the traditional interpretations defining the lit de justice assembly as a royal legislative weapon used to quell remonstrances of the Parlement of Paris.

[22]The choice of Rouen seems to have been an especially deliberate one; the Parlement of Rouen was of relatively recent creation, and prior to its establishment a delegation from the Parlement of Paris had rendered justice in the province; Shennan, *Parlement of Paris*, 213.

[23]Hanley, *Lit de Justice*, 121–24, 152, 172.

[24]Chantonnay to Philip II, August 19, 1563, cited from Hector de La Ferrière, *Le XVIe siècle et les Valois d'après les documents inédits du British Museum* (Paris, 1879), 164.

assembly at Rouen was based on mutual agreement between the queen mother and the chancellor.

The lit de justice was held at the Parlement of Rouen on August 17.[25] In his speech delivered on behalf of the king, L'Hôpital first declared that the victory of Le Havre was God's gift, given to recognize the king's merits and also to punish the adversaries of the throne.[26] Reminding the parlementaires of the constitutional prerogatives of the king, who had now attained his majority, the chancellor emphasized the authority of the pacification edicts promulgated in the king's name: "The king wishes that all his edicts and ordinances be observed and maintained, especially the Edict of Pacification of disorder … [and] that all his officers, those of his sovereign courts as well as baillis, sénéschaux, and others, to administer his justice with equity and without prejudice or passion."[27]

L'Hôpital's address was full of stinging accusations against the parlements' resistance to the will of the king, the sole legislator:

> You swear an oath at your appointment to the office to observe ordinances and to have others observe them. Do you observe them well? … [instead] you act as if you are above the ordinances and not obliged to follow them if they displease you. Messieurs, messieurs, the ordinances are above you. You are said to be sovereign courts, but the ordinance is the commandment of the king and you are not superior to the king.… The will of the judge must conform to the intention of the legislator. [But] the king makes an ordinance and you interpret it incorrectly, contrary to his intention, which is not your duty. Judges who do not obey the legislator are like sailors who do not follow the orders of the captain and thus imperil the ship.[28]

L'Hôpital specifically criticized the parlements' practice of iterative remonstrances: "If you find, in executing an ordinance, that it is too harsh, difficult, improper, and unfit for the region where you are judges, you nevertheless must observe it until the prince corrects it. You have no power to remove, change, or contaminate it, but are only to resort to remonstrances." The chancellor denied the magistrates' assertion of their right to hold secret deliberations:

[25]The lit de justice ceremony of Rouen is described in detail in Pierre Dupuy, *Traité de la majorité de nos rois et des régences du royaume, avec les preuves tirées tant du Trésor des Chartes du roy que des registres du parlement, ensemble un traité des prééminences du Parlement de Paris* (Paris, 1655), 356–97.

[26]August 17, 1563, *Discours pour la majorité de Charles IX*, 100; *Oeuvres complètes*, 2:56.

[27]*Discours pour la majorité de Charles IX*, 105–6; *Oeuvres complètes*, 2:64–66.

[28]*Discours pour la majorité de Charles IX*, 107–8; *Oeuvres complètes*, 2:67–68.

You complain that the secret deliberations of the court are revealed to the king.... [But] *l'oeil de justice veoit tout, le roy veoit tout, et le temps découvre tout*. Do nothing which you would not wish to be known.... In the past, royal *commissaires* and even councillors of the Grand Conseil, today's Conseil Privé, entered Parlement in order to see everything going on there and report it to the king.... His Majesty has the right to know how his justice is administered and whether or not his judges are properly discharging their duties ...; the king ought to know it because he is responsible for his judges to God.[29]

The Majority lit de justice of Rouen established an important precedent that kings could convoke lit de justice assemblies in any parlement of France, not just in Paris. By persuading the king to convoke lit de justice assemblies in provincial parlements, L'Hôpital effectively contested the prevailing theory of "union des classes," a doctrine which held that all parlements of France were united under the oldest and the most illustrious one, the Parlement of Paris.[30] This was a concept underscoring the Parlement of Paris' claim to preeminence among sovereign courts. As discussed above, L'Hôpital, as the president of the Chambre des Comptes, had refused to recognize the appellate jurisdiction of the Parlement of Paris. He strongly denied the concept of the unity of sovereign justice represented by the Parlement of Paris, and claimed the Chambre des Comptes' complete independence from and equality with the Parisian judicial court.

In the same vein, Chancellor L'Hôpital now challenged the pretensions of the Parlement of Paris as "la cour des pairs," the notion that the court represented royal justice and was superior to its provincial counterparts. L'Hôpital instead proposed the theory of the unity of all the parlements "in one class" under royal authority. He claimed in September 1560, not long after he became chancellor, that "if the king could administer his sovereign justice by one Parlement alone, as was done in earlier times, he would do so. [But in these days] the different parlements are only various

[29]*Discours pour la majorité de Charles IX*, 110; *Oeuvres complètes*, 2:74–75. The chancellor advocated the privileges of the members of the Conseil Privé to sit in the Parlement of Paris, with the vote of deliberation; Aubert, "Organisation," 72–73. For the conflict between the royal council and the Parlement of Paris in the sixteenth century, see Noël Valois, "Etude historique sur le conseil du Roi," *Inventaire des arrêts du Conseil d'Etat (Règne de Henri IV)* (Paris: Imprimerie Nationale, 1886), chap. 1.
[30]Hanley, *Lit de Justice*, 149–59, 197–98.

divisions [*classes*] of the royal Parlement."[31] Provincial parlements eagerly welcomed the chancellor's version of the theory of the union of classes. The Parlement of Rouen, the proud host of the Majority lit de justice, declared, "La court de Parlement de Paris n'estoit non plus la court des pairs que les autres."[32]

It is understandable that the Parlement of Paris was bitterly aggrieved by the innovation of convoking a Majority lit de justice assembly elsewhere. The Parisian parlementaires protested that the right of the court was ignored, recalling that it was at Paris that the ordinances of the king's majority had been published in 1375, 1392, and 1407.[33] Vehement remonstrances from the Parlement met only angry rebukes from the king and the chancellor's severe reprimand against its immoderation. After a bitter confrontation that continued throughout September and October, the Parlement was convinced of L'Hôpital's determination to subjugate the resistant Parlement of Paris to royal authority.[34] The long controversy over the Rouen lit de justice was clear evidence of the uncompromising position of the chancellor in defending royal authority.

In November 1563, at the Parlement of Paris, L'Hôpital expounded on his interpretation of the proper relations between the king and his officeholders. Reminding the magistrates that they "exercise the judgment of the king, and not their own," the chancellor admonished that they ought not to "oppose themselves directly to the will and commandment of kings, who are jealous of their power, without wanting to be defeated."[35] In particular, he warned that a young prince must not be irritated or displeased, since at his majority he would remember all the humiliation he had undergone. He remarked that a prince might be compared to a fine horse, which must be flattered constantly; those who would ill treat him would be kicked. L'Hôpital clearly pronounced that "it was not reasonable that the judges wanted legislative power, by observing some ordinances and not others." Such actions of the judges would only bring confusion in justice.

[31]September 7, 1560, *Discours pour la majorité de Charles IX*, 54; *Oeuvres complètes*, 1:360. Ironically, the Parlement of Paris in 1755 referred to this discourse of Chancellor L'Hôpital, to raise the Grand Conseil above the other sovereign courts; see Maugis, *Parlement de Paris*, I, 418; Hanley, *Lit de Justice*, 149–50; Shennan, *Parlement of Paris*, 84–85. See also Robert Villers, "Les Origines de la théorie parlementaire dite de "l'union des classes," *Revue historique de droit français et étranger* 62 (1984): 718–19.

[32]Amable Floquet, *Histoire du Parlement de Normandie* (Rouen: E. Frère, 1840–1842), 3:8.

[33]Maugis, *Parlement de Paris*, 1:608; *Lettres de Catherine de Médicis*, 2:xxiv-xxv.

[34]The Parlement's repeated remonstrances and the royal government's counterattacks are printed in Dupuy, *Traité de majorité*, 405–43, and analyzed in detail in Hanley, *Lit de Justice*, 183–98.

[35]November 12, 1563, *Oeuvres complètes*, 2:87.

Some complained, the chancellor noted, that the court did not have as much authority as before. But one should remember the difference between authority and power. Authority was something which "came *ex opinione virtutis.*" The kings could dispense power, but not authority. Judges must earn their own authority. L'Hôpital pointed out that there was also a clear difference between fear and respect. People feared one who had power over them, but they did not respect him, unless he was good and virtuous. "If those in this court did what their predecessors had done, they would still have the same authority among subjects and foreigners, who would willingly come to submit themselves to the Parlement's jurisdiction."[36] Finally, the chancellor flatly said that he thought that "the judges, in part, are the cause of the civil wars, because they have given encouragement to bold and wicked spirits."[37] He expressed his concerns that the parlements' remonstrances about the edicts of pacification would give false encouragement to disturbers of the peace, and that their resistance to royal authority rendered more difficult the enforcement of edicts. It is likely that he was specifically referring to the recent complaint the king received from Huguenots in Bas Languedoc that some judges at the Parlement of Toulouse were "trop passioné" and did not make fair judgments. Their petition requested that the king should not assign such judges to cases involving Huguenots.[38] L'Hôpital deplored that "tout n'est pas encore appaisé," despite the Peace of Amboise. He told the parlementaires that as many wrongdoings as before were being committed in the provinces.[39]

While he was preoccupied with subduing the judiciary to the crown, L'Hôpital could not neglect maintaining the shaky balance between Catholics and Protestants and preserving the uncertain peace after the First Religious War. L'Hôpital took caution not to provoke the Catholic population, who were still grumbling about concessions made to Huguenots by the Edict of Amboise in 1563. The squabble with England over the book of Walter Haddon is a good illustration of L'Hôpital's efforts not to stir up unnecessarily the hostile opinion of Catholics and the Parisian magistrates. In 1563, the famous Portuguese theologian Jerome Osorius wrote a book, later translated into French under the title *Lettre adressée à la reine Elisabeth.* In his book, Osorius detailed the errors and dangers of Anglicanism. The English scholar Walter Haddon immediately wrote a strong refutation and submitted the manuscript to Robert Estienne in Paris for

---

[36]*Oeuvres complètes*, 2:95.

[37]"Quia addidêre animos audacibus et improbis"; *Oeuvres complètes*, 2:96.

[38]"Request of the Huguenots in Bas Languedoc to Charles IX, October 17, 1563," printed in *Dokumenty po istorii grazhdanskikh voin vo Frantsii*, 319–22.

[39]November 12, 1563, *Oeuvres complètes*, 2:96.

publication, only to see it seized by French officials. When the English ambassador Thomas Smith complained to the chancellor about the incident and demanded the authorization to publish Haddon's work in France, L'Hôpital answered that the queen mother did not want to appear to favor the Huguenots, and the authorization would provoke fierce opposition from the Parlement of Paris. He added that although the government would not confiscate books of the new religion from private persons, it still would not officially authorize their publication in France. The English ambassador reported to his government that, apart from the misgivings of the French government, Chancellor L'Hôpital in particular "fears his judges and loath he would have him to take hurt."[40] Haddon's treatise was eventually published in Paris. But this incident attests to the difficulties L'Hôpital faced in sustaining the frail peace between Catholics and Protestants in the kingdom. Thanks to his policies defending Protestants, his own life was in constant danger. According to the Spanish ambassador, in October 1564 the rumor that the pope was considering hiring an assassin compelled the chancellor to strengthen the guard around himself.[41]

Through his conflicts with the Parlement of Paris, L'Hôpital firmly laid theoretical foundations for absolute authority of the crown, but his advocacy of absolute royal power inevitably incurred enormous hostility among the parlementaires. It almost seemed that the Parlement opposed the chancellor's policies just for opposition's sake and without any discretion. When the king issued the Edict of January 1564, ordering that, in the future, the year start on the first day of January instead of at Easter, the Parlement objected and adhered to the old computation.[42]

Charles IX and Catherine de Médicis embarked upon the royal "grand tour" across the kingdom in March 1564. In the course of their journey, which continued for twenty-seven months, the king held a lit de justice assembly at the Parlement of Dijon (May 1564), the Parlement of Toulouse (February 1565), and the Parlement of Bordeaux (April 1565).[43] On each

[40]Reports of Thomas Smith, March 6, 9, 10, April 14, and May 10, 1564, *CSP Foreign*, 7: 70, 73, 76, 111, 130.

[41]Alava and Beaumont to Philip II, October 25, 1564, *Archivo documental Español, Francia, 1559–1566* (Madrid: Real Academia de Historia, 1950–1954), 6:461–62.

[42]Article 59 of the Edict of Paris, January 1564. The English ambassador claimed that the Parlement's opposition to this measure was hardly more than an expression of its grievances against L'Hôpital; see Georges Tessier, "Parlement de Paris et style du 1er janvier," *Bibliothèque de l'Ecole des Chartes* 101 (1940): 233–36. Concerning the common mistake of attributing this measure to the Edict of Roussillon, issued in August 1564, see Alexandre Le Noble, "Note sur l'Edit de Paris de 1563," *Bibliothèque de l'Ecole des Chartes* 2 (1840–1841): 286–88.

[43]Jean Boutier, Alain Dewerpe, and Daniel Nordman, *Un tour de France royale: le voyage de Charles IX, 1564–1566* (Paris: Aubier, 1984), 241.

occasion, L'Hôpital, who accompanied the king on most of the tour, repri-
manded the provincial judges for neglecting their duties and for a tendency to defy royal will. At the lit de justice of Bordeaux on April 12, 1564,
L'Hôpital severely scolded the Parlement for not yet having published the
Ordinance of Orléans. The chancellor reminded the magistrates that their
business was primarily judicial and that they were not the king's tutors:

> You, messieurs, are commissioned specifically to execute justice.
> Do not imagine that [your position] is yours. You only hold bor-
> rowed positions, and must recognize that they belong to the
> king.... The law must be above the judges, not the judges above
> the law.... When you do not obey the king's ordinances, you
> remove from him his royal power, which is worse than taking
> away from him his domain.... You seem to assume that you are
> wiser than the king; but your expertise is limited to judging [par-
> ticular] cases. You are not wiser than the king, the queen, and the
> royal council. [The king] has achieved peace [in his kingdom] but
> now is at war with his Parlement....[44]

The chancellor gravely warned the judges: "Do not do anything for which
your king would hurl his anger against you."[45] L'Hôpital cited his own
conduct when he reproved the parlementaires' pretensions that they
could scrutinize royal legislation:

> You respect your own arrêts, and put them above royal ordi-
> nances. You receive ordinances and then interpret them as you
> wish. It is not you, but the king alone, who can interpret royal
> ordinances.... I have the honor to be the chief of the king's justice,
> but I would deserve death if I attempted to interpret his ordi-
> nances, without consulting with him. When I was president of the
> Chambre des Comptes, when some people wanted to put into
> deliberation an issue which was contrary to royal ordinances, I
> did not allow it. Likewise, you presidents must not do that.[46]

The chancellor specifically charged the Bordelais judges with permitting widespread factional strife within the court. Deliberations often
ended in brawling, and the judges were "more afraid of the governors
than of the king." Urging the magistrates not to be intimidated by powerful local seigneurs, the chancellor decided to show them a practical example. In Bordeaux, some nobles and their armed bands frequently pillaged
the city on the pretext of protecting the Catholic religion and openly

[44]*Oeuvres complètes*, 2:108–109.
[45]Ibid., 110.          [46]Ibid., 111.

defied the royal order prohibiting the carrying of arms in the city. Their notorious chief was a certain marquis de Trans, but no one dared bring him to justice. L'Hôpital summoned the marquis to the Parlement and harshly scolded him for brigandage. When the impudent marquis began to laugh, the chancellor roared: "What are you laughing for? You can laugh, but I can have your throat cut the moment I give sentence. You may thank Her Majesty that your head is still on your shoulders." The marquis, frightened, staggered and almost fainted. Brantôme, who witnessed this scene, wrote that "il ne falloit pas se jouer avec ce grand juge et rude magistrat."[47]

L'Hôpital's high-handed attitude towards the parlements, evident in his tirades against the judges, incurred their deep antagonism. Hélène Michaud points out that rarely had a chancellor before L'Hôpital employed such harsh and rigid language in his addresses to the parlements.[48] Behind this abrasive language lay L'Hôpital's fundamental goal to diminish the political authority of the sovereign courts. L'Hôpital explicitly wrote into the Ordinance of Moulins, issued February 1566, the prohibition of repeated remonstrance. Article 1 stipulates that all ordinances so far issued were to be observed, regardless of remonstrances or reservations attached to them. Article 2 prescribes that once remonstrances had been made and the wishes of the king were made known, the parlements should proceed to prompt registration without resort to any further remonstrances.[49] Together these articles marked the climax of the chancellor's campaign against the parlements' claim that they possessed legislative authority. In December 1566, after fierce opposition from the Parlement of Paris, the king withdrew the second article and confirmed that the parlements could reiterate remonstrances as many times as they wished. But the first article was preserved, and it was reaffirmed that an ordinance, once registered, no matter whether its publication was made by the king's "express command" (that is, by *lettres de jussion*), would be maintained regardless of further remonstrances.[50]

The conflict over the Parlement's remonstrance against royal edicts revolved around the question of the Parlement's legislative authority. Another important constitutional issue that was in equally serious contention was the doctrine of irremovability of royal officeholders. L'Hôpital attempted to challenge, or at least limit, the magistrates' lifetime tenure. The doctrine of irremovability constituted the basis of the judges' inde-

---

[47]Brantôme, *Oeuvres complètes*, 3:308–9.
[48]Michaud, *La grande Chancellerie*, 27.
[49]Isambert, *Recueil général*, 14:191–92.
[50]*Seconde déclaration des ordonnances de février 1566 faicte par le Roy sur les remonstrances à luy réitérée par les gens de sa cour de parlement à Paris: Actes Royaux*, BN, *Imprimé*, F. 46829 (11).

pendence from the crown, and along with the right of remonstrance, it was an issue crucial to defining the relationship between the king and his officials. Louis XI's ordinance of 1467 had established the general theory of irremovability of officials, prescribing that the king could not discharge officials except "par mort, forfaicture ou incompatibilité d'offices."[51] In the sixteenth century, however, the emerging concept of a royal monopoly on the authority to govern tended to restrict the right of judges to their offices. Since all royal officials merely exercised a part of the prerogative that remained unrestrained, according to the apologists for absolutism, they could be revoked at any time by the crown.[52] But the spread of sale of offices in the sixteenth century reinforced the principle of irremovability because, when the king wanted to dismiss an official, he now had to assume the obligation of reimbursement.[53] In practice, venality and irremovability together significantly increased the independence of officials and effectively limited the king's ability to dismiss freely his own officials.[54]

The Parlement of Paris, which regarded itself as a guardian of the constitution, maintained that its members should be protected by a law superior to the king. But L'Hôpital was never willing to accept such extreme pretensions of the parlementaires, which placed the principle of irremovability above royal authority. L'Hôpital had already written in 1556 that "all offices are at the king's disposal and only the king has the right to distribute offices."[55] At the lit de justice at Rouen in 1563, he declared that the doctrine of irremovability did not confer on the judges immunity for their actions. They were still accountable to the king, "from whom you hold your honors and magistracies for an indeterminate length of time, that is, as long as it pleases him. In contrast to other countries, you magistrates are perpetual. Do not abuse [the privilege], and do not change this legitimate honor into tyranny, and, finally, obey the king and his ordinances."[56]

[51]Doucet, *Les Institutions de la France*, 403–4. For an analysis of the Ordinance of 1467, see Christopher Stocker, "Office and Justice: Louis XI and the Parlement of Paris (1465–1476)," *Mediaeval Studies* 37 (1975): 360–86.

[52]William F. Church, *Constitutional Thought in Sixteenth Century France* (Cambridge, Mass: Harvard University Press, 1941), 53, 136.

[53]B. La Roche-Flavin, *Treze livres des Parlemens de France* (Geneva, 1621), vol. 2, cited in Aubert, "Organisation," 213, n. 2. "Et à présent," continued La Roche-Flavin, "une destitution ne se peut faire, à cause de l'édict de la paulette, qu'au seul cas de forfaicture, quand par crime ou délict un officier est privable ou privé de son estat."

[54]Irremovability and venality were indissolubly united, because offices became venal only after they had become irremovable; P. Louis-Lucas, *Etude sur la vénalité des charges et fonctions publiques* (Paris: Challamel ainé, 1883), 2:17.

[55]Epistle to Marguerite de Valois, *Poésies complètes*, 249. See chap. 2, p. 40, above.

[56]August 17, 1563, *Discours pour la majorité de Charles IX*, 111; *Oeuvres complètes*, 2:76.

Again in 1565 in Bordeaux, the chancellor stated that the judges were commissioned specifically to execute justice, and that they held only borrowed positions (*sièges empruntez*), since ownership belonged to the king.[57] L'Hôpital stressed that individual officeholders were always bound to the king, and that the security of the magistrates' position was to be guaranteed as long as they properly observed royal ordinances.[58]

L'Hôpital attempted to establish a broad foundation for the responsibility of royal officials.[59] He argued that irremovability did not guarantee the good administration of the state, because it often covered up incapacity on the part of *officiers*, or even their corruptions. L'Hôpital was particularly concerned about the unnecessarily lengthy procedure in convicting a judge and the increasing abuses of judges taking advantage of their permanent tenure. He spoke at the Parlement of Paris in June 1561: "Although some say that discharging judges, when necessary, seems as easy as changing one's mind, it is well known that it is not so promptly done, and that *nostris institutis*, a royal official is not dismissible except in certain cases. It is necessary to bring him to proceedings. It could take a year to get the result."[60]

According to L'Hôpital, irremovability, reinforced by venality, in practice prevented the king from dismissing culpable officials. He deplored the serious impact of venality on the good conduct of administration: "It is the fault, if there is any, of the past kings or their councils, who placed them, by money, for the exigence of the wars; no one can touch those officials because the offices sold to them are perpetual. Discharging them without their consent, and without proceedings, is not the

---

[57]April 12, 1564, *Oeuvres complètes*, 2:108.

[58]The ordinance of 1467 prescribing irremovability turned into dead letters; Loyseau pointed out such clauses in the letters of provision of office as "tant qu'il nous plaira," and "que le Roy est suffisamment informé de la capacité de l'officier." Charles Loyseau, *Les Oeuvres de Maistre Charles Loyseau contenant Les Cinq livres de droit des office* (Paris, 1678), book I, chapter 3:31. L'Hôpital wanted to restore the validity of these conditions which he considered to be essential for good administration.

[59]G. Martin-Sarzeaud, *Recherches historiques sur l'inamovibilité de la magistrature* (Paris: E. Duchemin, 1883), 140, 145, 161.

[60]June 18, 1561, *Oeuvres complètes*, 1:425. With the arrival of venality, even the regulation of forfeiture became less sustainable at the sovereign courts. The parlements distinguished the case in which an office was declared vacant and the officeholder deprived of his charge from one in which the accused officeholder was simply declared incapable of keeping his office. In the latter case, the officeholder lost only the right of exercising his office and still kept the right to resign the office for money. The second hypothesis was prevalent at the parlements, and offices were rarely declared vacant by reason of simple malversation of incumbents; see Jacques Kubler, *L'Origine de la perpétuité des offices royaux* (Nancy: Société d'Impressions Typographiques, 1958), 279.

way it is done in this kingdom."[61] But the chancellor's attempts to challenge the seemingly sacrosanct principle of irremovability inevitably made him the target of vehement criticisms.[62]

The Parlement of Paris counterattacked L'Hôpital's attempts to diminish their privileges by consciously challenging the authority of the chancellor, in whom it found a powerful rival. In 1565, the Parlement issued strong remonstrances when the king commissioned an official in the bailliage of Vermandois for three years, and not for life tenure.[63] In its remonstrances, the Parlement contended that continuity and stability of office, promoted by permanent tenure, were more useful to the kingdom than a frequent change of the incumbents. The longer officials stayed in their offices, the parlementaires argued, the more learned and experienced they would become about their functions. Besides, those who held only temporary appointments were more likely to commit malfeasance while in office, "not wishing to lose time."[64] The Parlement further argued that temporary commissions were a violation of the ordinance of Louis XI which, it maintained, could be revoked only by another ordinance. If the king still wanted to appoint officials on a temporary basis, therefore, it must be done in the form of an edict, which should be registered at the Parlement, and not by individual commissions.[65] Resentful as they were of Chancellor L'Hôpital's attempts to undermine the theory of irremovability, the magistrates chose to make an issue of the life tenure of the chancellor. In 1563, the Parlement had issued remonstrances that the office of the chancellor belonged to the domestic offices of the king and thus was revocable *ad libitum*. The chancellorship, contended the parlementaires,

---

[61]November 17, 1567, *Oeuvres complètes*, 2:126. "Some people say," L'Hôpital explained further, "that it is necessary to hold proceedings against [the judges], and they believe that, with their judicious minds, it can be done within an hour. I reply to them that it is not possible to do it within such a short time. It is not easy to find witnesses against the judges; also the courts of parlement do not simply review the judgment of the inferior and subordinate judges, but have the power to punish them [so it is difficult for subordinate judges to testify against their superiors]"; ibid., 126–27.

[62]Kubler, *L'Origine de la perpétuité*, 288–94, argues that L'Hôpital did not oppose the basic right of the magistrates to their offices; rather L'Hôpital simply attacked the effects of venality, which had rendered it difficult to dismiss an officeholder from his charge even when he was culpable and should suffer forfeiture. I remain unconvinced by Kubler's arguments that L'Hôpital denounced the difficulties in removing venal officeholders but still retained a fundamental belief in irremovability of the judges. Jean Bodin confirmed that the chancellor wanted to abolish the system of lifetime tenure among royal officials; see n. 78 below.

[63]BN, MS Fr. 3888, fols. 40–45, *Remonstrance faicte au Roy Charles IX par sa cour de Parlement de Paris, l'an 1565: Touchant les offices de judicature, et que les Rois en doubvent pourveoir des personnes capables à vie, & non à temps seulement.*

[64]Ibid., fol. 42.     [65]Ibid., fol. 43v.

had not become irremovable until the time of Charles VIII, whereas the irremovability of judicial officials dated to Philip of Valois.[66] Two years later, the magistrates argued: "To persuade the king to change his chancellor and other domestic officers, although it is still lawful, would be very undesirable. It would discourage all royal officials from fulfilling their duties...."[67] They warned that L'Hôpital's obstinacy would jeopardize the cooperation between the government and the Parlement; the Parlement flatly stated that "reciprocity of good will is necessary between the superior and the inferior."[68]

L'Hôpital's conflict with the Parlement of Paris over irremovability amply testifies to his commitment to an unchallenged royal authority and his absolutist belief. The issue of irremovability most clearly distinguishes L'Hôpital's constitutional stance from that of the sixteenth-century constitutionalists. For Claude Seyssel, for instance, the permanent tenure of judges was an important precondition of good administration. He believed that the court could limit the action of the king when he infringed the rights of his subjects. In order to assure that *la justice* acted as a check (*frein*) on royal power, the freedom and security of offices in the judiciary were indispensable. Seyssel therefore concluded that the magistrates ought to be irremovable except for offenses established by the court.[69] But L'Hôpital, as chancellor responsible for the affairs of state, was more concerned than Seyssel about the effects of the immoderate independence of the magistracy. L'Hôpital maintained that parlements had been instituted by the king and held their authority exclusively from him. Royal judges were mere agents of the king who retained an undiminished prerogative; the judges' powers were entirely dependent on those of the sovereign prince. The idea that the courts should enjoy complete freedom of action in administering justice, independent from royal power, was obviously incompatible with L'Hôpital's view of indivisible rulership. Since the king was the source of parlements' authority, L'Hôpital concluded, he should be able to withdraw their power of jurisdiction.

[66]Duchesne, *Histoire des chanceliers*, 636, cited in Michaud, *La grande Chancellerie*, 38, n. 6.

[67]BN, MS Fr. 3888, fol. 45; P. Guyot and P.-A. Merlin, *Traité des droits, fonctions, franchises, exemptions, prérogatives et privilèges annexes en France à chaque dignité* ... (Paris: 1786–1788), 4:128; Jean Le Féron, *Histoire des connetables, chanceliers et gardes des sceaux, etc....* (Paris, 1658–1688), 115; Pierre Henrion de Pansey, *De l'autorité judiciaire en France* ... (Paris, 1818), 160, n. 1; Kubler, *L'Origine de la perpétuité*, 187–88; Michaud, *La grand chancellerie*, 38.

[68]BN, MS Fr. 3888, fol. 45.

[69]Claude de Seyssel, *La Monarchie de France et deux autres fragments politiques*, ed. Jacques Poujol (Paris: Librairie d'Argences, 1961), 117–18. For Seyssel's constitutional thought, see Leon Gallet, "La Monarchie française d'après Claude de Seyssel," *Revue historique de droit français et étranger* 22 (1944): 1–34.

Among contemporary jurists, Charles Du Moulin's constitutional stance on royal authority most resembles that of L'Hôpital. Du Moulin contended that the magistrates' title to jurisdiction remained strictly in possession of the king, and that officeholders, as mere executors of royal authority, were removable at royal discretion.[70] Du Moulin and L'Hôpital were not strangers to each other. In May 1552, when Du Moulin found himself charged with heresy by the Sorbonne, L'Hôpital was among his judges at the Parlement of Paris.[71] In 1564, Du Moulin in his *Conseil sur le faict du concile de Trente* argued against the publication of the Tridentine decrees in France. Shortly after its publication, the Parlement of Paris questioned Du Moulin on his Protestant leanings, and imprisoned him until the king ordered his release; it is likely that L'Hôpital played an important role in securing this release.[72] It is possible to conjecture that L'Hôpital, finding in Du Moulin a brilliant theoretical justification for his royalist Gallican policies, willingly supported and protected this fiery polemicist from his adversaries.

Yet L'Hôpital could not adhere to an ultra-Gallican conviction as did Du Moulin. Afraid that the Council of Trent and the papacy would undo the precarious religious peace he had created in France, the chancellor sought conciliation and cooperation among Frenchmen, instead of stirring and dividing them by stormy political polemics. But L'Hôpital's call for an end to faction and a return to Gallican unity did not compromise his political authoritarianism. His advocacy of the crown's power seems to have been more a matter of deliberate choice than a response to immediate political concerns. Repeated opposition from the Parlement of Paris to the registration of edicts of toleration, in particular, convinced the chancellor that the obstruction of parlement presented the main obstacle to royal efforts to bring the civil conflict to a close.

L'Hôpital's absolutist opinion was, however, far from a passive response to the parlementaires' offensive. Many historians treat the chan-

---

[70]Church, *Constitutional Thought*, 123; Skinner, *Foundations of Modern Political Thought*, II, 266–67.

[71]See chapter 4, pp. 95–96, above.

[72]*Conseil sur le faict du concile de Trente* (Lyon, 1564) was the first formal Gallican statement on the Tridentine decrees, written at the solicitation of the Conseil Privé. Shaw, *Michel de L'Hospital*, 112, argues that it was L'Hôpital who "induced" Du Moulin, who was known for his intense Gallicanism, to write a treatise against the reception of the decrees. According to Thireau, however, Du Moulin later confirmed that Marshal François de Montmorency was one of those who solicited his scholarly authority; Thireau, 50, n. 187, 52; also see Crimando, "Du Moulin," 175. Martin, *Gallicanisme*, 49–51, 70, claimes that it was Admiral Gaspard de Coligny. While Shaw argues that L'Hôpital "intervened and rescued" Du Moulin from prison, Thireau again ascribes the main role in this incident to Montmorency. Kelley, *Hotman*, 195, argues that L'Hôpital "served as a protector" of Du Moulin.

cellor's absolutism with reservation. Julian Franklin argues that L'Hôpital's absolutist ideas "need not have been very deeply held," because they were not systematically developed and appeared instead in the course of the government's efforts to secure its political program.[73] L'Hôpital was, after all, not an abstract theorist, but a statesman reacting to political concerns. His political opinions and actions were influenced by the course of events during the religious wars. These considerations do not, however, provide sufficient reason to underrate the scope or the sincerity of L'Hôpital's absolutist convictions. His position could not be mistaken when he flatly declared that "the principal maxims of kingdoms and republics ... is that one person must command and all others obey."[74] For L'Hôpital, it was the duty of the king's subjects to obey all royal commands, "that is to say his laws, edicts and ordinances, which all must obey and are subject to, except for the king alone."[75] In Moulins in 1566, he again explicitly pronounced that ordinances emanating from royal authority must be observed "religieusement et inviolablement."[76] L'Hôpital's concept of the unchallenged sovereignty of the crown was the natural outgrowth of his strong patriotism and political realism. His penchant for strong royal power was reinforced, but not conditioned, by the exigencies of the civil wars. He was not simply blown by the force of circumstances towards a theory of absolutism. Just as L'Hôpital's devotion to the interests of the state dictated his religious policy, his fundamental *étatisme* drove him to his autocratic position towards the parlements.[77]

Jean Bodin testified to the chancellor's determination in the important constitutional question of irremovability, stating that L'Hôpital had endeavored by all means to change all the offices into commissions, to be held only at the king's pleasure, and that he "never had any other thing in his mouth," that is, it was his unvarying objective.[78] Bodin himself closely

[73]Franklin, *Jean Bodin and the Rise of Absolutist Theory,* 21.

[74]November 12, 1561. *Oeuvres complètes,* 2:9.

[75]December 13, 1560, *Discours pour la majorité de Charles IX,* 81; *Oeuvres complètes,* I, 392.

[76]*Remonstrance de monsieur le chancelier faite en l'assemblée tenue à Moulins, au mois de Janvier, 1566.*

[77]Maurice Taillandier called L'Hôpital a self-declared "partisan de la *monarchie absolue.*" He further wrote that L'Hôpital "never abandoned "the principle that "la souveraineté, qui est indivisible, appartient au monarque seul ..., *base* fondamentale de son système." Maurice Taillandier, *Des projets de réforme du chancelier de L'Hospital et de quelques réformes actuelles* (Arras, 1903), 14.

[78]Jean Bodin, *Les six livres de la république* (Lyon, 1593), 4.4:593; see *The Six Bookes of a Commonweal,* tr. Richard Knolles, and ed. Kenneth D. McRae (Cambridge, Mass.: Harvard University Press, 1962). From this passage, Sylvia Neely argued that Bodin "thought L'Hôpital had gone too far by trying to abolish the system of irremovable judges and replace it with a system of *commissaires* who would hold office at the pleasure of the king."

echoed L'Hôpital's opinion. He wrote that in France all "magistrates and commissioners" were "mere executors and ministers of the laws and of the princes, from whom they have their authority,"[79] and that a sovereign "may also take the power given them by vertue of their commission or institution, or suffer them to hold it so long as shall please him."[80]

It is indeed notable that L'Hôpital's constitutional views pronounced in the 1560s show striking parallels to those of Jean Bodin, expressed in his *Les six livres de la république* (1576). To be sure, Bodin's constitutional position underwent a fundamental metamorphosis because of the monarchomach theory of popular sovereignty.[81] In his earlier book, *Methodus ad facilem historiarum cognitionem* (1566), Bodin had argued that the king cannot properly be above the law, that the king "cannot destroy the laws peculiar in the entire kingdom or alter any of the customs of the cities or ancient ways without the consent of the Three Estates," and that "those who have been trying to overthrow the dignity" of the parlements "seek the ruin of the state, since in these is placed the safety of civil order, of laws, of customs, and of the entire state."[82] In *Les six livres*, Bodin abandoned his previous constitutional position and accepted a strong monarchy as the only means of restoring political unity and peace. Concerning the estates, Bodin argued that the king is not required to follow their advice. He wrote that "the king, understanding their opinions, may accept or reject as he sees fit the requests of the estates,"[83] and refuted as absurd the argument that "the sovereign prince cannot make a law without the authority or consent of the estates or the people."[84] Bodin seemed to be almost echoing Chancellor L'Hôpital's words, pronounced some ten years earlier, when he declared that, although an initial right to issue remon-

---

It does not seem, however, that Bodin entirely disapproved of L'Hôpital's efforts to challenge the issue of irremovability of office, for he added that L'Hôpital did not make any distinction "in what forme of commonweale this chaunge were, without harme to be received." Bodin was rather simply making it a point, as he wrote in the next paragraph, that "commeanweales in nature contrarie, are by contrarie lawes and meanes to bee also governed and maintained … so that the rules and orders proper to maintaine and preserve Popular estates, serve to the readie ruine and overthrow of Monarchies and sole governments."

[79]Bodin, *Les six livres*, 3.5.439; *The Six Bookes*, 3.5.333.

[80]Bodin, *Les six livres*, 1.8123; *The Six Bookes*, 1.8.85.

[81]For the influence of the monarchomachs on Bodin, see J.H.M. Salmon, "Bodin and the Monarchomachs," in *Jean Bodin: Verhandlungen der internationalen Bodin Tagung in München*, ed. Horst Denzer (Munich, 1972), 359–78.

[82]*Method for the Easy Comprehension of History*, tr. Beatrice Reynolds (New York: Columbia University Press, 1945), 204, 257.

[83]Bodin, *Les six livres*, 2.1.263; *The Six Bookes*, 2.1.192.

[84]Ibid., *Les six livres*, 1.8.149; *The Six Bookes*, 1.8.103.

strances was conceded and was clearly recognized, the parlement had no right to persist in them; when the ruler's will was shown to be inflexible, the magistrates were bound to yield.[85] L'Hôpital had admonished the Parlement of Paris in November 1561 that although remonstrances were always well received by the king the Parlement ought to accept the legislation of the king's council after remonstrances had been issued.[86] "Even if kings command anything which seems unjust," it remained the duty of the magistrates "not to oppose themselves directly to the will of the king."[87] Bodin argued, in strikingly similar terms, that even if the commands of the sovereign were neither just nor honest, it was still "not lawful for the subject to break the laws of his prince" or oppose him "under the color of honesty or justice."[88]

In contrast to Bodin, François Hotman could not accept L'Hôpital's centralizing, autocratic policy that emphasized a preeminent royal authority. Hotman unequivocally declared in *Francogallia* that "the highest administrative authority in the kingdom" was vested in "the assembly of the three estates."[89] Hotman's emphasis on the authority of the Estates General was hardly reconcilable with L'Hôpital's insistence that the Estates, along with the parlements, had a purely advisory and consultative role and that its authority never overrode that of the king.

Bodin's *Les six livres* marked a departure from the medieval tradition of kingship, which tended to treat the king primarily as a judge. Disowning his own stance in *Methodus*, Bodin attributed to the king legislative authority, "the first and chief mark of a sovereign prince."[90] While one can specifically trace this marked shift in Bodin's thought, one can at best presume in L'Hôpital's thought the occurrence of a similar evolution, piecing together fragmentary statements uttered in his public speeches on various occasions. L'Hôpital's was not a sudden shift but a gradual evolution. At the Estates General at Orléans in 1560, L'Hôpital seemed to hold to the fundamental belief that justice was the essential attribute of the kingship: "The kings are elected above all to dispense justice, and it is not as royal an act to go to war as to exercise justice.... Therefore, on the seal of France is engraved not the figure of the king armed and on the horseback, as in many other countries, but the king sitting on his royal throne, rendering and dispensing justice."[91] In August 1563, L'Hôpital accused the parle-

---

[85]Bodin, *Les six livres*, 3.4.423; *The Six Bookes*, 3.4.320.
[86]*Oeuvres complètes*, 2:12–13.
[87]Ibid., 87–88.        [88]Bodin, *Les six livres*, 1.8.151.
[89]*Francogallia by François Hotman*, ed. Ralph E. Giesey and tr. J.H.M. Salmon (Cambridge: Cambridge University Press, 1972), 291.
[90]Bodin, *Les six livres*, 1.10.221.
[91]December 13, 1560, *Discours pour la majorité de Charles IX*, 74; *Oeuvres complètes*, I, 380.

ments of "interpreting" royal ordinances.[92] When the chancellor pronounced in November 1563 that "it was not reasonable that the judges
wanted legislative power," L'Hôpital seemed to be unequivocally
acknowledging that the king was the sole legislator.[93] L'Hôpital fundamentally accepted the idea of the king as justiciar and guardian of the law,
but he combined it with the conception of a sovereign as the sole law-
making authority, who was prepared to override the established laws in
the interests of the commonwealth as a whole. Attributing both legislative
and judicial prerogatives to the king alone was not uncommon among sixteenth-century legists. L'Hôpital attained, it seems, this synthesis in his
opening speech at the assembly of notables held in Moulins in January
1566, when he declared, "Justice belongs to the king and not to private
individuals …; in this monarchy the authority to interpret justice belongs
to the king, who makes the laws, and not to others."[94]

Chancellor L'Hôpital envisaged a polity in which royal power, limited
only by divine and fundamental law, would effectively promote the interests of the subjects against opposition from the magistracy. L'Hôpital's
effort to undermine the parlements' resistance to royal policies brought
about another dramatic confrontation with the cardinal of Lorraine in the
royal council in 1566.[95] At the meeting of Conseil Privé on March 16, the
cardinal of Lorraine, who had not followed the royal journey and only
recently rejoined the court at Moulins, presented a petition from the Parlement of Dijon. The Dijonnais parlementaires protested against a recent
royal edict that allowed persons of the Reformed religion in cities to call
for their ministers to console them and teach their children and themselves. This was a violation of the Edict of Amboise, which had allowed
Protestant worship only in one designated town in a bailliage or
sénéchaussée.[96] The petition had been presented by the delegates of the
Parlement of Dijon to the maîtres des requêtes. But the maîtres did not
report it to the royal council, apparently afraid of defying the chancellor,
who had sent the edict to the provinces, bypassing the registration procedure at the Parlement of Paris. The matter came to the ear of the cardinal,
and he indignantly told the Conseil Privé that he was astounded that
Catholics had no means to have their grievances heard at court. He

[92]*Oeuvres complètes*, 2:56.

[93]November 12, 1563, *Oeuvres complètes*, 2:87.

[94]*Remonstrance de Moulins*, 1566, *Discours pour la majorité de Charles IX*, 124.

[95]BN, MS Fr. 3951, fols. 100–107; BN, Dupuy 86, fol. 158. This incident is described in
*Mémoires de L'Estoile*, in Petitot, series 1, 45:62; "Deux altercations entre le Cardinal de Lorraine et le Chancelier l'Hôpital," 412–15; Jean-Marie Constant, *Les Guise* (Paris: Hachette,
1984), 59–60.

[96]Isambert, *Recueil général*, 14:137.

severely criticized the maîtres des requêtes who had neglected to report the petition to the royal councillors. Upon listening to the cardinal of Lorraine, the cardinal of Bourbon said that it must be the chancellor who created the edict in question, because the council had never discussed it. L'Hôpital turned to the cardinal of Lorraine and dryly remarked, "Monsieur, you already came back to trouble us." The cardinal retorted that he had, on the contrary, come to prevent the chancellor from troubling the kingdom. L'Hôpital then calmly asked whether the cardinal wanted to "prevent those poor people, whom the king allowed to live in accordance with their conscience, from ever being consoled." "Yes, I want to prevent that," said the cardinal, "because we know very well that allowing those things would be tacitly permitting secret sermons...." Lorraine, in exasperation, then yelled at the chancellor: "You, who enjoy your position today thanks to me, dare to tell me that I came to trouble you." The cardinal of Bourbon rushed to L'Hôpital's seat and loudly asked whether it was he who passed the edict without the knowledge of the council. At that point, all the council members leapt up, plunging the meeting into complete chaos.[97] The disorder at the council required the queen mother to intervene; she ordered that the edict be destroyed, and that those of the religion be forbidden to frequent towns where any exercise of their religion and the teaching of the Protestant catechism were strictly prohibited. The chancellor was specifically forbidden to seal any edicts concerning religious matters without the consent of the royal council. This incident, which definitely marked the end of L'Hôpital's friendship with the cardinal of Lorraine, was clear evidence of the chancellor's determination to prevent repetitive remonstrances of the parlements, which he regarded as entirely pointless and time-consuming.

Confronted with the daunting task of ending the civil wars that were tearing the kingdom apart, L'Hôpital could not afford the optimistic constitutionalist doctrine in the 1560s that the parlements' voices represented justice, civil order, and safety of the state, and that the constitution would be best served when the king freely submitted to the dictates of justice. Inevitably, however, his centralizing, reformist actions, and especially his unyielding efforts to reduce the parlements' authority generated the magistrates' deep hostility. Humiliated, and threatened, the parlementaires resented his authoritarian approach and felt betrayed by a former colleague.[98] L'Hôpital was certainly aware of this resentment over his rigor-

---

[97]*Mémoires de Condé*, 3:52.

[98]Colin Kaiser, "Les Cours souveraines au XVIe siècle: morale et Contre-Réforme," *Annales: Economies, Sociétés, Civilisations* 37 (1982), 15–31, explains the intractable attitudes of the magistrates, especially against the toleration of Protestants, in terms of an externalization of values. This process, he argues, was a precondition for the formation of the robe nobility in the second half of the sixteenth century.

ous advocacy of royal power and his religious policy. L'Hôpital once candidly told the parlementaires that he had been of their opinion when he was a member of the court, but had since learned that "one profits more doing otherwise." "I believe," he told the judges, "that you too would have changed your opinion had you served the king close to the throne."[99] The magistrates were sympathetic neither to the chancellor's plea for obedience to the royal will nor to his call for religious moderation. The result was continuous clashes between them.

L'Hôpital's battle with the parlementaires cost him dearly by dangerously narrowing his political base. The magistrates' opposition to the chancellor eventually helped bring about his disgrace in 1568. L'Hôpital's exit from the political stage cleared the floor for the impending tragedy of the St. Bartholomew's Day massacre, in which fanatical forces decimated whatever hope was left for a peaceful resolution of the civil war.[100] L'Hôpital's uncompromising authoritarianism certainly frightened the judges. In 1580, the Parlement of Paris claimed in its remonstrances to Henry III that L'Hôpital, by then deceased, had openly conceded in his later years that he had been wrong to attempt to restrict the Parlement's right of remonstrance.[101] This allegation of the magistrates, hard to prove as it is, was in effect a posthumous testimonial to L'Hôpital's reputation as an opponent of the constitutional pretensions of the Parlement and as an advocate of unchallenged royal authority.

---

[99]November 12, 1563, *Oeuvres complètes*, 2:90.

[100]Bourgeon was apparently overstating when he argued that the Parlement of Paris played the role of "sorcerer's apprentice" in the St. Bartholomew's Day massacre; Bourgeon, "La Fronde parlementaire," 24–25.

[101]Maugis, *Parlement de Paris*, 1:620–21.

# Chapter 6

# A Solon of France

E TIENNE PASQUIER is among those contemporaries of L'Hôpital who provide us with insightful and discerning observations of the chancellor and his policy. Pasquier mostly mentions L'Hôpital with profound respect and affection. After the Colloquy of Poissy in 1561, Pasquier remarked: "Monsieur le Chancelier & Monsieur l'Admiral [de Coligny] control most of the affairs [at court]; the former, a *sage politique*, the latter, an agitator and a promotor of the new Religion." Five years later, in the spring of 1566, this Catholic parlementaire wrote: "Monsieur le chancelier does what he can, and not what he once wanted. He hopes that all the things maintain a balance, with good conscience and without dissimulation, between this muffled division, in order not to stir new troubles." Pasquier added, however, "I do not think that his opinion will be very well followed."[1] This comment is indeed a trenchant observation of the evolution of L'Hôpital's religious policy, and in a way a reflection of the increasing opposition to L'Hôpital's religious policy, not just in the Parlement of Paris but throughout the royal court.

Pasquier's reservations about L'Hôpital's toleration policy did not deter him from acclaiming the chancellor as the author of many remarkable ordinances and edicts. During his chancellorship, L'Hôpital sought not only to subdue religious struggle between Catholics and Protestants but also to instigate fundamental and far-reaching reforms through sweeping legislation. He was convinced that unchallenged royal power would be established throughout the kingdom only with a reorganized bureaucracy and improved judicial structure. Pasquier praised the reformist ideals of L'Hôpital, the "principal mediator" of the Ordinance of Orléans in 1561, and the "instigator, promotor, and author" of the Edict of

---

[1]Pasquier, *Lettres historiques*, 70-71.

Roussillon in 1563 and the Ordinance of Moulins in 1566. L'Hôpital made these excellent laws, Pasquier stressed, when "the weakness of [Charles IX's] young age" and "the extraordinary violence of the times did not allow any leisure for legislations." Pasquier added regretfully, "I wish that [those laws] had been observed with the same devotion as they were introduced."[2] Along with the highly unpopular pacification edicts, L'Hôpital's judicial and administrative reforms met with almost perennial opposition. Many powerful interest groups, including the magistrates at the Parlement of Paris, perceived L'Hôpital's reform efforts as intrusive innovations that had to be resisted in order to preserve their privileges. By the time of the issuance of the Ordinance of Moulins, the chancellor's influence at court had already significantly waned. The gradual erosion of L'Hôpital's position in the royal council, especially after the Protestant plot to seize Charles IX at Meaux in September 1567, thwarted the implementation of most of his reform edicts.

This chapter will examine L'Hôpital's reforming program and indefatigable legislative efforts, seen against the backdrop of his declining influence at court and his eventual disgrace in the fall of 1568. L'Hôpital's reform edicts represented a distinct political vision during the religious wars that perceived the uniform and equitable legal system and the restoration of the integrity of royal administration as an essential solution to the crisis. When his efforts to prevent religious conflict faltered, L'Hôpital, undaunted, resolutely pursued reforms of the judicial and administrative structure, which he believed would ultimately help establish lasting peace in the kingdom.

L'Hôpital made conscious attempts to gather public opinions on a broad basis and include them in his reform edicts. He was keenly aware of the deep-seated grievances of the people against the disarray of judicial administration, and thus devoted major efforts to the reformation of justice. The Ordinance of Orléans, drafted by the chancellor on the basis of the *cahiers de doléances* of the estates, was a faithful reflection of public opinion.[3] The preamble of the Ordinance confirmed that its 151 articles were drawn up "on the complaints, grievances and remonstrances of the deputies of the three estates of our kingdom." Lucien Romier, who was hardly generous in his assessment of L'Hôpital's chancellorship, asserted that L'Hôpital proposed the Ordinance only as a concession to the

---

[2]*Les Oeuvres d'Estienne Pasquier, contenant ses recherches de la France ...* (Amsterdam, 1723), 2:575-76.

[3]For the question of the administrative transformation during the Religious Wars and public opinion, see André Stegmann, "Transformations administratives et opinion publique en France (1560-1580)," *Beihefte Der Francia, Histoire comparée de l'administration* (Munich: Artemis Verlag, 1980), 594-612.

demands of the nobles and the Third Estate, from whom the government wanted to extract money.[4] But the Ordinance of Orléans was more than a temporary contrivance. The chancellor's persistent efforts for judicial reforms were confirmed by the Ordinance of Moulins, which was in many respects a reiteration of the Ordinance of Orléans.

L'Hôpital's judicial reforms were geared to restore the integrity of the judicature, by suppressing widespread corruption and abuses and delineating jurisdictional boundaries. One of the core targets was the suppression of venal judicial offices, whose number had drastically increased during the wars in Italy. L'Hôpital denounced sale of offices as the main cause of judicial degradation, condemning such "shameful traffic of justice."[5] Venality of office was an important cause for the declining morality of the judges who, he argued, sought to reimburse themselves quickly for the price they had paid for the office. They were thus prone to take excessive épices and interested only in lucrative cases. According to the chancellor, "these days the judges do not want to do anything without money."[6] L'Hôpital repeatedly urged the magistrates to perform their duties without excessive passion and prejudice. He admonished the parlementaires of Rouen in 1563: "Make sure that, when you render a judgment, you be not swayed by enmity, favor, or prejudice.... You are judge of the cases brought to justice; you are not judge of life, morals, or religion.... If you do not feel strong and fair enough to control your passion and love your enemies, as God commands, abstain from the duties of judge."[7]

L'Hôpital was particularly concerned about the growth of an excessive esprit de corps and independence of the law courts, which compromised royal power. The creation of new offices often promoted alliances among families within the parlements and allowed them to exert powerful influence, thus weakening royal control of the magistrates. L'Hôpital deplored the situation in which bribes and solicitation were a common usage for procuring an office for a relative or a friend of councillors and

---

[4]Romier, *Catholiques et Huguenots*, 180-85.

[5]"... afin que toutes choses soyent réduictes à la raison & aux anciennes moeurs, il faut regarder & chercher tous les moyens d'oster toute avarice & ambition, larrecin & malice des hommes. Et pour ce que c'est chose notoire que la multiplicité des juges est cause de grands procez"; *Remonstrance de Moulins*, 1566, in *Discours pour la majorité de Charles IX*, 124.

[6]Address of August 17, 1563, *Discours pour la majorité de Charles IX*, 109; *Oeuvres complètes*, 2:70. L'Hôpital denounced the profit-chasing tendency of judges: "Quand estoit question de rapporter ung procez pour avoir ung escu, chascung y estoit; mais quand estoit question d'un affaire publique, personne n'y voulloit venir"; address of September 7, 1560, *Discours pour la majorité de Charles IX*, 50-51; *Oeuvres complètes*, 1:353-54.

[7]Address of August 17, 1563, *Discours pour la majorité de Charles IX*, 108; *Oeuvres complètes*, 2:69.

presidents.[8] The judges also looked to prominent seigneurs for favors, L'Hôpital complained, and did not hide their efforts to promote their patrons' interests rather than royal interests. The chancellor told the magistrates of Paris in 1560 that "there are more solicitors than judges" in the parlement.[9] He pointed out again in 1566 that "many presidents and councillors are more devoted to the princes and seigneurs than to the king, to such an extent that they do not hesitate to compromise the interests of the king in order to serve their patrons; [the judges] attend to their patrons' affairs and law suits as if they were domestic servants, a situation very unworthy of their position."[10]

At the Estates General at Orléans in 1560, the three estates expressed their unanimous hostility to venality of office.[11] Responding to their grievances, the Ordinance of Orléans stipulated the general suppression of all judicial offices created since the reign of Louis XII (article 30). Article 32 banned the pluralism of judicial officials, and debarred fathers and sons, brothers, and uncles and nephews from sitting in the same parlement.[12] The Ordinance of Moulins modified this measure, which apparently was too unrealistic in the current situation, and stipulated that members of the same family already serving in the same parlement merely be forbidden to sit in the same chamber.[13] Article 39 prescribed measures for the election to, rather than purchase of, offices: once a vacancy occurred in a parlement, the court would elect three candidates, from among whom the king would make the final nomination.[14] Article 44 explicitly prohibited the magistrates from "accepting any pension or salary from seigneurs and dames of this kingdom."[15] In practical terms, the problem was that the king was far from being able to repurchase the offices that he, and his predecessors, had created and sold. Thus the king had to continue the practice, whether or not he had any intention of stopping the alienation of substantial parts of his prerogative in return for money. This was indeed a

---

[8]L'Hôpital told the parlementaires: "plusieurs [of the judges] se sont desbordez, usans de leurs offices comme d'un bien temporel & propre patrimoine, s'estudians plus à leur profit qu'à faire le service qu'ils doyvent au roy"; *Remonstrance de Moulins*, 1566, *Discours pour la majorité de Charles IX*, 122.

[9]Address of July 5, 1560, *Oeuvres complètes*, 1:329.

[10]*Remonstrance de Moulins*, in *Discours pour la majorité de Charles IX*, 127.

[11]Picot, *Histoire des Etats Généraux*, 2:230-67; Romier, *Royaume de Catherine de Médicis*, 2:36; Mousnier, *La vénalité des office*, 75-76.

[12]Isambert, *Recueil général*, 14:72-73. The ordinance of 1493 had prohibited receiving two brothers in the same chamber. The ordinance of 1499 extended the rule to include father and son; see Aubert, "Organisation," 235.

[13]Article 85; see Aubert, "Organisation," 212.

[14]Isambert, *Recueil général*, 14:72-74.

[15]Isambert, *Recueil général*,14: 76.

recurring dilemma throughout the Ancien Régime. The perennial penury of the royal treasury, especially severe during the civil wars, therefore required that the abolition of venal offices take place only when particular offices were vacated by the death of their incumbents.

When the government's lack of money made it difficult for L'Hôpital to launch an all-out abolition of venality as he would have wished, he sought instead to effect a tighter supervision over the existing system. He stiffened the regulations of resignation and *survivance* and took care not to let the limited venality allowed in financial offices pervade the judicial sector.[16] L'Hôpital also imposed stricter qualification requirements for officials. In February 1561, he refused to approve the resignation of a conseiller at the Parlement of Paris in favor of Antoine Loisel, the future author of *Institutes coutumières*, because Loisel was only twenty-three years old, apparently too young to assume as important a post as councillor.[17] L'Hôpital attempted, on the other hand, to prevent the senility of officials by strengthening the "quarante jours" clause, a rule which compelled many officials to resign before it was too late, in order not to lose their office in case they died before forty days lapsed after the completion of transaction.[18] The Ordinance of Moulins spelled out the eligibility of new officials: candidates for the office of conseiller in the parlements must be at least twenty-five years old and have passed an examination before the entire court (article 9); in cases of résignation, an investigation was required regarding the "capacity and prudence" of the beneficiary (article 12).[19] The chancellor retained the final right to examine the qualification of royal officials before their appointment.[20]

According to the abbé de Brantôme, L'Hôpital's tough standards for the judges, whether for their knowledge, competency, or conduct, made them fear him as school pupils feared their principal. Brantôme described in his Mémoires an interesting anecdote he had witnessed.[21] One evening, a new président and a conseiller paid a visit to the chancellor seeking his

[16]L'Hôpital wrote to Artus de Cossé, sieur de Gonnor, who in 1564 became *surintendant des finances*: "la roine m'escrit particulièrement de l'article des résignations, lequel fault passer attendu la nécessité du temps, mais gardez bien que l'argent ne soit donné et aussi ne tirés résignations aux officiers de judicature mais à ceux qui sont vénaulx seulement." August 30, 1562, BN, Cinq Cent de Colbert 24, fol. 159. *Survivance* was the practice of resignation in favor of a designee, a son or a relative in most cases, while in fact the *résignataire* and *résignant* were jointly holding the office until it eventually passed into the possession of the survivor at the death of the incumbent. Shennan, *The Parlement of Paris*, 114.

[17]Mousnier, *La vénalité des offices*, 46; Aubert, "Organisation," 218.

[18]Mousnier, *La vénalité des offices*, 45.

[19]Isambert, *Recueil général*, 14:192-93.

[20]Michaud, *La grande Chancellerie*, 51.

[21]Brantôme, *Oeuvres complètes*, 3:307-8.

approval of their candidacy for nomination. Upon receiving them, L'Hôpital opened a law code on the table to a page chosen at random and then asked his two guests to explain a legal clause on that page. Caught surprised and unprepared, each of the two judges trembled like "a leaf in the wind" and offered such incoherent and unsatisfactory answers that the chancellor had to give them an impromptu lecture on the question he posed. L'Hôpital harshly reproved them; although they were almost fifty years old, he said, they still needed to go back to school. After they left, L'Hôpital deplored the serious harm inflicted when such ignorant judges were made responsible for royal justice and told Brantôme that he would request the king not to confirm them to the offices. This incident testifies that L'Hôpital attempted to impose a closer control over qualifications for judicial office, when the abolition of venality was no longer an option, in order to reduce its harmful effects on royal justice. In 1560, soon after he became chancellor, L'Hôpital created a post of *contrôleur et garde des rôles* in the Chancellerie in charge of all the *rôles*, or registers, for the provision of offices, and appointed Gilbert Combaud, his secretary and confidant, to the position.[22] Such meticulous control over offices has led one historian to comment, half-seriously, that the chancellor exerted particular influence on the "systematic organization" of venality.[23]

L'Hôpital's judicial reform program reflected the remarkably broad spectrum of his reformist vision. A notable illustration of his extensive reform agenda was the creation of consular jurisdiction. The edict of November 1563 established a special court in Paris to adjudicate commercial disputes, allowing an expeditious form of justice to merchants who ought to "negotiate with each other in good faith without being constrained to the subtleties of laws and ordinances."[24] This measure was intended to provide merchants with a simplified recourse for their legal problems and reduce the number of lawsuits clogging the courts. L'Hôpital claimed that there were more proceedings at the Châtelet in Paris than

[22]BN, Dupuy 233, fol. 145; Abraham Tessereau, *Histoire chronologique de La grande chancellerie de France* (Paris: Pierre Emery, 1710), 1:134; P. Guyot and P.-A. Merlin *Traité des droits,* 412; Henri François Delaborde, *Etude sur la constitution du Trésor des Chartes* (Paris: Plon-Nourrit, 1909), clxix; Michaud, *La grande Chancellerie,* 81-82. Concerning the procedure of the provision of offices, see Mousnier, *La vénalité des offices,* 60-61.

[23]Michaud, *La grande Chancellerie,* 27, 282.

[24]Isambert, *Recueil général,* 14:153-54; *Registres des délibérations du bureau de la ville de Paris,* ed. François Bonnardot, et al. (Paris, 1888-1892), 5:352-54. The city government of Paris had made request in October 1563 to the king for formation of a consular court, conveying the local businessmen's desire to obtain a simplified form of justice; see *Registres des délibérations du bureau de la ville de Paris,* 5:321-22. The preamble of the edict of November indicates that it was a response to this request "for the public good and the simplification of all proceedings."

throughout Italy. The judges were being so fastidious about the subtleties of law as to cause the legal system nearly to stall. The chancellor pointed out in August 1563:

> A good judge is one who prevents crimes from being committed, rather than punishing them.... But [these days] the judges instead seek fame not by trying to decrease litigations but by rendering intricate and equivocal judgments, which simply prompt more legal wranglings. [As a result] although they are seated all year around on the bench, lawsuits never seem to diminish.[25]

L'Hôpital was also aware that the existing judicial institutions did not respond to the realities of commerce, posing instead serious obstacles to its growth. Jurisdictions of prévôt, bailli, présidial, seigneury, church, university, and municipality all intervened in commercial affairs. Contracts concluded between merchants in different places were often the object of conflicting legal interpretations. Once started, the proceedings were inextricable and seemed to last forever. Lawyers representing seigneurs frequently resorted to juridical subtleties in order to make their services indispensable, and the judges were often found negligent. By the time the case reached the parlements, both parties had already spent such huge sums of money that winning the case could hardly make up for their financial losses. L'Hôpital told the Parlement of Paris in September 1560 that intricate legal proceedings always brought devastating results, such as the bankruptcy of disputants, and that the collapse of credit among them threatened the entire system of commerce.[26]

L'Hôpital was convinced that the encouragement of arbitration and conciliation was the only way to spare both the disputants and the judges from lengthy, painful, and costly proceedings. This conviction led him to launch an initial reform in the summer of 1560, allowing merchants to resolve among themselves, without the intervention of ordinary justice, those disputes occurring during commercial activities.[27] The edict of August 1560 removed all commercial cases from the ordinary tribunals and required that merchants submit their differences to conciliation and

---

[25]*Discours pour la majorité de Charles IX*, 109; *Oeuvres complètes*, 2:71.

[26]*Discours pour la majorité de Charles IX*, 52-54; *Oeuvres complètes*, 1:356-59.

[27]L'Hôpital proposed in the same month a separate edict, that would require the disputants in certain cases, particularly in family lawsuits involving property, to exhaust all available arbitration procedures before they came to the court; Isambert, *Recueil général*, 14:49-50. If one still persisted in going to a courtroom, L'Hôpital told the Parlement of Paris, he would find there plenty of vicious people; address of September 7, 1560, *Discours pour la majorité de Charles IX*, 52; *Oeuvres complètes*, 1:356.

pure and simple arbitration, which would have the effect of sovereign judgment.[28] Introducing this measure to the Parlement of Paris, L'Hôpital boasted that for those who had pleaded their case for twenty or thirty years it would bring an alternative within three days.[29] This drastic edict creating forced arbitration was replaced three years later with the creation of a much more elaborate system of consular jurisdiction in Paris.

The first two articles of the edict of November 1563 prescribed the election of the judges of the new consular court. The prévôt des marchands and the échevins drew up a list of one hundred bourgeois notables who were French nationals and residents of Paris. These notables then gathered to choose five members among them, of which the first was nominated judge and the four others consuls. Their commission lasted one year. The new officials were sworn in before the prévôt des marchands. From the second year, however, the prévôt and échevins no longer played any role in the election. Three days prior to the expiration of their commission, the judge and consuls assembled sixty merchants, who elected thirty among them. The latter, in collaboration with the outgoing judge and consuls, nominated five new officials. Article 3 stipulated the competence of the judge and consuls: their jurisdiction extended to "the cognizance of all the cases between merchants over the matters of commerce only." Since the main purpose of the consular tribunal was to save merchants' time and money, all the procedures at this new court were designed specifically to avoid the delays and intricacies of regular court proceedings. The disputing parties were required to show up in court and be heard in person, without representation by attorneys or prosecutors (article 4). The judge and the consuls primarily served as arbitrators between them. If the two sides did not reach an agreement in the first court appearance, the court adjourned only once briefly to allow each party to produce evidence and/ or bring witnesses. When evidence and witnesses were presented, the judge delivered a verdict immediately (articles 5 and 6). Only disputes in excess of 500 livres in value were allowed to appeal to the Parlement of Paris (article 9).

The establishment of consular jurisdiction in Paris was an outcome of L'Hôpital's consistent efforts to simplify complicated trial procedures. Its elaborate and efficient system seemed to be an almost perfect exemplar of the reform ideals of the chancellor. First of all, the new consular court

---

[28]Merchants were to "elect three persons, or more if the case requires it, from among merchants or those of other quality, and resolve differences following their decision and arbitration, which will have the effect of transaction, or sovereign judgment, and will not be reversed by approximation or appeal or other means"; Isambert, *Recueil général*, 14:51.

[29]Address of September 7, 1560, *Discours pour la majorité de Charles IX*, 52-54; *Oeuvres complètes*, 1:356-59.

resolved disputes in equity through arbitration, instead of legal wranglings. L'Hôpital had declared in 1549 that "the ultimate goal of the laws" was "safeguarding common good, which diminishes with dispute and increases with concord."[30] Secondly, the judge and consuls were elected, and hence removable. While the royal judges were installed to their position after having obtained the letters of provision, the merchant judges were elected to their office by their fellow merchants and occupied the position for only one year. Unlike the regular judges, the consular judges rendered free justice and were strictly forbidden to receive the épices. It was well known that L'Hôpital was an outspoken critic of the épices and the permanent tenure of royal officials.[31] L'Hôpital further opposed venality of office because he was concerned that the widespread practice of selling offices would divert credit that might otherwise be available for commerce. L'Hôpital complained that the excessive infatuation with a legal career hampered the development of trade and business. He pointed out in 1565 that "there is nothing which is more harmful to commerce than the excessive number of men of long robe; because no sooner did a merchant have some money than he tries to make his son attorney or councillor."[32]

The establishment of consular courts thus reflected the reform-minded chancellor's intention to promote commercial activities by simplifying legal procedures and to boost, when possible, business careers shunned by many aspiring bourgeois. Finally, Chancellor L'Hôpital, who had frequently expressed his concerns about the qualifications of royal officials, must have found it desirable that the consular judges, who were themselves merchants, were well versed in commercial practices and therefore able to render equitable and informed decisions over those commercial cases brought before them.

When he deplored the fact that too many young men went into the robe rather than trade, L'Hôpital was not, it is important to stress, trying to prevent social mobility for the good of national production; he was rather expressing his concerns that sale of offices retarded the industry and commerce of France by deflecting money and talent from entrepreneurial pursuits. It is very likely that L'Hôpital had fundamental faith in the virtue of upward social mobility as a result of merit and hard work. His own career was a striking example of such: born as the son of an obscure doctor, L'Hôpital began his public career when he obtained the

[30]Epistle to Jacques du Faur, *Michaelis Hospitalii, Carmina,* 89, cited from Taillandier, *Nouvelles recherches,* 359.
[31]L'Hôpital's objection to the irremovability of royal officials is discussed below.
[32]*Oeuvres complètes,* 2:114.

post of conseiller at the Parlement of Paris, thanks to his wife's dowry. L'Hôpital, therefore, does not seem to have condemned a priori venality of office; he rather attempted to remedy systematically its destructive effects on the administration of justice and to prevent money from replacing knowledge and virtue as a necessary condition for obtaining judicial offices.[33]

Consular jurisdiction met, however, with vehement resistance from municipal, royal, and even seigneurial judges, who were all deprived of their jurisdiction over commercial cases. Frequent conflicts followed between the *Châtelet* of Paris and the consular tribunal in Paris.[34] The consular court's emphasis on the arbitration of disputes in equity rather than juridical subtleties and formalities was criticized from the beginning by the regular judges, in particular by those in the parlements, who criticized the merchant judges for their ignorance of law and jurisprudence. In a series of remonstrances sent to the king in December 1563, the Parlement of Paris argued that merchant judges were not only ignorant of the laws which they were supposed to apply but were also avid for profit, the last thing to be expected from judges.[35] Merchants were "basically not of good faith" and their artifices were so cunning that only experienced men could discern them. The parlement further argued that merchant judges would favor the members of their confraternities, thus causing the danger of monopoly and competition between various guilds: this would plunge Paris into confusion and chaos. The parlementaires were especially

[33]Some jurists indeed argued in favor of venality, because the venal system, by enabling an individual to overcome social barriers that would otherwise constrain him, was an important means of social mobility. Most notable among advocates of venality was Montesquieu in the eighteenth century, who maintained that the system of purchasing offices encouraged people to work hard and was hence beneficial to industry; see *De l'esprit des loix* (Geneva, 1750), 1.5.19.138-39: "Advancing oneself by way of wealth inspires and maintains industry, a thing badly needed in this kind of government". Montesquieu further argued that venality was desirable in monarchical states, because, "if the posts were not sold by a public regulation, the courtiers' indigence and avidity would sell them all the same; chance will produce better subjects than the choice of the prince." Montesquieu thus shared the opinions of Richelieu, who regarded venality as a lesser evil, since "if venality were abolished, the disorder which would result from intrigues and manoeuvres, by which one procured offices, would be greater than what would be borne from the liberty to sell and purchase them"; see Richelieu, *Testament politique*, ed. L. André (Paris: R. Laffont, 1947), chap. 5, sec. 1, p. 241. L'Hôpital was more idealistic than either of them: His zeal as a reformer sustained him fast in his vision of an efficient and purified judicature that would create good government.

[34]The offensives of the prévôt de Paris, prévôt des marchands, and prévôt de l'hôtel against the merchant judges are described in detail in M. G. Denière, *La Juridiction consulaire de Paris, 1563-1792* (Paris: Henri Plon, 1872), 8-12.

[35]AN, X1a, 1607, fols. 154, 156, and 203 (December 17, 18, and 31, 1563). The parlement's remonstrances are analyzed in Maugis, *Histoire du Parlement de Paris*, 1:336-38.

aggrieved by the fact that the consular court was empowered to judge "souverainement" and was not subject to appeal in the parlement. The Parlement of Paris perceived this limitation of its appellate jurisdiction as a serious curtailment of its authority. Finally, the magistrates remonstrated that the creation of the consular court was a violation of the principle of royal justice, because such a court would serve only the interests of a particular group. Aware of the fact that the chancellor was the instigator of the creation of consular jurisdiction, the parlement chose to bring up the memory of the Semestre system, a largely unsuccessful attempt that had been supported by L'Hôpital. New experiments were always dangerous, the magistrates contended, as had been proved by "the invention of the *Semestre*, from which one expected a lot, but which simply turned out to be a fiasco."[36] The antagonism of the regular judges against the consular court was, in large part, due to the conflict of financial interests. Since épices constituted an essential part of remuneration of judicial officials, they inevitably resented the initiative of Chancellor L'Hôpital which attempted to deprive them of a good proportion of their perquisites of office. The exclusion of prosecutors and attorneys from consular court understandably created strong hostilities among this auxiliary personnel of justice.[37] But L'Hôpital was not swayed by these complaints and opposition. Upon the reiterated royal command to register the edict of November 1563, the Parlement of Paris finally capitulated, and registered the edict in January 1564, although with reservations.[38] The election of a judge and four consuls on January 27 inaugurated the consular jurisdiction in Paris.

A form of consular jurisdiction was quickly extended to other cities, including Bordeaux (December 1563), Orléans (February 1564), Nantes (April 1564), Calais (April 1565), and Amiens (May 1567). The jurisdiction of the courts was extended by the royal declaration of April 1565 so that even royal officials or privileged members of the universities who were engaged in trade would henceforth be judged by consular judges.[39] The rapid growth of consular jurisdiction intensified the protests of the sovereign courts. Their offensive achieved a partial victory when the Ordinance of Blois (1579) limited the creation of consular courts to principal cities with major commercial activities and the regular judges recovered com-

---

[36]For the Semestre, see chap. 2, pp. 37–38, above.

[37]Jean Hilaire, *Introduction historique au droit commercial* (Paris: Presses Universitaires de France, 1986), 73; A. Lefas, "La Juridiction consulaire de Lille et le protocole d'Adrien Baillon," *Revue du Nord* 7 (1921): 263.

[38]AN, X1a, 1607, fol. 244 (January 10, 1564).

[39]Article 2 of Declaration of April 28, 1565, Isambert, *Recueil général*, 14:181. See Victor Legrand, *Juges et Consuls, 1563-1905* (Bordeaux: Imprimerie G. Delmas, n.d.), 53-57.

mercial jurisdiction in towns without a présidial court (articles 239 and 240).[40] But even Michelet, who derided L'Hôpital's reforms as mere paper fantasy, did not question the lasting effect of consular jurisdiction.[41]

The creation of consular jurisdiction constituted an integral part of L'Hôpital's reforms to streamline judicial structure and improve the efficiency of the legal system. No less important, however, was the chancellor's intention to diminish municipal administrative independence by depriving the municipal courts of their jurisdiction over commercial matters. In important commercial towns where consular courts were introduced, the activities of merchant judges inevitably encroached upon the jurisdiction of the municipal judges. Municipal jurisdiction had been in gradual decline since the thirteenth century, but it was during L'Hôpital's chancellorship that decisive actions were taken to diminish its role. Many of the functions of the municipal government in Paris, the Hôtel de ville, overlapped those of the officers of the Prévôté de Paris appointed by the king. Conflicts of competence between municipal judges and royal judges were frequent in the sixteenth century, and in most cases the parlement upheld the pretensions of royal officials, punishing the municipalities by imposing severe fines. In order to prevent further confusion and delay resulting from the equivocal judicial boundaries, the Ordinance of Orléans abolished municipal jurisdiction where it constituted an inferior jurisdiction; thereafter, the bailli possessed the right of adjudication over civil affairs, without assistance or intervention from the échevins, who were often deemed incapable of handling these cases (article 50).[42] It was the Ordinance of Moulins which brought a final blow to municipal jurisdiction. Article 71 stipulated that the municipal government's jurisdiction be henceforth limited to police and criminal matters, and not to extend over civil matters.[43] The abolition of municipal jurisdiction over civil matters was a confirmation of the exclusive competence of royal jurisdiction over all the affairs concerning the person or the rights of the king. Article 72 of the Ordinance of Moulins specifically stipulated that in unchartered towns criminal jurisdiction was entrusted to the elected members of the

---

[40]Isambert, *Recueil général*, 15:434-35. See Paul Dupieux, "Les Attributions de la juridiction consulaire de Paris, 1563-1793: L'Arbitrage entre associés, commerçants, patrons et ouvriers au XVIIIe siècle," *Bibliothèque de l'Ecole des Chartes* 95 (1934:, 118.

[41]Michelet, *Oeuvres complètes*, 8:185, 199.

[42]Isambert, *Recueil général*, 14:78.

[43]Isambert, *Recueil général*, 14:208. The échevins understandably resisted this measure, and demanded the return of their ancient privileges; see, for instance, the request made to Charles IX by the échevinage of Amiens in February 1568, in Augustin Thierry, *Recueil des monuments inédits de l'histoire du tiers état* (Paris, 1850-1870), 2:777-79; see also Georges Testaud, *Des Juridictions municipales en France, des origines jusqu'à l'ordonnance de Moulins* (Paris, 1901), 189.

bourgeoisie and citizens, thus reinforcing local communal responsibilities over police and order.[44] Considered alongside the establishment of consular jurisdiction in commercial matters, these measures clearly displayed Chancellor L'Hôpital's aim to delineate and integrate judicial hierarchy in the kingdom and to protect royal interests by diminishing the administrative autonomy of municipal government. Local privileges were significantly abrogated with the loss of civil jurisdiction; yet the vital interests of the merchant community in the cities were safeguarded by the special form of justice of the consular tribunals.

The attack upon the municipal privileges attested to L'Hôpital's intention to restrain the jurisdiction of those who held their office by privilege, whether municipal corporations, the royal *officiers*, or ecclesiastics. L'Hôpital fundamentally objected to perpetual privileges of any kind. He firmly believed that all privileges granted by the king had force only during the lifetime of the ruler; otherwise they tended to compromise the prerogative of his successors. For L'Hôpital, laws, ordinances, letters patent, or grants did not take effect during the reign of successor princes, unless they were ratified by their express consent, or at least by tacit permission. According to Bodin, L'Hôpital refused, despite the request of the queen mother, to approve the privileges granted by Charles IX to the abbey of St. Maur-des-Fossés, because they carried the right of permanent exemption from the taille.[45] A notable illustration of the perpetual grant of privileges was the irremovability of officials. L'Hôpital did approve, at the accession of Charles IX in 1560, the exemption of royal officials from the procedure of *confirmation*, a kind of tax the incumbents of royal and municipal offices were obliged to pay in order to be confirmed in their offices at the accession of a king.[46] Some historians view the exemption as inconsistent with the chancellor's objection to permanent tenure of officials, and have interpreted it as his official approbation of the system of venality of offices.[47] It is more likely, however, that the decision to excuse royal officials from payment was rather a result of practical considerations, because less than two years previously they had paid a confirmation tax at the coronation of Francis II. L'Hôpital's opposition to any grant of permanent privileges was, as Bodin pointed out, a clear example of the assertion of undivided royal sovereignty.[48]

In his letter to Chancellor Olivier in 1547, L'Hôpital, then conseiller at the Parlement of Paris, spoke of a project that he had undertaken, the com-

[44]Isambert, *Recueil général*, 14:208-9.
[45]Bodin, *Les six livres*, 1.8.132.
[46]AN, X1a, 1596, fol. 109, declaration of December 10, 1560.
[47]Maugis, *Parlement de Paris*, 1:3, 239.
[48]Bodin, *Les six livres*, 1.8.132.

pilation of legal precedents with commentaries. The judge wrote that it would "offer many advantages, as a simple and easy reference" in resolving "problems and obscure points" of law.[49] Unfortunately, this work is not extant, and it is not certain whether the book was ever completed. In 1548, a year after he wrote to Olivier, L'Hôpital regretted that "if I were not interrupted by trials and disputes ... I could finish my book within two or three years."[50] Yet Jacques Auguste de Thou, referring to some work of L'Hôpital on law which "still has not seen the light," wrote that "for the good of the kingdom, that book, truly deserving immortality, should be published some day."[51] It is difficult to determine whether the book De Thou mentioned was L'Hôpital's aforementioned legal commentaries. But, in any case, this evidence indicates that L'Hôpital had himself planned to provide a cohesive body of laws, a project which he later, as chancellor, carried on by drafting many ordinances and edicts.

The important objective of L'Hôpital was to create a new and simple legal code, adapted to the historical experience of France and also the special needs of the times. L'Hôpital directed his reforms in the framework of the contemporary Renaissance jurists' movement to reorganize the French jurisprudence. The second half of the sixteenth century witnessed the remarkable development of jurisprudence in France. Legal scholars attempted to expound the contents of the *Corpus Juris* and develop them into a veritable body of jurisprudence. In the process, they realized that a large part of the rules in the *Corpus* were peculiar to the special needs of Rome and were in fact irrelevant to legal practice in France. The jurists thus arrived at the conclusion that the French law should be based not on a blind exposition of the Roman law but on an independent synthesis of the French juridical and historical experience.[52] The leading legists, such as François Baudouin, the author of *De Institutione historiae universae et ejus cum jurisprudentia conjunctione prolegomenon* (1561), Jean Bodin, the author of *Methodus ad facilem historiarum cognitionem* (1566), and François Hotman, the author of *Antitribonian* (1567), all looked to Chancellor L'Hôpital as the ultimate source for their movement. Bodin and Hotman, in particu-

[49]Epistle to Olivier, *Poésies complètes*, 13.

[50]Epistle to the Cardinal du Bellay, *Poésies complètes*, 68.

[51]De Thou, *Histoire universelle*, 4:824.

[52]Concerning the Renaissance jurists' attack on the authority of Roman law, see John L. Brown, *The Methodus ad facilem historiarum cognitionem: A Critical Study* (Washington, D.C.: Catholic University of America Press, 1939), chap. 2; Julian H. Franklin, *Jean Bodin and the Sixteenth Century Revolution in the Methodology of Law and History* (New York: Columbia University Press, 1963), chap. 2.

lar, writing almost at the same period, composed their books in the context of the reformist ideas of L'Hôpital.[53] Hotman's *Antitribonian* bears in the title page the statement that the book was "fait par l'advis de feu Monsieur de l'Hospital chancelier en France en l'an 1567."[54]

In the preface to the *Methodus*, Bodin wrote that his intention was "to bring together and compare the legal frameworks of all states" to establish what laws any commonwealth needs to possess for a satisfactory legal system.[55] Bodin's rejection of the exclusive study of the laws of ancient Rome was largely shared by Hotman. Pointing out that "the difference between the existing state of our France and that of the Romans is so great and enormous," Hotman maintained that the basic aim of legal study in France should be the study of history, laws, and customs actually in force in France.[56] The two theorists thus agreed on the need for the combined study of law and history and upheld Chancellor L'Hôpital's call for a more uniform and equitable legal code in France. Hotman celebrated in the *Antitribonian* the chancellor's reformist undertaking, and indeed called him the French Solon:

> It will be very easy at this time, when it has pleased God to grant
> our France a Solon in the person of the great Michel de l'Hôpital,
> to bring together a number of jurisconsults, statesmen, and some
> of the more notable advocates and practitioners of the kingdom,
> and to charge them with bringing together what they can use in
> the books of Justinian as well as in the books of philosophy and in
> experience.[57]

Hotman's theory of popular sovereignty in *Francogallia* was, as explained in the previous chapter, in direct opposition to L'Hôpital's view of royal authority. It does not mean, however, that Hotman, when he wrote *Antitribonian* in 1567, should have found it difficult to align himself with the reformist effort of the chancellor. Aside from constitutional issues, there was an ample ground for Hotman's espousing L'Hôpital's reform program. Hotman unreservedly upheld L'Hôpital's call for simple and direct

[53]Beatrice Reynolds, *Proponents of Limited Monarchy in Sixteenth Century France: François Hotman and Jean Bodin* (New York: Columbia University Press, 1931), 108, indicates various points of reference between *Antitribonian* and *Methodus*, arguing that the two books are derived from the same source—Chancellor L'Hôpital. See also Salmon, *Society in Crisis*, 164, 217.

[54]*Antitribonian ou discours d'un grand et renommé jurisconsulte de nostre temps, sur l'estude des loix* (Paris, 1603).

[55]Bodin, *Method for the Easy Comprehension of History*, 1945.

[56]Hotman, *L'Antitribonian*, 12-13.

[57]Hotman, *L'Antitribonian*, 153.

justice, based on reason and experience. He also supported the chancellor's ambitious agenda for the extensive reform of the judicial system.[58]

Apart from his reforms in the public sphere, L'Hôpital endeavored to establish a national system of private law. A good illustration of many edicts formulated in the reformist spirit and the insight of Chancellor L'Hôpital was the Edict of "Secondes Noces," issued in July 1560. This edict, regulating donations by widows and widowers who remarried, was occasioned by a public scandal involving a rich widow named Anne d'Allegre. She fell in love with a young man, Georges de Clermont, but he refused to marry her "because she looked too old for him." Eventually he married her, and she turned over all her possessions to her new husband, "her foolish passion preventing her from seeing that he sought only her possessions and not her person." She had seven children from the previous marriage, and almost nothing was reserved of her property for them. Chancellor L'Hôpital drew up an edict which forbade wives or husbands who remarried to make any donation to their second spouse that was larger than the smallest portion given to one of the children from previous marriages.[59] A supplement to this widely acclaimed Edict of Second Marriages was the Edict of Mothers, issued in May 1567.[60] The Edit des Mères forbade mothers to inherit property of their children which had once belonged to the children's paternal line. The main purpose of this law was to prevent property, especially that of noble families, from passing into other families. Its impetus was provided by the case of Jean de Monluc, bishop of Valence. Jean designated Pierre, his nephew and the eldest son of Blaise de Monluc, as his heir, but Pierre died in 1565. The prelate was worried that if the only child of Pierre died young, Pierre's widow would take away all the property of the House of Monluc to her own family. At the instigation of Jean, the chancellor's favorite colleague and strongest supporter in the Conseil Privé, L'Hôpital prohibited mothers from touching any paternal property bequeathed from their children; mothers were allowed only a life interest in half of the property, the entire ownership of which would return to the nearest kin of the paternal line after they died.

In an article investigating the political culture in sixteenth and seventeenth-century France, Sarah Hanley proposes the edict of 1560 as an illustration of a tacit effort of the legists to maintain socioeconomic authority

---

[58]See the last chapter of *Francogallia*, "The Parlements as Courts of Law," in Giesey and Salmon's edition, 496-525.

[59]Isambert, *Recueil général*, 14:36-37; De Thou, *Histoire universelle*, 2:838-89; Diefendorf, *Paris City Councillors*, 289-90; René Filfol, "L'Application de l'Edit des Secondes Noces en pays coutumier," *Mélanges Roger Aubenas* (Montpellier: Université de Montpellier, 1974), 295.

[60]Isambert, *Recueil général*, 14:221; De Thou, *Histoire universelle*, 3:782.

under "patriarchal hegemony."[61] Although it is unlikely that L'Hôpital had a conscious agenda for controlling "family formation"—borrowing Hanley's term—at least one can detect in L'Hôpital the note of patriarchal values deeply embedded in general in early modern culture. L'Hôpital was interested not only in the inheritance arrangement between mothers and children but also in mothers' responsibilities for the proper upbringing of their children. As early as in 1558, he expressed concerns about the Parisian mothers who, "mellowed by the delight of the life in the capital, and enslaved by the cult of their [own] beauty," did not want to breast-feed their own babies, lest they should get fat and ruin their fine complexion. Those young women thus put their babies under wet nurses' charge. The practice had innumerable bad effects because, L'Hôpital argued, the babies, "nourished with mercenary milk, suck the germs of corruption ... and [consequently] their instincts degenerate."[62] From this passage, Dupré Lasale contended that L'Hôpital, two centuries before Jean-Jacques Rousseau, warned against the disastrous effects of women deserting their motherly obligations.[63] No matter whether L'Hôpital's theory, with its curious logic, justifies him as a precursor of Rousseauist child education, it does at least attest to the broad spectrum of the chancellor's interests. L'Hôpital seems even to have attempted to carry out a fundamental reform of society's morality and customs. In 1567, he went so far as to issue a mandatory dress code for citizens, a sort of sumptuary law, to regulate excessive luxury in clothing.[64]

It was France's misfortune during the religious wars, as implied by Pasquier above, that the fate of most of L'Hôpital's reforming edicts was closely linked to the chancellor's precarious political position, and that, as L'Hôpital's influence in the royal court diminished, so did the chances of the successful implementation of his laws. Following the conference between Catherine de Médicis and the duke of Alba at Bayonne in the summer of 1565, there was a visible sign of rapprochement between the French and the Spanish courts.[65] The prospect of the return of the ultra-Catholic faction to dominance at court was growing, and so was the suspicion of Protestants over the royal government's pledge to maintain religious toleration. According to Noël Valois, the Conseil Privé had been

[61]Sarah Hanley, "Engendering the State: Family Formation and State Building in Early Modern France," *French Historical Studies* 16 (1989): 12-15, 21-22.

[62]Epistle to Jean Morel, *Poésies complètes*, 162-63.

[63]Dupré Lasale, *L'Hospital*, 2:93-94.

[64]*Ordonnance du Roy concernant la police générale de son royaume*, February 4, 1567, *Actes Royaux*, BN, *Imprimé*, F. 27582 (6).

[65]About the Bayonne conference, see Bernard Weber, "The Conference of Bayonne, 1565: An Episode in Franco-Spanish Diplomacy," *The Journal of Modern History* 11 (1939), 1-22.

dominated by the moderate forces since the Peace of Amboise in March 1563, mainly due to the death of many prominent Catholic leaders, including the duc de Guise, during the First Religious War.[66] Jean-Marie Constant's analysis of the membership of the royal council between 1563 and 1567 indicated that the Conseil Privé consisted of sixteen councillors who could be categorized as "catholiques zélés," six Protestants, and twenty "modérés." The moderate party was led by Chancellor L'Hôpital, and included Artus de Cossé, surintendant des finances, the bishop of Orléans Morvillier, and the bishop of Valence Jean de Monluc.[67] This relative prevalence of the moderate forces at court no longer looked the same in 1567. Above all, the cardinal of Lorraine was rapidly regaining the king's favor. According to the despatch of the English ambassador Henry Norris, written in August 1567, the cardinal had "greatly entered into the favour of the king who will neither ride, go, nor eat without his good cousin...."[68] The Spanish ambassador Alava reported as early as March 1566 that the cardinal of Lorraine sent him a letter rejoicing over the fact that Charles IX strictly ordered the chancellor not to do anything concerning religion before it was communicated to the king in his chamber, and that the king also affirmed that no offices or benefices would be given to anyone who did not live *catholiquement*.[69]

L'Hôpital appeared at the Parlement of Paris on July 26, 1567. He had not come to the court for a long time, and that year marked the thirtieth anniversary of his installation at the Parlement as conseiller. The chancellor's address to the magistrates on this visit, which he predicted could be the "last one," was marked by an overall melancholic tone. It sounded like a final heart-rending admonition of an old chancellor, exhausted, and disillusioned, after a long and lonely battle to promote the well-being of the kingdom. L'Hôpital started by declaring to the parlementaires that "I have no intention to recall, argue, or blame on you anything ... but [want to] locate, through warm and brotherly discussions, the problems, and find their remedies." The chancellor then calmly stated: "I have come my way, and am near the end. I became chancellor at the time of trouble and extreme turbulence. I have not had a single hour of rest during the [past] seven years. I have encountered many troubles, and have met enmities for which I did not blame anyone. I nevertheless did not avoid them, in order to serve the king and the kingdom."[70]

---

[66]Noël Valois, *Le Conseil du roi aux XIVe, XVe, XVIe siècles* (Paris, 1888), 181-95.

[67]Constant, *Les Guises*, 58-59.

[68]Norris to Elizabeth, August 23, 1567, *CPS Foreign*, 7:327.

[69]Alava to Secretary Gonzalo Pérez, March 18, 1566, *Archivo documental Español, Francia, 1559–1566* (Madrid: Real Academia de Historia, 1950–1954), ;8:274.

[70]*Oeuvres complètes*, 2:124.

L'Hôpital again urged the judges to rid themselves of the prejudices and religious passion which swayed their judgment: "[The kingdom] is divided over religion, and there have been complaints as well as challenges to judges, because people feared to be tried by someone of the opposite religion. I cannot believe it—how can it be possible that judges are swayed not only by particular factional hostilities but also by certain hatred resulting from their religious belief...."[71]

Finally, L'Hôpital admonished the magistrates for refusing to admit a Protestant conseiller. He flatly said: "if he is not capable, he must not be received; if he is, he must be received."[72] The chancellor's effort was to no avail. Only a month later, a royal proclamation ordered all judicial officials to attest their Catholic faith, and to profess their faith subsequently at least once a year.[73]

Protestants' misgivings that the king was contemplating the revocation of the pacification edicts were mounting daily.[74] Norris reported in August the "appearance of civil tumults."[75] According to De Thou, the prince of Condé received a letter from "un grand personnage de la cour," favorable to Protestants, warning that "a secret resolution has been made to arrest [Condé] and the Admiral ... and to revoke immediately the edict of pacification and complete the extermination of their party."[76] Henri Martin argues, though without evidence, that this letter was from L'Hôpital.[77] In fact, this was not the first time that he was suspected of being responsible for giving out secret information to Protestant leaders. In 1563, the Spanish ambassador Chantonnay reported that four secretaries of finance under the control of the chancellor leaked to Admiral Coligny some classified information to the advantage of Huguenots.[78] This incident caused such a scandal that the chancellor requested the queen mother to allow him to retire from court, citing his old age and poor health. But Catherine assured the chancellor that she did not have any intention of dismissing him. According to Chantonnay, the queen mother would have been forced to accept L'Hôpital's resignation if the incident

---

[71]*Oeuvres complètes*, 2:134. L'Hôpital, ibid., 135, emphasizes that "les judges sont judges de la cause, et non de la nation ou religion." He told the parlementaires: "vous estes judges de ce qui appartient à la court, non du reste.... Jugez seulement de ce qui est en la cognoissance, et non des qualitez des personnes, ne estant de la cause pour vous mettre hors de suspicion; et rendez la justice, quand ce seroit le plus malheureux homme du monde."

[72]*Oeuvres complètes*, 2:149.

[73]Adolph Blyleven to Gresham, August 30, 1567, *CSP Foreign*, 8:331.

[74]Norris to Elizabeth, August 23, 1567, *CSP Foreign*, 8:328.

[75]Norris to Elizabeth, August 29, 1567, *CSP Foreign*, 8:330-31.

[76]De Thou, *Histoire universelle*, 4:xlii.

[77]Martin, *Histoire de France*, 9:213.

[78]Chantonnay to Philip 2: August 14, 1563, *Archivo documental Español*, 5:355.

had happened before the Peace of Amboise, because at that time the constable of Montmorency was quite displeased with the chancellor. But since he had returned to court after his captivity, added the apparently disappointed Spanish ambassador, the constable became very friendly to L'Hôpital, and they became allies.[79] In any case, it is difficult to prove, as Martin argues, that L'Hôpital wrote the letter in question to Condé in 1567. He must have had deep concerns about the royal court leaning more and more to the Catholic side. It is unlikely, however, that he was so imprudent as to act in such a highly risky way.

In the midst of the escalating tension between the religious factions, in September 1567, the prince of Condé and other Protestant leaders planned to seize the person of the king, who happened to be at Meaux, in order to demand complete liberty of conscience and the banishment of the cardinal of Lorraine from court. The initial warnings of this "incident de Meaux" were received with suspicion by both the constable of Montmorency and Chancellor L'Hôpital.[80] The constable said that no army could be raised that he would not know about, and L'Hôpital roundly accused those who warned of the plot of giving a false alarm.[81] But the rumor was confirmed, and Protestant forces actually blockaded Paris, where the king had been forced to retire when he escaped the Protestant strike at Meaux on September 26. Catherine, deeply disillusioned by the Protestants' intended capture of the king, blamed L'Hôpital for the situation, reportedly telling him, "C'est vous qui par vos conseils nous avez conduits où nous sommes!"[82] The new Pope Pius V instructed the papal nuncio to advise the king to dismiss the chancellor.[83] The English ambassador reported in October that the Parisians during the siege "have the Constable and the Chancellor in such mistrust that they may not without peril ride in the streets."[84]

Catherine de Médicis soon despatched L'Hôpital to St. Denis to persuade the Huguenots to lay down arms.[85] The chancellor brought back from the prince of Condé ten articles, which, according to the English ambassador, "stirred up a fire which will hardly be quenched."[86] Contending that Protestants had been driven into action in self-defense,

---

[79]Chantonnay to Philip II, August 17, 1563, *Archivo documental Español*, 5:380-81.

[80]*Lettres de Catherine de Médicis*, 3:ix.

[81]Castelnau, *Mémoires*, in Michaud, 10:516.

[82]*Lettres de Catherine de Médicis*, 3:xi.

[83]Pius V to the papal nuncio Michel della Torre, October 16, 1567, in Charles Hirshauer, *La Politique de St. Pie V en France (1566-1572)* (Paris: Fontemoing, 1922), 101-3.

[84]Norris to Cecil, October 10, 1567, *CSP Foreign*, 8:354.

[85]Norris to the queen, September 30, 1567, *CSP Foreign*, 8:349.

[86]Norris to the queen, October 10, 1567, *CSP Foreign*, 8:353.

Condé demanded that he take over the control of the government, that all foreigners—apparently implying the Guises—be banished from court, that preaching and liberty of conscience throughout the realm be guaranteed, and that one of the king's brothers be given to the prince's camp as a hostage.[87] None of these conditions were acceptable to the government. The negotiations failed, and the first military skirmish took place at St. Denis on November 10 between the Protestant forces and the royalists. It marked the beginning of the Second Religious War, after less than five years of fragile peace.

L'Hôpital's influence at court was rapidly declining. The line he had taken at Meaux cost him dearly by doubling hostility among Catholics, who accused him of conniving with the Huguenots. More important, the queen mother's trust in her chancellor seemed to diminish fast. Catherine blamed L'Hôpital for the resumption of civil war as well as for the ill-fated toleration policy. But by doing so, as Héritier pointed out, she was condemning her own policy, a situation that revealed the extent of her confusion and frustration.[88] It is difficult to estimate to what extent L'Hôpital, or Catherine, was responsible for the policy of the government in the 1560s. What is certain is that the overall policy of religious toleration, however precarious, was based on the close collaboration between the two, and hence completely depended on the queen mother's confidence in her chancellor. During his chancellorship, L'Hôpital relied exclusively on royal support for the power he wielded. When that support seemed to be withdrawn, the entire policy of toleration was at stake. To be sure, after the Edict of Longjumeau of March 23, 1568, which ended the second civil war by confirming the Peace of Amboise, Catherine in large measure maintained a toleration policy toward Protestants. It seemed, however, that she was no longer willing to listen to her chancellor. Evidence indicates that L'Hôpital, "finding himself striving against the stream, and willing to eschew [*sic*] that no decay should fall in this state as long as he is in government," in May 1568 requested to be discharged of his office.[89] His request was not accepted at this point, but he ceased to appear in the Conseil Privé in late June.[90] The English ambassador commented that this was what the cardinal of Lorraine had been waiting for, because "this one man's authority has been the greatest countermand of his devices."[91]

---

[87]Norris to the queen, October 10, 1567, *CSP Foreign*, 8:353.

[88]Héritier, *Catherine de Médicis*, 264.

[89]Norris to the queen, May 12, 1568, *CSP Foreign*, 8:454.

[90]The *comptes rendus* of the Conseil Privé sessions were signed by Chancellor L'Hôpital until June 25, and thereafter by Morvillier. Michaud, *La grande Chancellerie*, 27-28, n. 3.

[91]Norris to the queen, May 12, 1568, *CSP Foreign*, 8:454.

L'Hôpital's policy of pacification, religious or political, was rapidly reversed. Most notable was the increase of the pope's intervention in French affairs. Pius V issued a papal bull on August 1, allowing the king to alienate church properties amounting to an annual revenue of 150,000 livres. The pope dictated, however, that this money be used only to suppress "the uprisings of heretical and rebellious Huguenots."[92] The opinion of the Conseil Privé was sharply divided. L'Hôpital, who was apparently back at court, argued in the royal council on September 19, in the presence of the queen mother, that the papal bull infringed the privileges of the Gallican Church, and asserted that the king had the right in time of need to close all the churches and use the income without permission from the pope. According to the English ambassador,

> the Cardinal being herewith much stirred reproached him to be a hypocrite, and that his wife and daughter were Calvinists, and that he was not the first of his race that had deserved evil of the king. The Chancellor replied that he had as honest a race as he, whereupon the Cardinal gave him the lie, and rising incontinently out of his chair to take him by the beard, the Marshal Montmorency stepped between them. The Cardinal in great choler turning to the Queen said that he was the only cause of the troubles in the realm, and that if he were in the hands of the parlement his head should not tarry on his shoulder twenty-four hours. The Chancellor said contrariwise that the Cardinal was the original cause of all the mischiefs that had chanced as well to France within these eight years as to the rest of Christendom.[93]

Despite L'Hôpital's efforts to block the publication of the papal bull, the king issued letters patent on September 25, confirming the content of the papal bull.[94] This declaration further included a royal command that all officials of justice and finance professing the "nouvelle prétendue religion" be deprived of their offices. Realizing that he no longer exerted any influence on royal policies, L'Hôpital preferred retiring from court to being forced to place the royal seal on this law he opposed.[95] He again asked the queen mother to relieve him, old and in ill health, from the burden of the chancellorship, and his request was finally accepted. The circumstances surrounding his retirement from court are largely unclear. Sources differ on the exact date of his departure from court. Hélène

---

[92]Félix Rocquain, *La France et Rome pendant les guerres de religion* (Paris: Champion, 1924), 80; De Thou, *Histoire universelle*, 4:136.

[93]Norris to Cecil, September 25, 1568, *CSP Foreign*, 8:554.

[94]Isambert, *Recueil général*, 14:228.

[95]Norris to the queen, September 30, 1568, *CSP Foreign*, 8:557.

Michaud argues that L'Hôpital retired to Vignay immediately after the issuance of the papal bull on August 1, but the squabble with the cardinal of Lorraine in the Conseil Privé provides confirmation that he was still present at court in September.[96] Historians are also in disagreement as to when he actually gave up the royal seals.[97] L'Hôpital's letter written on October 7, 1568, indicates that he returned to the king the royal seals he had carried with him to Vignay on that date, or not long before. The letter reads:

> Sire, in your letter you told me that it would be very inconvenient that each time you had to send the things to seal to me, who stay in my house far from you, during your proposed trip. For this reason you ordered that I send you the seals through Monsieur Brulart, secretary of finance. Sire, my wish is, as has always been, to render you very humble service during all my life, not to leave or desert you, and I greatly regret that I cannot take this trip with you and serve you in important matters. I left, following your command, the Great Seals of France and Dauphiné in the hands of the Sieur Brulart so that he could take them to you. However, I will try to recover my strength so that, upon your return, or when you wish, I go find you and continue the service I owe you. I ask you very humbly to take me in your grace, which is more important than anything else to me.[98]

According to Michaud, the proposed royal trip to Lorraine actually did not take place until several months later.[99] In any case, this letter suggests that L'Hôpital probably thought, or at least did not give up the hope, that the king would recall him soon. The seals he returned were entrusted to the bishop of Orléans, Jean de Morvillier. Even after the king removed the royal seal from him, L'Hôpital still kept his title and privileges as chan-

[96]Michaud, *La grande Chancellerie*, 28.

[97]Constant, *Les Guises*, 64, apparently was mistaken when he wrote that L'Hôpital returned the royal seals on May 24, 1568. According to Héritier, *Catherine de Médicis*, 193, L'Hôpital left for Vignay on October 7, 1568. Rocquain, *La France et Rome*, 81, argues that October 7 was actually the date that the king sent someone to Vignay to ask for the seals. The same incident is attributed to October 17 in *Mémoires de Condé*, 1:197. The Spanish ambassador wrote to Philip II on October 2 that "esta mañana" the chancellor sent the seals to the king; *Archivo documental Español*, 9:478. It is doubtless wrong when both Taillandier, *Nouvelles recherches*, 205, and Baguenot de Puchesse, *Morvillier*, 210, state that "the letter of discharge" of L'Hôpital was issued on February 6, 1568.

[98]BN, MS Fr. 18271, fol. 27. This letter is printed in Musée des Archives Nationales, *Documents originaux de l'histoire de France exposés dans l'Hotel Soubise*, ed. G. Saige (Paris: Plon, 1872), 385.

[99]Michaud, *La grande Chancellerie*, 28.

cellor, since the post of chancellor was given for life and was irremovable. Unlike the case of other royal officials, the letters of provision of chancellor did not contain the clause "tant qu'il nous plaîra."[100]

The reasons for L'Hôpital's fall can be analyzed in various ways. First of all, it is possible to conjecture that Catherine de Médicis, who had kept him in office for so many years against serious criticism and opposition from various forces, concluded that the presence of L'Hôpital at court was no longer desirable. Painfully disillusioned by the strike of Protestants that started the second war, Catherine had reason to feel, as pointed out by the Venetian ambassador Giovanni Correro, that no one could serve the monarchy with more devotion than the Guises, because it was their interests, next to those of the king, that had been most compromised by the Protestant forces. The Venetian ambassador also argued that "Her Majesty understood that no one else could find much-needed money as well as the cardinal of Lorraine, because no one had better credit in Paris."[101] It is also likely that Catherine concluded that war against Protestants was the lesser evil, and that peace at any price would mean the uprising of Catholics against the monarchy. Finally, it is conceivable that Catherine de Médicis and Charles IX lost faith in their chancellor's ability to produce an enduring peace. It is also possible that the queen mother simply became weary with defending L'Hôpital from haunting charges of Calvinist sympathies. Henri Amphoux argues that Catherine was jealous of L'Hôpital's influence over the king, but this interpretation, reminiscent of the now largely discredited theory that Catherine wanted to get rid of Admiral Coligny in 1572 for the same reason, appears unconvincing.[102]

When L'Hôpital found himself abandoned by the king and the queen mother, he realized that he was at the end of his lonely journey, throughout which he had been driven by the desire to achieve fundamental reforms of judicial and administrative structure that would be capable of establishing, ultimately, a lasting peace. The outbreak of the Second Religious War, which prompted L'Hôpital's fall, undid most of the judicial reforms he had undertaken during the eight years of his chancellorship. In January 1568, Charles IX flatly disclosed that the current financial exigencies forced him to resume the creation and sale of royal offices.[103] In June 1568, the king furthermore permitted *survivances*, the practice L'Hôpital had fought so hard to suppress, to all officials in return for payment of the

---

[100]Michaud, *La grande Chancellerie*, 38.
[101]Tomasseo, *Relations des ambassadeurs vénitiens*, 2:151.
[102]Amphoux, *Michel de L'Hôpital*, 386–87.
[103]Edict of January 22, 1568, Isambert, *Recueil général*, 14:226.

*tiers denier*, a tax amounting to one third of the value of office.[104] It is possible to speculate that L'Hôpital's opposition to the king's resumption of sale of offices on a large scale made the king impatient with his stubborn chancellor, and that it contributed to his disgrace. In December 1568, not long after L'Hôpital's departure from court, all Protestant officials were deprived of their offices.[105] Witnessing all his efforts crumble before his eyes, L'Hôpital submitted himself during his last years to a kind of curious fatalistic self-righteousness. He explained his own disgrace in his testament: "When I perceived that my policy was no longer pleasing either to the king or the queen, and that the king was so circumscribed that he could not have his own way nor even dare to express what he himself thought, I thought it better not to wage a hopeless fight any longer but to yield the state to new rulers."[106]

The departure of the chancellor from court marked the end of any efforts of the government in the 1560s to grapple with the troubles in the state and in society at large by restoring probity and integrity in the judicature and administration. Yet the reformist ideals of L'Hôpital were not completely wasted. L'Hôpital's crusade for reforms failed to achieve much practical effect during his chancellorship. Yet it established the reform traditions that were to be revived in the seventeenth century.[107] In the meantime, finally freed from the onus of a lonely battle against fanaticism and discord, the once embattled chancellor now seemed willing and ready to go back to the career of poet he so much missed.

---

[104]Aubert, "Organisation," 211-12; Doucet, *Les Institutions de la France*, 1:415; Mousnier, *La vénalité des offices*, 48. As John Salmon, *Society in Crisis*, 160-61, aptly describes, "instead of fulfilling his hope of reducing venality, it was his misfortune to preside over the reaffirmation and extension of the system."

[105]*Déclaration ... contenant suppression de tous et chacuns les estatz et offices, tant de judicature, de finance que autres ... de présent tenuz et exercez par personnages estants de la nouvelle prétendue religion*, issued in December 1568, *Actes Royaux*, BN, *Imprimé*, F. 46837 (30).

[106]Testament, *Oeuvres complètes*, 2:509.

[107]For insightful comparisons of L'Hôpital and Pomponne de Bellièvre, Henry IV's chancellor, in terms of the French reform traditions, see Salmon, *Society in Crisis*, 300, 318-20.

# Chapter 7

# Si J'estois Personne Privée

T HE LAST FIVE YEARS OF L'HÔPITAL'S LIFE, from 1568 to 1573, are largely overlooked. Many of L'Hôpital's biographers repeat a sentimental apology for the disgraced chancellor and his ill-fated religious policy, while paying little attention to the historical reality of his post-chancellor years. After his departure from court, L'Hôpital was completely removed from the politics of the government and apparently never left the vicinity of his estate in Vignay. But his retirement years are of peculiar importance because they provide rare opportunities to listen to the old chancellor's appraisal of his own politics and career in the twilight of his life. Following his retreat into private life, L'Hôpital resumed his once-prolific writing activities. He regretted at the beginning of his chancellorship that his official duties no longer allowed him time to compose Latin verses: "No longer able to enjoy the charm of writing poems, I seek solace in reading others' poems, hoping," he added amusingly, "that they are worse than mine."[1] In many poems written during his retirement, L'Hôpital discusses the achievements and failures of his career, his loyalty, his religious beliefs, and his philosophy, all in strikingly candid terms. Furthermore, his extant correspondence with Charles IX, Catherine de Médicis, and a few friends at court is a remarkable witness to his current concerns, and they reveal lesser known aspects of L'Hôpital's life. A rounded appreciation of L'Hôpital's life and political career requires an encounter with him in retirement, when he was least remembered by contemporaries.

\*  \*  \*

AFTER HIS DISGRACE, L'Hôpital appeared strikingly self-composed and self-assured. When his friends tried to console him, L'Hôpital answered that "such discharge and exile from court are no sorrow"; having "tossed

---

[1]"Aux Muses," *Poésies complètes*, 292.

around in the sink of wickedness," he was finally free to occupy himself with the cultivation of his little estate and the education of his grandchildren.[2] He could find solace in the belief that his fall was due to the intrigues of his adversaries, not his own faults: "[My enemies] chased me away because I demanded peace, because I was the faithful and vigilant guardian of laws and was not willing to tolerate their dilapidation."[3] He wrote to his friend Guy du Faur: "The parasites and the debauched have better chance to succeed, and they chase away the man who is right and irreproachable.... [But] the purity of his conscience, the noble motives of his retirement dissipate his regrets.... Every disgrace has its advantage, because, as the king's favor diminishes, jealousy and hatred also decrease."[4]

L'Hôpital deplored the fact that the king and the queen mother were swayed and controlled by a few powerful seigneurs who were fighting with each other to dominate the court: "Our king is noble, and his mother loves France and cares for her son; but people disdain his age and her sex; all the great noblemen seek to monopolize power; neither infamy nor assassination can stop them; I, who unfortunately have no means of action in this struggle, am compelled to suppress the outburst of my heart and my curses; my power remains chained by the hands of several audacious people."[5]

L'Hôpital stressed that his unswerving loyalty to the king incurred violent hostility from his adversaries, and added haughtily that as chancellor he never faltered in fulfilling his duties to the crown. He wrote in a memoir dedicated to Charles IX and Catherine de Médicis: "If I were a private man, all I would ask for would be to live in peace with everyone.... [But as] chancellor, the chief of justice of France under Your Majesties, the first councillor of the king, and the protector of your properties, your rights, your greatness and authority, your laws and ordinances, and your subjects, I inevitably offended everyone who infringed your authority, rights, domains, laws and ordinances, but I never feared to incur hostility and enmity...."[6] L'Hôpital recalled that "the Parlements" and "many men of the church ... wanted my death," because they believed that his call for

---

[2]"Sur sa disgrace," *Poésies complètes*, 352.
[3]Epistle to Antonio Vacca, *Poésies complètes*, 336.
[4]Epistle to Guy du Faur, *Poésies complètes*, 323–24.
[5]*Poésies complètes*, 326.
[6]BN, Dupuy 491, fols. 48–51, titled "Harangue de M. de l'Hospital lorsqu'on luy osta les sceaux." Concerning the question of the date of this treatise, see Atkinson, *L'Hospital*, 192–96. Atkinson's conclusion that it was composed sometime in October 1568, and not in 1562 as Duféy suggests, seems to be convincing. The treatise is printed in Taillandier, *Nouvelles recherches*, 200–204; P. D. L., *Eclaircissement*, 58–62.

negotiation with the Huguenots to end the Second Religious War was only a disguised effort to favor them. Some people also "incited the pope and the seigneurs against me."[7] But all these perils left L'Hôpital undaunted. What distressed him most, he said, was his no longer being able to offer the king his loyal service. Could he have done so, L'Hôpital asserted regretfully, he "would have quenched the flames which are devouring the country."[8]

Despite his heartfelt declaration of loyalty to the king, many of L'Hôpital's poems written after his disgrace indicate a deep disillusionment. He lamented that "the favor of kings is as fragile and inconsistent as the enthusiasm of the people."[9] Sometimes he went so far as to state explicitly that "kings detest rigid councillors and prefer slaves and flatterers,"[10] and that "nothing will remain solid and durable so long as the world depends as today on the caprice of a king."[11] "Why would one burn with ridiculous ardor for the public good," L'Hôpital asked, "if such devotion only brings about disgrace?"[12] To be sure, he pledged that "I will protect the interests of the king, even against his will, no matter if I might get as the reward for my work nothing but ingratitude."[13] Yet "[although] I dare not say that my disgrace was unjust, ... it surely brought the alienation of a faithful guardian of the law, a sincere friend of the crown, a citizen dedicated to the well-being of the country, devoted to the preservation of harmony and peace."[14]

L'Hôpital confirmed that "most people ... think that I terribly offended LL. MM. [*Leurs Majestés*]." But, he stressed, any offenses inflicted on them were simply the result of his efforts to make peace with the Huguenots in order to end the war and ensure the preservation of the royal edicts. "Now that God and LL. MM. declare that they want peace and that my opinion was right," L'Hôpital plaintively uttered, "one cannot but wonder what makes them continue this rigorous injustice against me."[15]

Even though L'Hôpital had completely given up his official duties, he still held the title of chancellor, and the royal seals were provisionally

---

[7]BN, Dupuy 491, fols. 48–51.  [8]*Poésies complètes*, 353.
[9]"Entretien avec ses amis," *Poésies complètes*, 339.
[10]*Poésies complètes*, 349.  [11]*Poésies complètes*, 323.
[12]*Poésies complètes*, 339.  [13]*Poésies complètes*, 345–46.
[14]To Jacques Corbinelli, *Poésies complètes*, 326.

[15]L'Hôpital to Madame de Belesbat, [n.d.], BN, Dupuy 194, fol. 14. This letter is printed in Taillandier, *Nouvelles recherches*, 226–30. L'Hôpital protested faithfulness on his part to the king and the queen mother: "Everyone knows that my service to LL. MM. was loyal and consistent from the beginning to the end, and that it was always geared to render them honor and to preserve their estates, as the truth and the outcome have demonstrated."

entrusted to Jean de Morvillier, the bishop of Orléans, without commission.[16] The choice of Morvillier, a longtime friend of L'Hôpital and also his loyal supporter in the royal council, indicates that Catherine de Médicis was not yet willing to reverse entirely the direction of the royal policies taken during L'Hôpital's chancellorship.[17] In 1569, Catherine seriously considered establishing an official garde des sceaux. When she sent Claude Pinart, the secrétaire d'état, to Vignay on September 20 to ask for the chancellor's opinion, L'Hôpital did not present any objection but expressed his disappointment that the king and the queen mother "could not defend me against my enemies in this matter of garde des sceaulx."[18] In a letter to Morvillier, written around the same time as the letter to Catherine, L'Hôpital plainly stated: "Since LL. MM. want to establish a garde des sceaulx, I neither can nor want to resist them. They want to be surrounded by their men."[19] A. H. Taillandier argues that Catherine wanted to appoint Morvillier to the post.[20] Morvillier's own letter written in October reveals, however, that there was an understanding between him and Catherine, when he took over the seals from L'Hôpital, that he would serve only as an interim minister until she and the king were "resolved" on the future of the chancellorship. Morvillier told L'Hôpital that Catherine complained of the difficulties in finding a suitable candidate to whom to entrust the royal seals, since "what they [Charles IX and Catherine] consider most important is to choose someone that is loyal to the king and to no one else, one who has no other goal than good service in his office."[21] Apparently because of this problem, Catherine gave up the plan to appoint a garde des sceaux, at least for the time being. Morvillier warned L'Hôpital, however, that "[it is] her nature, as you know, to be easily influenced. If someone discovers that she has the intention to establish a garde des sceaux, a thousand people will try to sway her, and the decision will be made before she has given much thought to it." Morvillier stressed that the only reason he agreed to take over the royal seals was to

[16]Tessereau, *Histoire chronologique de la grande Chancellerie*, 1:149.

[17]Héritier, *Catherine de Médicis*, 279.

[18]Catherine to L'Hôpital, September 20, 1569, BN, Dupuy 491, fol. 35. This letter is printed in Taillandier, *Nouvelles recherches*, 209; *Lettres de Catherine de Médicis*, 3:273–74. L'Hôpital's response to Catherine, BN, Dupuy, 194, fol. 12 [n.d.]. This letter was probably written between September 20 and October 22, 1569 (when Morvillier's reply to L'Hôpital was dated).

[19]L'Hôpital to Morvillier, [n.d.], BN, Dupuy 194, fol. 12v.

[20]Taillandier, *Nouvelles recherches*, 207.

[21]In his reply to L'Hôpital's letter cited above, Morvillier, October 22, 1569, BN, Dupuy 647, fol. 44v, explains that "le point où elles en sont demeurées est qu'elles m'ont commandé les suivre en ce fâcheux voyage, durant lequel elles se résoudront; à quoy je prie Dieu les bien inspirer"; this letter is printed in P. D. L., *Eclaircissement*, 171–74.

prevent such an unfortunate situation.[22]

It is unlikely that L'Hôpital had any realistic expectation of being called back to court. In fact he had more pressing problems to be concerned about: not long after his disgrace, the old chancellor found himself worrying about his financial situation. He learned in September 1569 that he "should be content with 10,000 or 12,000 livres per year, so that the rest would go to someone who would become garde des sceaux."[23] Apparently, this amount was much less than what he received in office; a receipt dated July 30, 1560, indicates that his salary when he first became chancellor was 18,000 livres, not counting various perquisites that accompanied the office.[24] L'Hôpital was therefore compelled to write to Catherine de Médicis and to Morvillier, requesting that he be allowed to receive his full wages and emoluments as chancellor. He asked the queen mother not to treat him "worse than what the late king did my predecessor, and do to me what one used to do to those who were excused from their service because of old age or ill health...." L'Hôpital sounded rather bitter when he wrote: "It is not very considerate of the king to deprive me of five or six thousand francs. I am sixty-five or sixty-six years old; the rest of my life is plagued by illness. My life is short and I will not be able to enjoy those monies for long.... My predecessor maintained his title and pension as if he had been in office ...; you should not begin this new policy with me."[25] But he resignedly told Morvillier: "If they wish the retrenchment of my position and begin this novelty with me, I will remain patient and consent to it as I have done to all the other wishes of Their Majesties."[26]

Evidence suggests that L'Hôpital's fortune was meager for a man of his standing. He had bought the estate at Vignay in 1546 for 5,000 livres, probably with the money he received by selling to his brother Pierre the land in La Roche that he had inherited from his father.[27] In August 1560,

---

[22]Morvillier, October 22, 1569, BN, Dupuy 647, fol. 44v, according to his own word, feared that if he refused to consent "j'ouvrirois une grande porte aux pratiques des ambitieux, et osterois le loysir à la Reyne de bien penser à faire eslection"; Morvillier to L'Hôpital, BN, Dupuy 674, fol. 44v; Morvillier's intention was never misunderstood by L'Hôpital. Until he finally submitted the royal seals in March 1571, Morvillier constantly sought and listened to L'Hôpital's advice, and the two kept their old friendship intact. Baguenault de Puchesse, *Jean de Morvillier*, 218.

[23]L'Hôpital to Catherine, BN, Dupuy 194, fol. 12. [24]BCF, 740, fol. 66.

[25]BN, Dupuy 194, fol. 12, [n.d.]; printed in Taillandier, *Nouvelles recherches*, 210–12.

[26]BN, Dupuy 194, fol. 12 v, [n.d.]. printed in Taillandier, *Nouvelles recherches*, 205–207; Baguenault de Puchesse, *Jean de Morvillier*, 213–15.

[27]A. Deverre, "Les dernières années de Michel de L'Hôpital, sa retraite au Vignay et sa mort au château de Belèbat," *Bulletin de la société historique et archéologique de Corbeil, d'Etampes et du Hurepoix* (1903), 39. L'Hôpital described his estate of Vignay in a poem written during his first retirement in 1562; *Poésies complètes*, 133–34. For the transaction with Pierre, see Anselme, *Histoire généalogique*, 6:489.

L'Hôpital purchased the seigneury of Champmoteux, two miles from Vignay, for 2,000 livres.[28] Judging from the amount paid, Champmoteux was not of great value. In July 1565, Charles IX granted L'Hôpital the right of high, middle, and low justice in Vignay and in the adjacent seigneury of Gandevilliers,[29] and in August 1565 the king authorized the "establishment of two fairs a year and a weekly market" in Champmoteux.[30] That certainly improved the condition and value of the estate. Meanwhile, the Spanish ambassador Alava reported in February 1567 that Chancellor L'Hôpital was severely reproached by the prince of Montpensier in front of the entire royal council for opposing some minor grants of the king, when he himself had received a few days earlier a royal gift of 50,000 livres.[31] If this report is credible, L'Hôpital's purchase of the seigneuries of Bû and Vert-le-Grand was probably funded from this royal gift.[32] In addition to the property surrounding Vignay, Catherine de Médicis granted L'Hôpital in February 1564 a house and land in Saint-Maur-des-Fossés, a property that had once belonged to Cardinal Jean du Bellay, who had allowed L'Hôpital to use it for a vacation in the 1540s.[33] Finally, Charles IX conferred on the chancellor *in commendam* the abbey of Crêté, located near Chaumont, on the border of Champagne and Lorraine. The abbey of Crêté, because of its distance from L'Hôpital's estate, could not have been of great use to him. Hence, after his retirement, L'Hôpital requested of Charles IX permission to exchange Crêté for the abbey of Ferrière, located near Vignay.[34] Again in 1571 he instructed his daughter, Madame de Belesbat, to ask the queen mother to arrange that exchange of the two lands, but no evidence is extant to indicate whether his request was accepted.[35] At any rate, all these possessions of L'Hôpital apparently were not of much help to his straitened finances after his retirement. L'Hôpital

[28]Deverre, "Les dernières années," 39; Duféy's introduction to L'Hôpital's *Oeuvres complètes,* 1: 274–75, 294, n.

[29]AN, X1a, 8626, fol. 61–62; see also AN, P/8, no. 83, "Hommage de la justice du château de Vignay et de la seigneurie de Gandevilliers, July 6, 1567." Epistle to Corbinelli, *Poésies complètes,* 327, L'Hôpital referred to Gandevilliers: "I live in and cultivate a small land Charles gave to me...."

[30]*Lettres patentes* of August 15, 1565, AN, X1a, 8626, fol. 79v-80.

[31]Alava to Philip II, February 18, 1567, *Archivo documental Español, Francia, 1559–1566 (Archivo general de Simancas)* (Madrid: Real Academia de Historia, 1950–1954), IX, 144–45.

[32]AN, P8, no. 215, "Hommage de la terre et seigneurie et châtellerie de Bû, January 141568"; AN, P16, no. 392, "Hommage de la terre et seigneurie de Vert-le-Grand, July 23, 1568."

[33]AN, Y105, fol. 37; Lasale, *L'Hospital,* 1:107.

[34]L'Hôpital to Catherine, BN, Dupuy 194, fol. 12; L'Hôpital to Morvillier, BN, Dupuy 194, fol. 12v.

[35]L'Hôpital to Madame de Belesbat, April 8, 1571, BN, Dupuy 194, fol. 13. This letter is printed in Taillandier, *Nouvelles recherches,* 225–26.

sounded undisguisedly bitter and disillusioned about his situation after disgrace, when he painfully deplored that he could not even afford a modest house in Paris: "When I get tired of the countryside [in Vignay], I do not have any place to go and stay in Paris. I remain condemned to my muddy land of refuge and exile, where my destiny has assigned me."[36] L'Hôpital was compelled to appeal to Catherine that he had nine grandchildren to support, and that "my fortune is so small that I cannot even afford to pay my servants."[37] According to Morvillier, Catherine, upon hearing that 6,000 livres was cut off from L'Hôpital's pension, said that she "wanted [him] to be content," and promised that she would talk to the king about the matter.[38] It is not clear whether L'Hôpital subsequently obtained any increase in his pension.

In retirement, L'Hôpital devoted himself to the study of the Bible and delved into the subjects of Christian piety and divine providence. He wrote in one of his poems:"I will always regret that the best years of my life had been spent on the study of words rather than on things: I sought, like a parrot, to imitate the Latin poets, to set my verses in the rhythms of the Greeks; and the reality escaped me.... I no longer see any glory in being able to write in Greek or Latin."[39] Instead, he had come to realize that,

> it is God alone who gives us virtue like all other things. Worldly virtues are nothing more than the pale gleam of truth, and hardly deserve the name. Where would the reading of ancient authors lead me if their wisdom does not come from God and cannot take me to God through the right path? St. Paul knew what he was talking about when he maintained that all knowledge was in

---

[36]Epistle to Barthélemy Faye, *Poésies complètes*, 355.

[37]L'Hôpital to Catherine, BN, Dupuy 194, fol. 12. L'Hôpital wrote in a poem that his family was already worried, while he was in office, about his indifference to money matters: "My children, my wife, and my relatives ... blame my negligence; they are afraid that I am too indifferent to my own interests to profit from the advantages offered by fortune; they believe that some day I will regret, but too late, my foolish scrupulousness.... They ask me 'will it not be a shame for you and your family if you die in debt, if you leave your heirs nothing but mourning and poverty?'" *Poésies complètes*, 346.

[38]Morvillier to L'Hôpital, October 22, 1569, BN, Dupuy 647, fol. 44v. In a letter written a month earlier, Morvillier wrote: "[The queen mother] told me that to her great regret she knew several things by which she could well understand the means taken to harm you, which she considered proceeded from the hatred certain people felt for you and the ambition of others; but that you can rest assured that neither she nor the king will ever withdraw their protection from you"; Morvillier to L'Hôpital, September 21, 1569, BN, Dupuy, 647, fol. 44.

[39]Epistle to Corbinelli, *Poésies complètes*, 330–31.

Christ, in Christ who died on the Cross. The most simple and the most ignorant men will be God's elect, and will go to heaven.[40]

L'Hôpital declared that "human wisdom is nothing more than a void pomposity; the true philosophy is that of heaven." Lamenting that "for almost six hundred years Aristotle reigned in the temple of Christ while St. Paul was chased away from it," he urged, "Do not let ourselves, therefore, be deceived at all by sophisms." L'Hôpital was increasingly convinced of man's inability to provide his own salvation. Because of the fundamental privation in human beings, he maintained, they could not perceive the truth. Only the illumination of divine grace and a complete submission to providence could guide them. Christ was the only way to redemption. L'Hôpital thought it deplorable that some people "want to go to heaven through a path other than the one revealed to them," when "it is from Jesus Christ, and no one else, that we must ask grace."[41]

L'Hôpital's emphasis on God's infinite transcendence and man's utter insignificance led him to a sort of determinism: "Nothing is fixed and stable in this world; each one follows sooner or later his destiny, and no one escapes from it."[42] The realization that our will is determined by external force then inclined him to articulate a theory of predestination. In a letter to his former benefactress Marguerite, the duchess of Savoy, L'Hôpital expounded his views of salvation: "No one reaches heaven by his own virtue, regardless of piety and innocence; no one can be his own guide. It is the grace of God that summons us and directs us. All that we receive is from him who chose at the beginning of the world the elect whom he would admit into his empire."[43]

This letter, written only a few months before his death, did not fail to conjure up the old suspicion concerning L'Hôpital's religious belief. But his rudimentary expression of predestinarian views rather appears simply to underscore L'Hôpital's belief that every human being has a place in the universal scheme of things arranged by God. The absolute acceptance of divine order seems to evidence, not negate, the Catholic faith he consistently professed. It is important to point out that confessional lines were remarkably fluid in the sixteenth century. With the exception of hard-liners and extremists in both camps, many in the broad middle ground held beliefs that are often impossible to pin down. Just as attempts to explain L'Hôpital's political opinions in categorical terms bring more confusion than clarity, so efforts to characterize his religious views as exclusively Catholic or Protestant risk distorting the true nature of his religious

[40]Epistle to Corbinelli, *Poésies complètes*, 331–32.
[41]Ibid., 330–31.                                   [42]Ibid. 330.
[43]Epistle to Marguerite, *Poésies complètes*, 367.

beliefs. All evidence suggests that L'Hôpital was sympathetic to the Protestant church and in particular to the plight of the Huguenot minority, but that he was not a convert himself. The best support for L'Hôpital's denial of the Protestant faith comes from none other than the eminent Calvinist leader Theodore Beza, who stated that L'Hôpital "held the torch to enlighten others but not himself."[44] At any rate, L'Hôpital's fundamental belief in Providence enabled him to accept his disgrace with almost Stoic aloofness. L'Hôpital believed that "God gives everyone enough force and courage to fight the pain with which he tests us." Thus he wrote about his disgrace: "God allowed me more than what my enemies could take away from me. In return for such a small loss, I have an eternal life, and the promises of God are not false.... Nothing will trouble me as long as I follow the traces of Jesus Christ on the road to heaven, no matter how wearisome and dangerous it might be.[45]

If L'Hôpital's policy of tolerating Protestants was initially dictated by practical considerations based on political necessity, it was after he had returned the royal seals and stepped down from office that he expounded a cohesive argument against religious persecution. L'Hôpital had earlier asserted that "if religious passion was our sole motive, our sole reason to sound the trumpet of war, we would still displease God.... We are victims of a fatal error which turns us away from the right path...."[46] In his retirement, with his deepened belief in providence, L'Hôpital denounced every kind of religious conflict as a result of human folly. The emergence of heresy was, according to him, God's punishment for human arrogance, specifically for the corruption and moral laxity of the clergy. Those who were "clad in black, violet, or red robes ... seek gold and opulence ... [and] are no longer even slightly concerned with teaching the people."[47] The persecution of the Huguenots was then not only contrary to the spirit of Christianity, but was also a sheer sign of human presumption. "Are these the teachings God gave you? When he rose towards heaven, did he tell his disciples to suppress violently the unbelievers and rule with iron and fire?"[48] Besides, it was wrong to call the Huguenots heretics, because "they believe in God, the Trinity, confessing to holy scripture, and seek salvation only in God, Jesus Christ."[49] L'Hôpital believed, therefore, that it was better to leave the religious schism to work out its own solution than to persecute the Huguenots and fight against them in civil war. All one

[44]Quoted in Bayle, *Dictionnaire historique et critique*, 2:807.
[45]Epistle to Corbinelli, *Poésies complètes*, 326.
[46]Epistle to the cardinal of Lorraine, written in 1562, *Poésies complètes*, 287.
[47]Epistle to the cardinal of Lorraine, written in 1562, *Poésies complètes*, 300–301.
[48]To Barthélemy Faye, *Poésies complètes*, 370.
[49]Address of September 1 [*sic*], 1561, *Oeuvres complètes*, 1:472–73.

could do was to try to extirpate the evils and abuses that were within the sphere of human power. L'Hôpital pleaded "que d'abord on réforme les moeurs, on réformera plus tard les croyances."[50] For him, after all, religious war was not only wrong in itself but also futile in its outcome. L'Hôpital the realist statesman and L'Hôpital the Christian humanist were never strangers to each other.

*     *     *

CATHERINE DE MÉDICIS once again attempted to reconcile opposing factions. After the Treaty of St.-Germain ended the Third Religious War in August 1570, the Protestant forces were visibly in the ascendant. It was at this time that there was talk of the chancellor's comeback. The concerned papal nuncio Frangipani reported that "the Queen just told me yesterday that [the chancellor] would not return, but I am doubtful of that promise, to which I do not give much credence."[51] On September 30, Frangipani reported the arrival at court of the duchess of Ferrara, the well-known patroness of the French Protestants in Italy, and wrote that "her visit seems to present a great danger, and announces perhaps the return of L'Hospital and even the Châtillons."[52] But the rumor of L'Hôpital's return remained a rumor. L'Hôpital later confided his mixed feelings in a letter to Arnauld du Ferrier:

> People talked about me, and it was not totally groundless. I do not know what the king said to stir such agitation at court; but the guile [of my enemies] dissipated the rumor. I can thus again enjoy freedom which I am given from heaven. The wicked and the selfish make fun of [my retirement] but the friends of the king mourn it. Ah! there are so few who worry about the kingdom and the public good![53]

In the same letter, L'Hôpital expressed hope for the growing prospect of Admiral Coligny's return:

> If M. de Châtillon found a chance to kiss the hands of the king, he would whisper two or three words in [the king's] ear and let him realize that he has fallen victim to so many intrigues that even his throne is being threatened. Oh!, if he could awaken the king from deep sleep, he would regain his authority, govern people who

---

[50]Epistle to the cardinal of Lorraine, *Poésies complètes*, 291.

[51]Fabio Mirto Frangipani to Cardinal Rusticucci, August 19, 1570, in *Acta Nuntiaturae Gallicae*, ed. A. Lynn Martin (Rome: Université Pontificale Grégorienne, 1975–1984), 16:74.

[52]Fabio Mirto Frangipani to Cardinal Rusticucci, September 30, 1570, in Charles Hirshauer, *La Politique de St. Pie V en France (1566–1572)* (Paris: Fontemoing, 1922), 120–21.

[53]*Poésies complètes*, 321–22.

loudly called for him, and take over the control of the state, which cannot yet be left to the weak hands of the young prince. This prospect drives the great seigneurs desperate.[54]

Coligny indeed returned to court and the royal council in September 1571.[55] Coligny's return probably had something to do with the aborted attempt of Protestants in October 1571, as reported by the papal nuncio, "to bring Chancellor L'Hôpital back to court."[56]

On March 2, 1571, Morvillier remitted the royal seals to the queen mother and retired from court.[57] The situation surrounding Morvillier's resignation is not clear; perhaps Morvillier thought his departure would open the way for Chancellor L'Hôpital to regain his office. In the previous fall, when the rumor of L'Hôpital's comeback was widespread, Morvillier had to endure the malignant suggestion that he was obstructing the chancellor's return in order to retain his position at court. He may have felt it was necessary to clarify the allegation: he wrote to L'Hôpital on October 29, 1570, that no one wanted L'Hôpital's reinstallation and dignity more than he did, and that he would immediately give up the royal seals if only he were allowed to do so.[58] Morvillier's intention was not mistaken by L'Hôpital, who assured his old friend that there was never any misunderstanding on his part. L'Hôpital also declared that he had no intention to return to court for ambition or greed. Having finally decided to step down, Morvillier wrote to L'Hôpital in February 1571 that "those who love the country regret your absence." He tried to convince L'Hôpital that "Their Majesties have never thought that you employed someone near them to work for your return, and if someone mentioned it to them, they would not in my opinion think that it came from you."[59]

According to the report of the Florentine ambassador, it seemed that L'Hôpital would immediately be recalled to court, so no one wanted to accept the royal seals.[60] It is not certain, however, whether L'Hôpital was officially asked by the king to return to court. In a letter to his daughter, written probably in March or April that year, L'Hôpital made it clear that "I do not want to make myself a laughing stock of my adversaries by

---

[54]*Poésies complètes*, 321.

[55]Liliane Crété, *Coligny* (Paris: Fayard, 1985), 408.

[56]Frangipani to Rusticucci, October 14, 1571, *Acta Nuntiaturae Gallicae*, 16:166–67.

[57]Baguenault de Puchesse, *Morvillier*, 218.

[58]Morvillier to L'Hôpital, October 29, 1570, BN, Dupuy 647, fol. 47. This letter is analyzed in Tessereau, *Histoire chronologique de la grande Chancellerie de France*, 1:149.

[59]Morvillier to L'Hôpital, February 10, 1571, BN, Dupuy 647, fol. 49v; printed in P. D. L., *Eclaircissement*, 175–77.

[60]*Négociations avec la Toscane*, 3:643.

presenting myself [at court] and resuming the chancellorship for three or four days," only to be left out in the cold again. He also declared, "I do not have any wish to return to the labyrinth from which I have escaped, to serve LL. MM. against their wishes, and to abandon the repose which they gave me, no matter whether my enemies might call it escape or exile."[61] In the end, the chancellor's return never came about, and the royal seals were instead given to René de Birague.[62]

L'Hôpital's relationship with the Guises seemed to be worsening. It was generally believed in the court circle that the chancellor's fall was in part a result of the cardinal's antagonism. In 1569, Mary Stuart, the queen of Scots and niece of the cardinal of Lorraine, was accused of abetting the murder of her husband, Lord Darnley, the count of Lennox. Pierre de L'Estoile alleged that L'Hôpital composed a poem accusing Mary[63] of intrigues: "She ambushes like brigands and gathers around her unworthy people."[64] This allegation by L'Estoile, hard to prove since the poem is not extant, attests to the deteriorated relationship between L'Hôpital and the house of the Guise. Despite his alienation from the cardinal of Lorraine, however, L'Hôpital still maintained friendship with Anne d'Este, widow of François de Guise. It was Anne who saved the life of L'Hôpital's daughter, Madeleine, who happened to be in Paris on the day of the St. Bartholomew's Day massacre. In a letter of gratitude, L'Hôpital spoke regretfully of his estrangement from the cardinal of Lorraine, but consoled himself in his friendship with Anne, who had not been affected by the quarrels with the Guises: "Although I have been struggling with the accusation of my enemies and the wrath of your family, whom I always loved and respected, I never considered that you share the anger and resentment of your brothers. Rather, have you not done all you could do to calm their spirits, to touch their hearts, and to revive their extinct affection?"[65]

L'Hôpital's departure from court apparently did not improve his relationship with the Parlement of Paris. To be sure, many presidents and senior judges at the Parlement had supported, at least in part, the chancel-

---

[61]L'Hôpital to Madame de Belesbat, [n.d.], BN, Dupuy 194, fol. 14; Taillandier, *Nouvelles recherches*, 229.

[62]Isambert, *Recueil général*, 14:232. According to Michaud, *La grande Chancellerie*, 28, Birague was chosen to keep the royal seals, mainly because the king and Catherine, having experienced the inconveniences of having a stubborn and uncompromising figure in the chancellorship, wanted someone who would be more docile and obedient. The Venetian ambassador Giovanni Michiel commented that Birague was "incapable"; cited in Doucet, *Institutions de la France*, 1:104.

[63]Eleven years earlier L'Hôpital had written a lavish ode to Mary at her marriage to Francis II.

[64]*Mémoires-Journaux de Pierre de L'Estoile* (Paris: Alphonse Lemerre, 1896), 12:374.

[65]Epistle to Anne d'Este, *Poésies complètes*, 362.

lor's policy, and L'Hôpital maintained friendship with them. In retirement, he exchanged letters with his friends at the court and wrote many epistles to such people as the presidents Pierre Séguier, Christophe de Thou, and Barthélémy Faye.[66] Other friends of L'Hôpital at the Parlement included Paul de Foix, Christophe du Harlay, and Jean-Baptiste du Mesnil. Among L'Hôpital's protégés, Henri de Mesmes, maître des requêtes during L'Hôpital's chancellorship, gratefully recalled in his memoirs the gracious favor he enjoyed from the old chancellor.[67] Despite the sympathy and admiration these judges held for L'Hôpital, the Parlement as a whole persisted in its hostility towards the chancellor, whose judicial reforms were perceived as a threat to its privileges and authority.

A letter from L'Hôpital to Charles IX written in 1571 is a conspicuous testimony to the old chancellor's bitter resentment against the Parlement's alleged iniquitous treatment of him. The Edict of St.-Germain in August 1570 reversed the preceding royal declarations and prescribed the reinstallation of Protestant officials who had lost their offices since 1568. On February 12, 1571, L'Hôpital appealed to the king, charging that, contrary to the royal order, the Parlement of Paris willfully refused to readmit to his office a Bonault, his relative.[68] The register of the Parlement of October 1, 1569, records that Jean Bonaud, conseiller since 1566, resigned on account of his religion and was replaced by Pierre Bouguier.[69] Bonaud, or Bonault in L'Hôpital's letter, had obtained the post of conseiller through the good offices of the chancellor, as shown by the letter to Charles IX: "It is the only office that you gave me upon my request during my service as your chancellor." Although the king allowed all Protestant officials to regain their posts, complained L'Hôpital,

> Bonault alone cannot reenter [the Parlement] although you and your conseil privé have ordered that he re-enter, despite the [parlementaires'] remonstrances. But I can see clearly that my fierce and wearisome enemies are more in favor. All the power in this

[66]L'Hôpital to Séguier, [n.d.], 1568, BN, Dupuy 491, fol. 34, and Dupuy 459, fol. 478; L'Hôpital to de Thou, October 16, 1569, BN, Dupuy 491, fol. 36; L'Hôpital to Barthélemy Faye, December [n.d.], BN, Dupuy 491, fol. 33, and Dupuy 459, fol. 478.

[67]*Mémoires inédits de Henri de Mesmes* (Paris, 1886; reprinted Geneva: Slatkine Reprints, 1970), 165–66. The Collection Baluze, 209, at the Bibliothèque Nationale has several letters in Latin that were exchanged between L'Hôpital and Mesmes after L'Hôpital's retirement: L'Hôpital to Mesmes, September 4, 1570 (fol. 250); Mesmes to L'Hôpital, [n.d.] (fol. 250v); Mesmes to L'Hôpital, December 29, 1570 (fol. 251); L'Hôpital to Mesmes, January 4, 1571 (fol. 251v); and L'Hôpital to Mesmes, January 1, 1572 (fol. 252).

[68]L'Hôpital to Charles IX, February 12, 1571, BN, MS Fr. 21147, fols. 4–4v (fols. 2–2v contains a copy from a later period).

[69]Cited in Maugis, *Parlement de Paris*, 1:263.

court comes from you; I dare say that if the justice and equity of you and your conseil privé has no more power to make this order obeyed and to have the said Bonault received than my name does a disservice to him so as not to be received, your Majesty is offended more than I feel outraged personally.... Everyone will say that because I am so estranged from and disfavored by you that I alone cannot obtain from you what you and your edicts have granted to all others for their relatives and friends.[70]

L'Hôpital's point was obvious: Bonaud was being unfairly punished by the Parlement because of his relationship to the former chancellor. This letter was indeed a bitter indictment of the Parlement, which remained L'Hôpital's public enemy throughout, and even after, his chancellorship. Bonaud was reinstated on March 19, apparently thanks to L'Hôpital's appeal.[71] Whether the delay in Bonaud's reinstatement was related to his connections with L'Hôpital, as contended the chancellor, or to the Parlement's usual strong antipathy towards Protestant members in the law court is hard to decide. In either case, this incident attests to the deep grudge L'Hôpital held against the Parlement even years after his retirement.

Perhaps the biggest crisis L'Hôpital encountered during these years was the frightful threat of violence in the aftermath of the St. Bartholomew's Day massacre. L'Hôpital described in a letter to the duchess of Savoy the terrifying ordeal he suffered:

I barely escaped the horrible attempts on my life by a crazy mob, and the fury of young peasants in the neighborhood.... It would be a long story to tell you how this ignoble populace pursued me

[70]L'Hôpital to Charles IX, February 12, 1571, BN, MS Fr. 21147, fol. 4–4v.

[71]Cited in Maugis, *Parlement de Paris*, 3: 232. Hélène Michaud, *La grande Chancellerie*, 101, 102, nn. 1, 2, mentions a Michel Bonnaud, a secrétaire du Roi who lost his office in December 1568, and argues that this Bonnaud was the secretary of L'Hôpital. It does not seem that Jean Bonaud and Michel Bonnaud are the same individual. A manuscript describing the "Estat de la maison de la monseigneur de chancelier," BN, Dupuy 491, fol. 123, lists two different individuals, "Monsieur Bonaud, l'avocat," and "Monsieur Bonaud, secrétaire." Probably adding to our confusion, Pierre Bayle in the seventeenth century wrote that L'Hôpital had a secretary named Bouvaut. According to Bayle, *Dictionnaire histoire et critique*, 810 (article "L'Hospital," note M), L'Hôpital "fut blasmé de ce qu'estant de son naturel fort severe aux expeditions de justice, & revesche à ceux qui luy venoient parler, toutefois il n'estoit pas tel à l'endroit de ses domestiques, & principalement de son Secretaire Bouvaut, qui le surprenoit aussi souvent qu'il vouloit, ce qu'il continua jusques à ce que la plainte en estant venue au Conseil, sur l'occasion d'une Lettre fort incivile, ce Chancelier eut la honte d'avoir esté surpris, & fut contraint de chasser avec mille injures & reproches un serviteur qu'il avoit beaucoup aimé auparavant."

with incredible vexation, pillaging my farms, and detaining my tenants. One of my tenants brought this matter to the law court, which had been long closed ... but the judge who was supposed to be in charge of punishing the attackers was their accomplice; if it had not been for the soldiers the king sent to protect me, it would surely have been my last day.[72]

L'Hôpital was apparently so appalled by this incident that he seriously considered retiring to Montargis, where the duchess of Ferrara was offering a sort of asylum to those who were under suspicion because of their religious views. Charles IX's letter of September 2, 1572, shows that L'Hôpital even obtained the king's permission.[73] Instead of going to Montargis, however, L'Hôpital and his wife withdrew to Belesbat, the estate of his daughter, Madeleine, and son-in-law, Robert de Hurault, maître des requêtes. Belesbat was about five miles from Vignay, which made it easier for the L'Hôpitals to depend on the care of their children, while still staying close to Vignay. Madeleine had already been taking care of much of her father's business. L'Hôpital's extant letters to her evidence his complete trust in his daughter.[74]

By the time he was considering seeking the protection of the duchess of Ferrara, L'Hôpital seems to have been almost resolved to resign officially from the chancellorship. In January 1573, Catherine de Médicis sent Cheverny, chancellor of the duke of Anjou, to Vignay to negotiate with L'Hôpital the terms of his resignation. L'Hôpital's reply to Catherine was a heart-rending self-vindication of the old minister, who placed himself completely at the disposal of the king and the queen mother: "Madame, when I left court, I foresaw well this tempest and that its fierce and impetuous ferment would bring you a greater storm, but ... I hoped ... that perhaps the heart of those who were incensed with me would grow soft, seeing me absent from the court and without the position I held; truthfully I only thought about sparing you from the pain you suffered because of me...." He wanted only to wait quietly for his last day, "without looking

---

[72]Epistle to Marguerite de Valois, *Poésies complètes*, 365–66.

[73]Charles IX to L'Hôpital, September 2, 1572, BN, Dupuy 491, fol. 37. The letter reads: "Monsieur le chancelier, je désire votre bien et conservation, autant que vous-même, et ai pouvoir et très-bonne volonté de vous maintenir avec tout ce qui vous appartient, étant tel que vous êtes et vous aimant, comme je le fais. Toutefois, puisque avez délibéré d'aller à Montargis, je désire que ce soit avec votre contentement. Je écris à ma tante, Madame la duchesse de Ferrare, de vous recevoir et accommoder, ainsi que méritez. J'aurai à plaisir que vous soyez en bonne santé et me faites entendre ce dont vous aurez besoin." This letter is printed in Taillandier, *Nouvelles recherches*, 238–39; Jean Marie, *Essai sur la vie & les ouvrages du Chancelier Michel de L'Hospital* (Rennes: Oberthus & Fils, 1868), 78; *Oeuvres complètes*, 2:493.

[74]BN, Dupuy 194, fols. 13–19.

for any ways to return to my status and post," but "my enemies are not contented," because they could not remove him from the chancellorship before his death or without his voluntary consent. Impatient, they incited the king to put him on trial: "To wait for my death seemed to them too long; they are uncertain about my wish, so they pretend to be informed of my life and say they want to start proceedings against me. Taking proceedings against me, who has conducted his office with more sanctity and integrity than any other chancellors, who has loved the king and you more than himself? Madame, Madame, you know that well...."[75]

His enemies accused him of many hideous crimes, but his only fault, if there was any, was "that I upheld the royal edicts of pacification: the chancellor takes an oath to uphold the edicts of the king and to have them obeyed by others; if he did otherwise he would deserve serious blame." Some people charged that he prevented the king from revoking the Edict of Amboise. "I confess that I wanted the edict to remain intact," but, L'Hôpital protested, it was only because he feared "the long war and the troubles which we have now." L'Hôpital bitterly swore that his enemies "can neither intimidate me to give up the office to them, nor have you persuade me to do so." But he did not intend to resist the queen mother's will. "You ask me to return to you what you have given me," L'Hôpital calmly stated, and "the office is not mine; it is yours, one which I can no longer keep and carry on due to my age and ill health." Finally, L'Hôpital concluded his lengthy and emotional letter by asking Catherine to remember that "I have always been a loyal and true servant of yours, and I loved you singularly and honored you at all times, without ever swerving."

On February 1, 1573, L'Hôpital signed in Belesbat the "Acte de consentement de résignation de la charge de chancelier." The document stipulates that the chancellor consented "freely and voluntarily that the said seigneur roy provides for the exercise of the said post of chancelier in the best way as he sees fit, either by simple commission of garde des sceaux or by the establishment and creation of the office of garde des sceaux."[76] It was specified that L'Hôpital voluntarily agreed to forego the right of irremovability vested in his office, "expecting the said seigneur roy and the reyne, his mother, to keep and maintain the promises which they have made to the said seigneur chancelier in the letters that have been or will be written at the discharge of the exercise of his said office." Charles IX, by the lettres patentes of February 6, discharged L'Hôpital from "the exercise

[75]L'Hôpital to Catherine, [n.d.], BN, Dupuy 194, fol. 11; printed in Taillandier, *Nouvelles recherches*, 240–45; P. D. L., *Eclaircissement*, 159–64.

[76]BN, Dupuy 672, fol. 7; Dupuy 847, fol. 270; Dupuy 851, fol. 111. The text is printed in P.D.L., *Eclaircissement*, 179–81.

of his said office regarding the seal and our conseil privé," preserving for him the title of chancellor, his wages, and the other prerogatives attached to the office of chancellor.[77] The same day, the king appointed René de Birague to the office of garde des sceaux.

L'Hôpital did not enjoy for long the privileges promised by the king; he died on March 13, less than six weeks after his resignation. It seems that L'Hôpital knew that his last day was approaching when he wrote to Catherine de Médicis on January 22 that he was "almost at the end of my long voyage," and asked her to take his wife and children under her protection.[78] In a letter to Charles IX, dated January 12, L'Hôpital declared that he had "always followed the great high road of the king, without turning to right or to left, and without joining myself to any private faction." Finally, wrote the old chancellor: "I pray to God to grant you His grace, and guide you by His hand in all your affairs and in governing this beautiful kingdom with all gentleness and clemency towards your good subjects, in imitation of Him who is good and patient to bear our offenses and prompt to forgive our faults."[79]

On March 12, L'Hôpital drafted his will and had it copied by his grandson Michel.[80] He passed away the next day, on March 13, in Belesbat. The cause of his death is unknown, but in his will he mentioned that he had suffered from "an infinity of diseases for six months."[81] The king appointed Birague to the vacant chancellorship on March 17.[82]

*       *       *

L'HÔPITAL'S TESTAMENT is an epitome of his principles, his motives, and his own assessment of his political career. It is indeed the veritable political manifesto of a statesman who resolutely tried to prevent, to the utmost of his power, the tragedy of civil conflict: "I always advised and per-

---

[77]AN, X1a, 8630, fol. 275v, fol. 309. The text is printed in P.D.L., *Eclaircissement*, 183–87. The royal letters were verified at the Parlement of Paris on March 11, 1573, two days before L'Hôpital's death; see Tessereau, *Histoire chronologique*, I, 173.

[78]L'Hôpital to Catherine, January 22, 1573, BN, MS Fr. 3956, fol. 253; 23358, fol. 13; 4743, fol. 18; 4766, fol. 174. This letter is printed in Taillandier, *Nouvelles recherches*, 246–47; *Oeuvres complètes*, 2:495.

[79]L'Hôpital to Charles IX, January 12, 1573, BN, MS Fr. 3956, fol. 253; 23358, fol. 11; 4743, fol. 18; 4766, fol. 174. This letter is printed in Taillandier, *Nouvelles recherches*, 245–46.

[80]Only this copy made by Michel, not the original, is extant. L'Hôpital added the subscription in his own hand, and Robert de Hurault also added his signature. BN, Dupuy 491, fol. 38.

[81]Testament, *Oeuvres complètes*, 2: 525. It seems that L'Hôpital had already suffered from hemorrhoids since he was in office. Henri de Mesmes, *Mémoires inédits de Henri de Mesmes*, 165–66, recalled that sometimes the Chancellor, "having lost blood and unable to sit," authorized de Mesmes to seal documents in his lieu in his chamber.

[82]AN, X1a, 8630, fol. 349.

suaded [people] to seek peace, believing that there was nothing more regrettable in a country than civil war, and nothing more beneficial than peace, no matter in what condition it might be."[83] After eight years of uphill battle, he found his pacification policy being charged with having caused all the problems in the kingdom. L'Hôpital was convinced that he had fallen victim to those who were aware that "as long as I stay in office, they could neither destroy the royal edicts nor pillage the finance of the king and his subjects."[84] His ill-fated toleration policy was, L'Hôpital believed, being used only as a pretext for his enemies to get him out of the way. L'Hôpital lamented in one of his poems that he was simply overpowered in his endeavor to defend the authority of the crown and to protect the people under the laws: "Would it be necessary to remind me that there is a law, if I could employ them effectively? It is not that I lack courage; but law is without authority. Those who implement them have no force and no power. They tremble and do not want at all to hear the grievances of the oppressed. The tribunals, the only dike against the torrent, remain demolished and silent, overwhelmed by terror."[85] But L'Hôpital could still declare at the end of his life: "I can call God, all the angels and all the people as witness that … I never considered anything more important than the well-being of the king and the preservation of my country."[86]

L'Hôpital's testament underscores his profound devotion to his wife, Marie. She appears to have been a capable woman, to whom L'Hôpital entrusted domestic affairs. It was she who supervised the reconstruction of a château in Vignay in 1562 while her husband was preoccupied with the First Religious War. According to one source, she took care to include the Italian style in the reconstruction in order to allow her weary husband to reminisce about his happy days at the universities of Padua and Bologna.[87] In one of his poems, L'Hôpital credited his wife for her thoughtful and delightful ways of running their estate in Vignay and expressed gratitude; she even directed the landscaping of the estate and had thick elm trees planted by the château, under the shade of which he used to "take a walk, write poems, or read the passages of Horace and Virgil, until the voice of my wife announced that dinner was served."[88] In his will, L'Hôpital made Marie the administrator of all his properties, stating that he was confident that her management would be beneficial to his children.[89]

L'Hôpital's tolerance of Protestantism in France was reflected in his silent approval of the Protestant views of his wife, daughter, and son-in-

[83]Testament, *Oeuvres complètes*, 2:522.      [84]Testament, *Oeuvres complètes*, 2:524.
[85]*Poésies complètes*, 348.                    [86]Testament, *Oeuvres complètes*, 2:524.
[87]André Bondu, "Un grand libéral: La véritable figure du Chancelier Michel de L'Hospital," *La Revue Libérale* 3 (1953): 70.
[88]"A mes hôtes," *Poésies complètes*, 134.     [89]Testament, *Oeuvres complètes*, 2:525–26.

law. There apparently existed no tensions over religious beliefs in L'Hôpital's household. L'Hôpital specifically praised his wife for her "singular piety." As for L'Hôpital's own religious stance, Etienne Pasquier personally confirmed that after "having the honor to see [L'Hôpital] and talk to him," he did not believe that the chancellor was Huguenot.[90] In fact, one can find some noticeable parallels between L'Hôpital and Guillaume Budé in that both were suspected of Calvinism because of the religious beliefs of their family members. Furthermore, their funerals incited suspicion about their own beliefs. L'Hôpital asked his wife and domestics to take care of his funeral and burial, which "seems silly to Christians,"[91] and was buried quietly at night in the cemetery of the village chapel of Champmoteux.[92] Budé specifically requested in his testament a quiet funeral at midnight without the usual pomp of a Catholic burial, and after his death Budé's widow and several children took refuge in Geneva.[93] Despite their certain sympathy for their family members' confessional allegiance, however, there is simply not enough evidence to prove that either L'Hôpital or Budé was Calvinist. According to Pierre de L'Estoile, L'Hôpital's widow abjured Protestantism in 1585.[94] Madeleine and Robert Hurault were buried in the abbey of Morigny. Some historians assume that they also renounced their Calvinist belief.[95]

L'Hôpital willed that his grandsons among his eight grandchildren add his family name to their surname Hurault.[96] Only two of them, Michel and Robert, had offspring to carry on this new line as the Hurault de L'Hôpital.[97] Another grandson, Paul, became maître des requêtes and later archbishop of Aix.[98] Michel Hurault de L'Hôpital became conseiller at the Parlement of Paris, and married Olympe, the daughter of Guy du Faur de Pibrac, president of the Parlement of Paris and the long-time friend of Chancellor L'Hôpital.[99] Catherine de Médicis had promised in 1573, in return for the chancellor's dismissal, to grant a post of secrétaire du roy to one of his grandchildren. L'Hôpital pleaded with Catherine in his last letter to keep this promise. It is possible that Paul obtained his

---

[90]Pasquier, *Lettres historique*, 314, n. 5.    [91]Testament, *Oeuvres complètes*, 2:530.

[92]Deverre, "Les dernières années," 45–46.    [93]Diefendorf, *Paris City Councillors*, 75.

[94]Cited in P. D. L., *Eclaircissement*, 104.

[95]P. D. L., *Eclaircissement*, 104–5; Deverre, "Les dernières années," 51.

[96]Testament, *Oeuvres complètes*, 2: 526.

[97]Concerning the genealogy of the Hurault de L'Hôpital, see Anselme, *Histoire généalogique et chronologique*, 514–16; Deverre, "Les dernières années," 51.

[98]Among other grandsons, Charles and François died without having been married; Jean died without children.

[99]For Michel's marriage, see Le Père Anselme, *Histoire généalogique et chronologique*, 515. Guy du Faur became president of the Parlement of Paris in 1577.

position of maître des requêtes through this arrangement.[100] It was grandson Michel to whom the chancellor bequeathed his library. Michel was
attached to the king of Navarre, future Henry IV, who made him his chancellor. Michel was delegated on various missions to England, Holland,
and Germany.[101] It was probably this Michel who was among François
Hotman's students at the academy of Geneva in 1578.[102] He died in 1592,
a Protestant.[103] According to genealogists, Michel Hurault de L'Hôpital's
line ended in 1706, and his brother Robert's branch was also extinguished
sometime after 1787.[104] But the name L'Hôpital was preserved through
the chancellor's brother Pierre. Pierre, seigneur of La Roche, was gentilhomme ordinaire of the duc de Lorraine in 1546. His son, Michel, served
as maître d'hôtel du roi. Among Michel's sons was Gilbert, who in 1642
appealed to the Conseil d'Etat to claim the noble pedigree of the L'Hôpital.

*          *          *

JEAN BODIN HARDLY EXAGGERATED when he acclaimed Chancellor L'Hôpital to be a notable illustration of one who overcame an adverse background through virtue and erudition. Bodin attested that his
contemporaries, especially the common people, were "ravished with an
incredible pleasure to feel themselves all honored" when they saw "a poor
physician's son [become] chancellor of a great kingdom."[105] Trite eulogies
of L'Hôpital often impede a sound understanding of his life and his place
in history. Nevertheless, revolt against the profuse panegyrics of L'Hôpital
should not obscure his rightful claim for recognition, that is, an exile's son
who courageously confronted the tragic turbulence of the civil war and
resolutely defended the interests of the kingdom, "without turning to
right or to left."[106] The French historian J.-H. Mariéjol commented that
"there is a history and there is a legend of L'Hôpital." L'Hôpital's history
should not be eclipsed by his own legend.

---

[100]L'Hôpital to Catherine, January 22, 1573, BN, MS Fr. 3956, fol. 253.

[101]Anselme, *Histoire généalogique et chronologique*, 515.

[102]Kelley, *Hotman*, 272; Pierre Mesnard, "François Hotman (1524–1590) et le complexe
de Tribonien," *Bulletin de la Société de l'histoire du protestantisme français* 101 (1955): 135. Neither Kelley nor Mesnard provide evidence.

[103]Brantôme, *Oeuvres complètes*, 3:324; P. D. L., *Eclaircissement*, 104–6; Deverre, "Les
dernières années," 51–52.

[104]P. D. L, *Eclaircissement*, 104–6, Deverre, "Les dernières années," 52.

[105]Bodin, *Les six livres*, 6.6.1055.

[106]L'Hôpital's last letter to Charles IX, January 12, 1573. See n. 79 above.

# Chapter 8

# L'Hôpital's Legacy

C RITICAL EXAMINATION OF L'HÔPITAL'S CAREER dispels a number of misconceptions. Instead of being a lonely preacher of religious toleration, L'Hôpital was a statesman who conceiveda policy of religious tolerance as an inevitable precondition for peace and made unyielding efforts to stop the persecution of Protestants. He did not propose the enlightened ideal of freedom of conscience as a positive moral value in the society of the sixteenth century; rather he viewed the coexistence of two religions as the only alternative to endemic civil strife. Far from upholding the cause of "moderation" in politics, or a general compromise, he was a dedicated advocate of the theory of absolutism. He unapologetically proclaimed the unchallenged power of the king, and he resolutely adhered to his position against vehement opposition from the magistrates of the Parlement of Paris. If he was a pacifist denouncing violence, he was also a confirmed patriot, who believed that wars were sometimes proper when they served the national interest. Often described as a man of incorruptible virtue and unwavering principle, or a heroic foe of fanaticism and factionalism, L'Hôpital was in fact an individual with his own aspirations and ambitions who knew how to cultivate and employ friendship and patronage to promote his political career. L'Hôpital had his share of inconsistencies and contradictions.

L'Hôpital's political actions ought to be viewed as particular responses to the dilemmas of the religious wars, but the scope of his ideals surpasses the confines of his times. L'Hôpital was a striking representative of the Gallican royalists, who were confronted with the double tasks of fending off intervention from Rome and effecting necessary reforms of the church institution to prevent the alienation of the Huguenots as well as moderate Catholics. Above all, L'Hôpital and his government were charged with the urgent task of ending the civil wars. L'Hôpital tried to resolve these crises by stubbornly refusing to view the current situation from a religious angle, and by insisting on dealing with the troubles only in political terms. He was one of the first statesmen in France who envisioned the separation of politics and religion. Divorcing politics from religion was indeed an unrealistic and unlikely idea in the sixteenth century. Yet L'Hôpital pursued his religious policy of separating seditious Huguenots from Huguenots of conscience when, for almost everybody else in his time, such a separation was inconceivable. Even after his patron, the cardinal of Lorraine, turned to persecution of Protestants following the failure of a policy of concord, L'Hôpital consistently argued for legal coexistence of Catholics and Protestants. L'Hôpital maintained that one could live in peace with those of different religious opinions in one kingdom, and further stated that even a non-Christian did not cease to be a good citizen. These bold statements, spoken by the chancellor of France, were contrary to fundamental assumptions of the period.

Why was L'Hôpital so unable to see the impracticability of his idea of separating politics and religion? Why was he unwilling to acknowledge the profundity of the contemporary mentality that simply prevented most French Catholics from being able to distinguish politics from religion? All available evidence shows that L'Hôpital was not a naive visionary who blindly sought to bring about, overnight, the unity of Catholics and Protestants in France. Nor was L'Hôpital an aloof idealist preaching religious toleration. He was rather a pragmatic statesman whose main concern was to end the civil war. Yet his struggle for his cause demonstrates his fundamental faith that religious coexistence could work in France. This indeed seems to be the key to understanding L'Hôpital's policy of toleration. L'Hôpital's belief in the prospect of separating politics from religion, which he rightly considered to be the only alternative to civil war, indicates that his views were too far ahead of his time. L'Hôpital was illuminated by the light of the sixteenth century and should be understood as such. He was not an advocate of liberty of conscience in the mode of the nineteenth century. At the same time, however, L'Hôpital's vision transcended the bounds of his age. Pursuing steadfastly his ideal until his disgrace, even after Catherine de Médicis and the majority in the court of Charles IX lost belief in religious toleration as a permanent solution, L'Hôpital was in one sense immersed in a distinct idealism of his own.

It is important to distinguish L'Hôpital's policies from those of Catherine de Médicis in this crucial period of the religious wars. After the debacle of the Colloquy of Poissy, the queen mother realized the folly of a policy of religious concord and pushed the peace edicts merely out of political necessity. Although her wish for peace was genuine, Catherine did not believe in coexistence of Catholics and Protestants and, like many of her contemporaries, envisaged the reunification of the kingdom under "une foi" and "une loi." In contrast, L'Hôpital pursued a policy in the direction of separating politics from religion. His religious policy was based on the sound judgment that the only option left for the French government was to give up religious unity for the sake of peace in the kingdom. Without denying the fundamental value of religious agreement in France, L'Hôpital was convinced that the unity of the kingdom was more imperative than religious uniformity under Catholicism, and he believed that peaceful coexistence of Catholics and Protestants would reunite France under one king. L'Hôpital remained loyal to his principle to not forsake the Huguenots by excluding them from the community of France, and L'Hôpital's vision of religious tolerance was thus indissolubly integrated with his vision of the French national interests. But such a view by the chancellor, however sensible, could not carry the day.

L'Hôpital has justifiably been regarded as a precursor of the Politique party. The connections between L'Hôpital's ideas and the late-sixteenth-century Politiques appear particularly prominent in the political realm. The Politique settlement of the French religious wars recognized the need to rearrange the relationship between the king and his *officiers*, and thus implied stronger power of the crown. L'Hôpital was a staunch defender of unchallenged royal authority. The kingdom could be freed from the threats of both internal conflict and papal intervention, he believed, only when the prince wielded power strong enough to suppress all centrifugal forces and ensure the unity of the realm. L'Hôpital's chancellorship was thus expended upon a relentless struggle to secure obedience to royal power.

In his quest to restore the power of the crown, L'Hôpital sought to create a reformed judiciary. His crusade to create sound judicial and administrative systems, which he hoped would provide a basic remedy to the problems confronting the monarchy, illustrates his vision as an idealist reformer. L'Hôpital asserted that justice was not a sort of private possession, but that it belonged instead to the crown, who would guarantee the dispensation of uniform and impartial justice. L'Hôpital rightly judged that obstruction against the crown by officeholders, increasingly entrenched in their offices, was the main predicament of the monarchy. L'Hôpital's efforts to attack this self-protective caste and tackle the widespread and rapidly worsening stagnation in administration heralded the so-called "administrative revolution" of the first half of the following century. His judicial reforms failed to achieve much practical effect during his chancellorship. Whether these reforms, had they been successful, would have produced a lasting peace is a difficult question to answer. At least, however, L'Hôpital's reformist ideals created precedents upon which later reforming ministers could base their work. L'Hôpital's chancellorship can therefore be regarded as the beginning of the reform tradition in ancien régime France. If L'Hôpital's dual vision of religious toleration and raison d'État was too advanced to create any impact on sixteenth-century politics, his ideas foreshadowed arguments for religious toleration and contributed to the formulation of the "absolutist" monarchy of the seventeenth and the eighteenth centuries. L'Hôpital was indeed a rare blend of pragmatist statesman and idealist reformer.

L'Hôpital was in many respects a prototype of the eminent royal ministers in the seventeenth century. Indeed, comparison between L'Hôpital and Cardinal Richelieu is illuminating. Besides their common "étatiste" beliefs, their rise to power bears some similarity. Both owed their swift promotion at court to the extraordinarily generous patronage they enjoyed, L'Hôpital from the Guises and Richelieu from Marie de Médicis. But profound devotion to the interests of the king drove each of them to break with their original patron. A major difference is that L'Hôpital, unlike Richelieu, was not always able to count on royal support. L'Hôpital stood almost alone: he was suspected by Catholics as a Huguenot sympathizer and frequently distrusted by Huguenots as a former henchman of the Guises. L'Hôpital encountered the bitterest hostility from his former colleagues at the Parlement of Paris because he personified for the parlementary opposition the authoritarian government they sought to resist. The constitutional tensions between the royal government that L'Hôpital headed and the parlements were aggravated by the religious issue as the conservative judges strongly opposed the chancellor's toleration policy. L'Hôpital was hence entirely dependent on Catherine de Médicis's support, and it was only as long as she was inclined to follow her chancellor's policy that he was able to keep his position.

When the discontented opponents dared not attack the king and the queen mother personally, the chancellor became an ideal scapegoat. Eventually, Catherine de Médicis concluded that the presence of L'Hôpital at court was no longer desirable for the royal interests when balanced against the continued opposition of many Catholics and the magistrates. Upon subjection to disgrace, L'Hôpital realized that he had been defeated in his campaign to defend royal authority. The consolidation of royal absolutist power was to wait several decades, for the arrival of the Bourbon monarchs.

The visions L'Hôpital espoused were unconventional and perhaps too advanced for his time. After his fall from grace, L'Hôpital was quickly forgotten, as is often the fate of men whose causes are shunned by their contemporaries. And therein lay the agony of the reformist chancellor.

# Bibliography

## MANUSCRIPT SOURCES

Archives Nationales, Paris (AN)
  JJ 265
  KK 940
  P 3, 8, 16
  X 1A 1577, 1596–1607, 8626, 8630
  Y 105
Bibliothèque nationale, Paris (BN)
  *Collection Baluze,* 209, 186, 509
  *Collection Clairambault,* 341, 355
  *Collectin Dupuy,* 31, 137, 194, 246, 358, 459, 472, 475, 491, 647, 672, 689, 846, 854
  *Fonds français,* 2881, 3876, 3888, 3951, 3952, 3955, 3956, 4743, 4766, 6618, 6620,
    15519, 15871, 15875, 15881, 15882, 18271, 18281, 18282, 21147, 23110, 23159,
    23358
  *Nouvelles acquisitions,* 1470, 7225, 7236
Bibliothèque municipale et interuniversitaire de Clermont-Ferrand, Clermont-Ferrand (BCF). MS 740

## PRINTED MATERIAL

*Acta Nuntiaturae Gallicae.* Vols. 12–16. Rome: Université Pontificale Grégorienne, 1975–1984.

*Actes royaux: Catalogue général des livres imprimés de la Bibliothèque nationale.* Edited by Albert Isnard. Paris: Imprimerie nationale, 1910–1960.

Akademiia nauk SSSR, Institut istorii. *Dokumenty po istorii grazhdanskikh voin vo Frantsii, 1561–1563 (Documents pour servir à l'histoire des guerres civiles en France, 1561–1563).* Edited by A. Lublinskaya. Moscow, 1962.

Allen, John William. *A History of Political Thought in the Sixteenth Century.* 2d ed. London: Methuen, 1941.

Amphoux, Henri. *Michel de l'Hôpital et la liberté de conscience au XVIe siècle.* Paris, 1900; reprinted, Geneva: Slatkine Reprints, 1969.

Anchel, Robert. "Michel de L'Hôpital." In *Hommes d'Etat.* pp. 299–401. Edited by A. B. Duff, and F. Galy. Paris: Desclée de Brouwer, 1937.

Anquez, L. *Le chancelier de L'Hospital.* Paris, 1881.

Anselme de Sainte-Marie, Le Père. *Histoire généalogique et chronologique de la maison royale de France, des Pairs, grands officiers de la couronne, etc.* 9 vols. Paris, 1726–1733.

*Michel de L'Hôpital*

Antoine, Michel. *Le dur métier de roi.* Paris: Presses Universitaires de France, 1986.
———. "Genèse de l'institution des intendants." *Journal des savants* (1982): 283–317.
Archivo General de Simancas. *Archivo documental Español, Francia, 1559–1566.* 9 vols. Madrid: Real Academia de Historia, 1950–1954.
Armstrong, Edward. *The French Wars of Religion.* 2d ed. Oxford: Blackwell, 1904.
Aubert, Félix. *Histoire du Parlement de Paris de l'origine à François Ier.* 2 vols. Paris, 1894.
———. "Le Parlement de Paris au XVIe siècle." *Extrait de la Revue des études historiques.* Paris: Alphonse Picard, 1905.
———. "Recherches sur l'organisation du Parlement de Paris au XVIe siècle (1515–1589)." *Extrait de Nouvelle revue historique du droit français et étranger.* Paris: Sirey, 1912.
d'Aubigné, Théodore Agrippa. *Mémoires.* Edited by Ludovic Lalanne. 4 vols. Paris, 1854.
———. *Histoire universelle.* Edited by André Thierry. Geneva: Librairie Droz, 1981.
Aucoc, Léon. *Le conseil d'estat: avant et depuis 1789.* Paris, 1876.
Aymon, J. *Tous les synodes nationaux des églises réformées de France, auxquels on a joint des mandemens royaux, et plusieurs lettres politiques du Cardinal de Sainte-Croix au Cardinal Borromée, sur ces matières synodales.* The Hague, 1710.
———. *Oeuvre en rime de Ian Antoine de Baif.* Edited by Ch. Marty-Laveaux. Paris, 1883.
Baguenault de Puchesse, Gustave. *Jean de Morvillier: Evêque d'Orléans, garde des sceaux de France 1506–1577.* Paris, 1869; reprinted, Geneva: Slatkine-Megariotis Reprints, 1977.
Barbiche, Bernard, and Ségolène de Dainville-Barbiche. "Les légats *a latere* en France et leurs facultés aux XVIe et XVIIe siècles." *Archivum Historiae Pontificiae* 23 (1985): 93–165.
Barrillon, Jean. *Journal.* Edited by Pierre de Vaissière. 2 vols. Paris, 1897–1899.
Baschet, A. *Journal du Concile de Trente, rédigé par un secrétaire vénitien présent aux sessions de 1562 à 1563.* Paris, 1870.
Baumgartner, Frederic J. *Change and Continuity in the French Episcopate: The Bishops and the Wars of Religion 1547–1610.* Durham: Duke University Press, 1986.
———. *Henry II: King of France 1547–1559.* Durham: Duke University Press, 1988.
Bayle, Pierre. *Dictionnaire historique et critique.* 4 vols. Amsterdam, 1740.
Beame, Edmond M. "The Development of Politique Thought During the French Religious Wars (1560–1595)." Ph.D. dissertation, University of Illinois, Urbana, 1957.
———. "The Politiques and the Historians." *Journal of the History of Ideas* 54 (1993): 355–79.
Bellay, Joachim. *Oeuvres françaises de Joachim du Bellay.* Edited by Ch. Marty-Laveaux. Paris, 1867.
Benoist, Charles. *L'influence des idées de Machiavel.* Paris: Academy of International Law, 1926.
Bernandi, Joseph Elzear Dominique de. *Essai sur la vie, les écrits et les lois de Michel de L'Hôpital, chancelier de France.* Paris, 1807.

Berthoud, G., et al. *Aspects de la propagande religieuse.* Geneva: Librairie Droz, 1957.

Bèze, Théodore de. *Correspondance de Théodore de Bèze.* 14 vols. Geneva, Librairie Droz, 1960–1990.

———. *Les vrais portraits des hommes illustres en piété et en doctrine....* Geneva, 1581; reprinted, Geneva: Slatkine Reprints, 1986.

Blanchard, François and Jean-Baptiste L'Hermite-Souliers. *Catalogue de tous les conseillers du Parlement de Paris.* Paris, 1645.

Bodin, Jean. *Les six livres de la république.* Lyon: G. Cartier, 1593.

———. *The Six Bookes of a Commonweale.* Translated by Richard Knolles. London, 1606.

———. *Method for the Easy Comprehension of History.* Translated by Beatrice Reynolds. New York: Columbia University Press, 1945.

Boislisle, Arthur Michel de. *Chambre des Comptes de Paris: Pièces justicatives pour servir à l'histoire des premiers présidents (1506–1791).* Nogent-le Rotrou, 1873.

Bondois, Paul. "Catalogue des actes de François II." *Positions des thèses de L'Ecole Nationale des Chartes,* pp. 19–29. Paris, 1908.

Bondu, André. "Un grand libéral: La véritable figure du chancelier Michel de L'Hospital." *Revue libérale* 3 (1953): 59–83.

Bordonove, Georges. *Les rois qui ont fait la France: les Valois.* Paris: Pygmalion, 1987.

Bouillet, Jean Baptiste. *Nobiliaire d'Auvergne.* 7 vols. Clermont-Ferrand, 1846–1853.

Boulet-Sautel, Marguerite. "Le Contrat de Poissy, acte de droit privé." *Droit privé et institutions régionales: études historiques offertes à Jean Yver,* pp. 77–85. Paris: Presses Universitaires de France, 1976.

Bourgeon, Jean-Louis. "La Fronde parlementaire à la veille de la Saint-Barthélemy." *Bibliothèque de l'Ecole des Chartes* 148 (1990): 17–83.

———. "Les Régendes ont la vie dure: A propos de la Saint-Barthélemy et de quelques livres récents." *Revue d'histoire moderne et contemporaine* 34 (1987): 102–16.

Boutier, Jean, Alain Dewerpe, and Daniel Nordman. *Un tour de France royal: Le Voyage de Charles IX (1564–1566).* Paris: Aubier, 1984.

Brantôme, Pierre de Bourdeille, seigneur de. *Oeuvres complètes.* Edited by Ludovic Lalanne. 11 vols. Paris, 1867.

Brown, Frieda S. *Religions and Political Conservatism in the "Essais" of Montaigne.* Geneva: Librairie Droz, 1963.

Brown, John L. *The Methodus ad facilem historiarum cognitionem, A Critical Study.* Washington, D.C.: Catholic University of America Press, 1939.

Buisseret, D. J. "A Stage in the Development of the French Intendants: The Reign of Henry IV." *Historical Journal* 9 (1966): 27–38.

Buisson, Albert. *Michel de L'Hospital 1503–1573.* Paris: Hachette, 1950.

Butler, Charles. "Life of L'Hôpital." *Philological and Biographical Works of Charles Butler,* pp. 149–215. London, 1817.

*Calendar of State Papers and Manuscripts Relating to English Affairs Existing in the Archives and Collections of Venice and in Other Libraries of Northern Italy.* 38 vols. London: Longman, 1864–1947.

*Calendar of State Papers, Foreign Series of the Reign of Elizabeth (1558–1589).* 28 vols. London: Longman, 1861–1950.

*Calvini opera quae supersunt omnias.* Edited by Guillaume Baum, Eduard Cunitz, and Eduard Reuss. 59 vols. Brunswick, 1878–1879.

Caprariis, Vittorio de. *Propaganda e pensiero politico in Francia durante le guerre di religione (1559–1572).* Vol. I. Naples: Edizioni Scientifiche Italiane, 1959.

Carey, John. A. *Judicial Reform in France before the Revolution of 1789.* Cambridge, Mass.: Harvard University Press, 1981.

Castelnau, Michel de. *Mémoires.* In *Nouvelle collection des mémoires pour servir à l'histoire de France,* series 1, vol. 9, pp. 401–554. Edited by Joseph François Michaud and Jean Joseph François Poujoulat. Paris, 1838.

*Catalogue des actes de Henri II.* Collection des ordonnances des rois de France. 2 vols. Paris: Imprimerie nationale, 1979–1986.

Centre National de la Recherche Scientifique. *La Cour des Comptes.* Paris, 1984.

Chabrol, Guillaume Michel, ed. *Coutumes générales et locales de la province d'Auvergne.* Riom, 1784–1786.

Champion, Pierre. *Catherine de Médicis présente à Charles IX son royaume (1564–1566).* Paris: Bernard Grasset, 1937.

———. *Paris au temps des Guerres de Religion: Fin du règne de Henri II, régence de Catherine de Médicis.* Paris: Calmann-Levy, 1938.

———. *Charles IX.* 2 vols. Paris: Bernard Grasset, 1939.

Cheruel, Adolphe. *Histoire de l'administration monarchique de la France.* 2 vols. Paris, 1855; reprinted, Geneva: Slatkine-Megariotis Reprints, 1974.

Cheverny, Philippe Hurault, comte de. *Mémoires.* In *Nouvelle collection des mémoires pour servir à l'histoire de France,* series 1, vol. 10, pp. 461–576. Edited by Joseph François Michaud and Jean Joseph François Poujoulat. Paris, 1838.

Church, William F. *Constitutional Thought in Sixteenth-Century France.* Cambridge, Mass.: Harvard University Press, 1941; reprinted, New York: Octagon Books, 1969.

Cimber, L. and F. Danjou, eds. *Archives curieuses de l'histoire de France depuis Louis XI jusqu'à Louis XVIII.* 27 vols. Paris, 1834–1840.

Cloulas, Ivan. "Les aliénations du temporel ecclésiastique ordonnées par les rois Charles IX et Henri III de 1563 à 1588." *Positions des thèses de l'Ecole nationale des chartes.* Paris, 1957.

———. *Catherine de Médicis.* Paris: Fayard, 1979.

Condorcet, Jean-Antoine-Nicolas de Caritat, marquis de. *Eloge de M. de l'Hôpital.* Paris, 1777.

Constant, Jean-Marie. *Les Guise.* Paris: Hachette, 1984.

Crimando, Thomas I. "Two French Views of the Council of Trent." *Sixteenth Century Journal* 19 (1988): 169–86.

Damas, P. "Comment fur enregistré l'édit de décembre 1563 créant la juridiction consulaire de Bordeaux." *Revue historique de Bordeaux* 2 (1953): 113–18.

Dareste, R. *Histoire de France depuis les origines jusqu'à nos jours.* 2 vols. Paris, 1865–1879.

Davis, Natalie Zemon. *The Return of Martin Guerre.* Cambridge, Mass.: Harvard University Press, 1983.

Degert, Antoine. "Procès de huit évêques français suspects de calvinismse." *Revue des questions historiques* 76, n.s. 32 (1904): 61–108.

Delaborde, Henri François. *Etude sur la constitution du Trésor des chartes*. Paris: Plon-Nourrit, 1909.

Delachenal, Roland. *Histoire des avocats au Parlement de Paris, 1300–1600*. Paris, 1885.

Denault, Gerald Francis. "The Legitimation of the Parlement of Paris and the Estates General of France, 1560–1614." Ph.D. dissertation, Washington University, 1975.

Denière, Georges. *La juridiction consulaire de Paris, 1563–1792: Sa création, ses luttes, son administration intérieure, ses usages, et ses moeurs*. Paris, 1872.

Denzer, Horst, ed. *Jean Bodin. Verhandlungen der internationalen Bodin Tagung in München*. Munich: Verlag, 1973.

Desjardins, Abel, ed. *Négociations diplomatiques de la France avec la Toscane*. 4 vols. Collection de documents inédits sur l'histoire de France. Paris, 1859–1886.

*Despatches of Michele Suriano and Marc' Antonio Barbaro, Venetian Ambassadors at the Court of France, 1560–1563*. Edited by Henry Layard. Lymington, 1891.

"Deux altercations entre le Cardinal de Lorraine et le Chancelier L'Hôpital." *Bulletin de la Société de l'histoire du protestantisme française* 10 (1975): 409–15.

Deverre, A. "Les dernières années de Michel de L'Hôpital, sa retraite au Vignay et sa mort au château de Belèbat." *Bulletin de la société historique et archéologique de Corbeil, d'Etampes et du Hurepoix* (1903): 39–55.

Didier, Noël. "Paul de Foix à la mercuriale de 1559." *Mélanges d'archéologie et d'histoire de l'école françois de Rome* 56 (1939): 402–35.

Diefendorf, Barbara B. *Paris City Councillors in the Sixteenth Century: The Politics of Patrimony*. Princeton, N.J.: Princeton University Press, 1983.

———. *Beneath the Cross: Catholics and Huguenots in Sixteenth-Century Paris*. New York: Oxford University Press, 1991.

———. "Prologue to a Massacre: Popular Unrest in Paris, 1557–1572." *American Historical Review* 90 (1985): 1067–1091.

Doucet, Roger. *Etude sur le gouvernement de François Ier dans ses rapports avec la Parlement de Paris*. 2 vols. Paris: E. Champion, 1921–1926.

———. "L'état des finances de 1567." *Bulletin philologique et historique* (1926–1927): 1–32.

———. *Les institutions de la France au XVIe siècle*. 2 vols. Paris: A. et J. Picard, 1948.

Duchesne, François. *Histoire des chanceliers et gardes des sceaux de France distingués....* Paris, 1680.

Du Moulin, Charles. *Conseil sur le faict du Concile de Trente*. Lyons, 1564.

Dupieux, Paul. "Les attributions de la juridiction consulaire de Paris, 1563–1792: L'arbitrage entre associés, commerçants, patrons et ouvriers au XVIIIe siècle." *Bibliothèque de l'Ecole de Chartes* 95 (1934): 167–48.

Dupont-Ferrier, Gustave. "Le role des commissaires royaux dans de gouvernement de France, spécialement du XIVe au XVIe siècle." In *Mélanges Paul Fournier*. Paris, 1929.

Dupré Lasale, Emile. *Michel de L'Hospital avant son élévation au poste de chancelier de France*. 2 vols. Paris, 1875–1899.

Dupuy, Pierre, ed. *Instructions et lettres des rois très-chrestiens, et de leurs ambassadeurs, et autres actes concernant le concile de Trente*. Paris, 1654.

————. *Traité de la majorité de nos rois et des régences du royaume, avec les preuves tirées tant du Trésor des Chartes du roy que des registres du parlement, ensemble un traité des prééminences du Parlement de Paris*. Paris, 1655.

Duranthon, Antoine, ed. *Collection des procès-verbaux des assemblées générales du clergé de France*. 9 vols. Paris, 1767–1768.

Ellul, Jacques. *Histoire des institutions de l'époque franque à la Révolution*. 5th ed. Paris: Presses Universitaire de France, 1967.

Erlanger, Philippe. "Machiavelique Catherine." *Historama* 27 (1986): 50–57.

d'Este, Hyppolito. *Négociations ou lettres d'affaires ecclésiastiques et politiques écrites au Pape Pie IV et au Cardinal Borromée*. Paris, 1658.

Evennett, Henry Outram. *The Cardinal of Lorraine and the Council of Trent*. Cambridge: Cambridge University Press, 1930.

————. "The Cardinal of Lorraine and the Colloquy of Poissy." *Cambridge Historical Journal* 2 (1927): 133–50.

————. "Claude d'Espence et son 'Discours' du Colloque de Poissy." *Revue historique* 163–164 (1930): 40–59.

Fédou, R. *Les Hommes de loi lyonnais à la fin du Moyen Age: Etude sur les origines de la classe de robe*. Paris: Société d'Edition Les Belles Lettres, 1964.

Filhol, René. "L'application de l'Edit des secondes noces en pays coutumier." In *Mélanges Roger Aubenas*, pp. 295–99. Montpellier: Université de Montpellier I, 1974.

————. *Le premier président Christofle de Thou et la réformation des coutumes*. Paris: Recueil Sirey, 1937.

Floquet, Amable. *Histoire du Parlement de Normandie*. 7 vols. Rouen, 1840–1842.

Fontanon, Antoine. *Les édits et ordonnances des rois de France*. 4 vols. Paris, 1580.

Ford, Franklin. *Robe and Sword: the Regrouping of the French Aristocracy after Louis XIV*. Cambridge, Mass.: Harvard University Press, 1953.

Forneron, H. *Les ducs de Guise et leur époque*. 2 vols. Paris, 1877.

Fournier de Flaix. "L'Hospital, son temps et sa politique." *Comptes-rendus de l'Académie des Sciences Morales et Politiques* 153 (1900): 433–54.

François, Michel. *Le cardinal François de Tournon*. Paris: E. de Boccard, 1951.

Franklin, Julian. *Jean Bodin and the Rise of Absolutist Theory*. Cambridge: Cambridge University Press, 1973.

————. *Jean Bodin and the Sixteenth Century Revolution in the Methodology of Law and History*. New York: Columbia University Press, 1963.

Gadoffre, Gilbert. "Joachim du Bellay et Michel de L'Hospital." In *Les Angevins de la littérature, Colloque*, pp. 79–91. Angers, 1979.

Gallet, Léon. "La monarchie française, d'après Claude de Seyssel." *Revue historique de droit français et étranger* 22 (1944): 1–34.

Garcin, Paul. "Michel de L'Hospital et les tribunaux consulaires." *Revue des deux mondes* 17 (1963): 118–25.

Garrisson, Janine. *Guerre civile et compromis 1559–1598*. Paris: Éditions du Seuil, 1991.

Girard, Etienne, and Jacques Joly. *Trois livres des offices de France*. Paris, 1658.

Givan, Walker. "The Politiques in the French Religious Wars (1560–1595): Advocates of Religious Toleration and Strong Monarchy." Ph.D. dissertation. Yale University, 1950.

Glasson, Ernest-Désiré. *Histoire du droit et des institutions de la France.* 6 vols. Paris, 1887–1903.

———. "Les juges et consuls des marchands." *Nouvelle revue historique de droit français et étranger* 21 (1897): 5–38.

———. *Le Parlement de Paris: son rôle politique depuis le règne de Charles VII jusquà la Révolution.* 2 vols. Paris: Hachette, 1901; reprinted ed., Geneva: Slatkine-Megariotis Reprints, 1974.

———. *Précis élementaire de l'histoire du droit français.* Paris: F. Pichon, 1904.

Godefroy, Théodore. *Le cérémonial françois.* 2 vols. Paris, 1649.

Graham, Victor E., and W. McAllister Johnson. *The Royal Tour of France by Charles IX and Catherine de Médicis: Festivals and Entries, 1564–1566.* Toronto: University of Toronto Press, 1979.

Guyot, Pierre-J., and P.-A. Merlin. *Traité des droits, fonctions, franchises, exemptions, prérogatives et privilèges annexés en France à chaque dignité, & à chaque état, soit civil, soit militaire, soit ecclésiastique.* 4 vols. Paris, 1786–1788.

Haag, Eugene, and Emile Haag. *La France protestante ou vies des protestants français.* 10 vols. Paris, 1846–1859.

Hanley, Sarah. *The Lit de Justice of the Kings of France: Constitutional Ideology in Legend, Ritual, and Discourse.* Princeton, N.J.: Princeton University Press, 1983.

———. "Engendering the State: Family Formation and State Building in Early Modern France." *French Historical Studies* 16 (1989): 4–27.

Hauser, Henri. *Les sources de l'histoire de France: XVIe siècle (1494–1610).* Paris: Picard, 1912; reprinted, Nendeln, Liechtenstein: Kraus Reprints, 1967.

———. *La Modernité du XVIe siècle.* Paris: F. Alcan, 1930.

Heller, Henry. *Iron and Blood.* Montreal: McGill-Queen's University Press, 1991.

Henrion de Pansey, Pierre. *De l'autorité judiciaire en France.* 3d ed. Paris, 1827.

Héritier, Jean. *Michel de L'Hospital.* Paris: Flammarion, 1943.

———. *Catherine de Medici.* Translated by Charlotte Haldane. New York: St. Martin's Press, 1963.

Hilaire, Jean. *Introduction historique au droit commercial.* Paris: Presses Universitaires de France, 1986.

Hirschauer, Charles. *La politique de St. Pie V en France (1566–1572).* Paris: Fontemoing, 1922.

*Histoire ecclésiastique des églises réformées au royaume de France.* Edited by Guillaume Baum and Eduard Cunitz. 3 vols. Paris: Librairie Fischbacher, 1883–1889; reprinted, Nieuwkoop: B. de Graaf, 1974.

Holt, Mack P. *The Duke of Anjou and the Politique Struggle during the Wars of Religion.* Cambridge: Cambridge University Press, 1986.

———. "The King in Parlement: The Problem of the *Lit de Justice* in Sixteenth-Century France." *Historical Journal* 31 (1988): 507–23.

Homais, Maurice. *De la vénalité des offices sous l'ancien régime.* Paris: Librairie de la société du recueil général des lois et des arrêts, 1903.

Hotman, François. *L'Antitribonian, ou Discours d'un grand et renommé sur l'estude des loix.* Paris, 1603.

———. *Le tigre de 1560.* Edited by Charles Read. Paris, 1875.

———. *Francogallia by François Hotman.* Edited by Ralph E. Giesey. Translated by J. H. M. Salmon. Cambridge: Cambridge University Press, 1972.

Hunt, Richard A. "Religion and Law: The Chancellorship of Michel de L'Hospital, 1560–1562." Ph.D. dissertation, University of Pennsylvania, 1973.

Jardonnet, Marcel. "Michel de L'Hospital: poète néo-Latin et humaniste." *L'Auvergne littéraire.* 158–159 (1958): 1–127.

———. "Michel de L'Hospital." *Bulletin historique et scientifique de l'Auvergne* 83 (1964): 136–50.

Isambert, François André, et al. *Recueil général des anciennes lois françaises depuis l'an 420 jusqu'à la Révolution de 1789.* 29 vols. Paris, 1822–1833.

Jeanvrot, Victor. *La magistrature.* Paris, 1882.

Jedin, Hubert, Joseph Glazik, and Erwin Iserloh. *History of the Church.* Translated by Anselm Biggs and Peter W. Becker. 10 vols. New York: The Seabury Press, 1980.

———. *A History of the Council of Trent.* Translated by Dom Ernest Graf. 2 vols. Edinburgh: Nelsol, 1957.

Kaiser, Colin. "Les Cours souveraines au XVIe siècle: morale et contre-réforme." *Annales: économies, sociétés, civilisations* 37 (1982): 15–31.

Kelley, Donald R. *Foundation of Modern Historical Scholarship.* New York: Columbia University Press, 1970.

———. *François Hotman: A Revolutionary's Ordeal.* Princeton, N.J.: Princeton University Press, 1973.

———. *The Beginning of Ideology: Consciousness and Society in the French Reformation.* Cambridge: Cambridge University Press, 1981.

———. "Fides Historiae: Charles Dumoulin and the Gallican View of History." *Traditio* 22 (1966): 347–402.

Kim, Seong-Hak. "The Chancellor's Crusade: Michel de L'Hôpital and the Parlement of Paris." *French History* 7 (1993): 1–29.

———. "Dieu nous garde de la messe du chancelier: The Religious Belief and Political Opinion of Michel de L'Hôpital." *Sixteenth Century Journal* 24 (1993): 595–620.

———. "Michel de L'Hôpital Revisited." *Proceedings of the Annual Meeting of the Western Society for French History* 17 (1990): 106–22.

Kingdon, Robert M. "Some French Reactions to the Council of Trent." *Church History* 33 (1964): 149–56.

Knecht, Robert J. *The French Wars of Religion 1559–1598.* London: Longman, 1989.

———. *Francis I.* Cambridge: Cambridge University Press, 1982.

Kubler, Jacques. *L'Origine de la perpétuité des offices royaux.* Nancy: Société Impressions Typographiques, 1958.

La Boétie, Estienne de. *Mémoire sur la pacification des troubles.* Edited by Malcolm Smith. Geneva: Librairie Droz, 1983.

La Cuisine, Elisabeth François. *Le Parlement de Bourgogne depuis son origine jusqu'à sa chute.* 2 vols. Dijon, 1864.

La Faye de L'Hôpital, Paul (P. D. L.), *Quelques éclaircissements historiques et généalogiques sur M. de L'Hospital et sa famille.* Clermont-Ferrand, 1862.

La Ferrière, Hector de. *Le XVIe siècle et les Valois d'après les documents inédits du British Museum.* Paris, 1879.

Laferrière, Julien. *Le Contrat de Poissy 1561.* Paris: J.-B. Sirey, 1905.

Lafon, Jacqueline-Lucienne. *Juges et consuls: à la recherche d'un statut dans la France d'Ancien Régime.* Paris: Economica, 1981.

La Place, Pierre de. *Commentaires de l'estat de la religion et république soubs les rois Henry et François secondes et Charles neufième (1565).* In *Choix de chroniques et mémoires sur l'histoire de France,* vol. 13, pp. 1–201. Edited by J. A. C. Buchon. Paris, 1836.

La Planche, Louis Regnier, sieur de. *Histoire de l'estat de France, tant de la république que de la religion, sous le règne de François II.* Edited by Edouard Mennechet. 2 vols. Paris, 1836.

La Roche-Flavin, Bernard de. *Treze livres des parlemens de France.* Bordeaux, 1617.

Lavisse, Ernest., ed. *Histoire de France.* 9 vols. Paris: Hachette, 1904. Vol. 7: *La Réforme et la Ligue: l'Edit de Nantes, 1559–1598,* by Jean-H. Mariéjol.

Le Noble, Alexandre. "Note sur l'Edit de Paris de 1563." *Bibliothèque de l'Ecole des Chartes* 2 (1840–1841): 286–88.

Lecler, Joseph. *Toleration and the Reformation.* 2 vols. Translated by T. L. Westow. London: Longmans, 1960.

Lefas, Alexandre. "De l'origine des juridictions consulaires des marchands de France." *Revue historique de droit français et étranger* 48 (1924): 83–120.

Le Féron, Jean. *Histoire des connétables, chanceliers et gardes des sceaux, etc....* Paris, 1658–1688.

Legrand, Marie-Dominique. "Michel de L'Hospital: Éléments pour une poétique de la liberté de conscience." *La liberté de conscience (XVIe-XVIIe siècle: Actes du colloque de Mulhouse [Haut-Rhin] et Bâle (1989).* Geneva: Librairie Droz, 1991: 85–91.

Legrand, Victor. *Juges et consuls 1563–1905.* Bordeaux: Imprimerie G. Delmas, [1905].

Lemaire, André. *Les lois fondamentales de la monarchie français d'après les théoriciens de l'ancien régime.* Paris: A. Fontemoing, 1907.

Lescuyer, J. *Le nouveau stille de la chancellerie de France et des chancelleries establies prèz les parlements.* Paris, 1622.

L'Estoile, Pierre de. *Mémoires-Journaux.* 12 vols. Paris, 1896.

*Lettres de Catherine de Médicis.* Edited by Hector de La Ferrière. 11 vols. Paris: Imprimerie nationale, 1880–1943.

L'Hôpital, Michel de. *Oeuvres complètes de Michel de L'Hospital.* Edited by P. J. S. Duféy. 3 vols. Paris, 1824–1825.

———. *Discours pour la majorité de Charles IX et trois autres discours.* Edited by Robert Descimon. Paris: Imprimerie Nationale, 1993.

———. *Michaelis Hospitalii, Carmina: Editio a prioribus diversa et auctior.* Edited by P. Vlaming. Amsterdam: B. Lakeman, 1732.

———. *Poésies complètes du chancelier Michel de L'Hospital.* Translated by Louis Bandy de Nalèche. Paris, 1857.

————. *Essai de traduction de quelques épîtres et autres poésies latines de Michel de l'Hôpital.* Edited by J. M. L. Coupé. 2 vols. Paris, 1778.

————. *Remonstrance faite de M. le chancelier [M. de L'Hospital], à l'assemblée tenue à Moulins, au mois de janvier 1566.* BN 80 Lf24.40.

Liaussau, A. "Un tétracentenaire oublié: celui de Michel de l'Hospital." *Marseille, revue municipale* 104 (1976): 78–82.

Livet, Georges. *Les guerres de Religion.* Paris: Presses Universitaires de France, 1962.

Lot, Ferdinand, and R. Fawtier. *Histoire des institutions françaises au Moyen Age.* 3 vols. Paris: Presses Universitaires de France, 1957–1962.

Louis-Lucas, Paul. *Etude sur la vénalité des charges et fonctions publiques.* 2 vols. Paris, 1883.

Loyseau, Charles. *Les oeuvres de Maistre Charles Loyseau contenant les Cinq livres de droit des offices.* Paris, 1678.

Major, J. Russell. "The Third Estate in the States General of Pontoise, 1561." *Speculum* 29 (1954): 460–76.

————. *The Estates General of 1560.* Princeton, N.J.: Princeton University Press, 1951.

————. *Representative Government in Early Modern France.* New Haven: Yale University Press, 1980.

Maimbourg, Louis de. *Histoire de la Ligue.* Paris, 1686.

Marie, Jean. *Essai sur la vie & les ouvrages du Chancelier Michel de L'Hospital.* Rennes: Oberthus & Fils, 1868.

Mariéjol, Jean-H. *Catherine de Médicis.* 2d ed. Paris: Taillandier, 1979.

Martin, Henri. *Histoire de France: depuis les temps les plus reculés jusqu'en 1789.* 17 vols. 4th ed. Paris, 1855–1860.

Martin, Victor. *Le gallicanisme et la réforme catholique: essai historique sur l'introduction en France des décrets du Concile de Trente (1563–1615).* Paris: Alphonse Picard, 1919.

————. *Les origines du gallicanisme.* 2 vols. Paris: Bloud & Gay, 1939.

Martin-Sarzeaud, G. *Recherches historiques sur l'inamovibilité de la magistrature.* 2d ed. Paris, 1883.

Maugis, Edouard. *Histoire du Parlement de Paris de l'avènement des rois Valois à la mort d'Henri IV.* 3 vols. Paris: Alphonse Picard, 1913–1916.

Maury, Alfred. "L'administration française avant la révolution de 1789." *Revue des deux mondes* 107 (1873): 832–59.

Melin, Joseph Roserot de. "Rome et Poissy (1560–61)." *Mélanges d'archéologie et d'histoire* 39 (1921–1922): 47–151.

*Mémoires de Condé, pour servir à l'histoire de France, & d'éclaircissement à celle de Mr. De Thou.* 6 vols. The Hague, 1743.

Merle, Pierre. "Jean de L'Hospital, père du chancelier et médecin du connétable de Bourbon." *L'Auvergne littéraire, artistique et historique* 37 (1960): 3–17.

Mesmes, Henri de. *Mémoires inédits.* Edited by Edouard Fremy. Paris, 1886; reprinted ed., Geneva: Slatkine Reprints, 1970.

Mesnard, Pierre. *L'essor de la philosophie politique au XVIe siècle.* Paris: Furne, Boivin & Cie, 1936.

————. "François Hotman (1524–1590) et le complexe de Tribonien." *Bulletin de la Société de l'histoire du protestantisme français.* 101 (1955): 117–37.

Michaud, Claude. "Finances et guerres de religion en France." *Bulletin de la société d'histoire moderne* 16 (1979): 3–10.

————. "Finances et guerres de religion en France." *Revue d'histoire moderne et contemporaire* 28 (1981): 572–96.

————. "Les aliénations du temporel ecclésiastique dans la seconde moitié du XVIe siècle: quelques problèmes de méthode." *Revue d'histoire de l'eglise de France* 67 (1981): 61–75.

Michaud, Hélène. *La grande chancellerie et les ecritures royales au seizième siècle (1515–1589).* Paris: Presses Universitaires de France, 1967.

————. "Les registres de Claude Pinard, secrétaire d'état (1570–1588)." *Bibliothèque de l'Ecole des Chartes* 120 (1962): 130–52.

Michelet, Jules. *Oeuvres complètes.* Edited by Paul Viallaneix. Paris: Flammarion, 1980.

Miquel, Pierre. *Les guerres de religion.* Paris: Fayard, 1980.

Molinier, Alain. "Aux origines de la Réformation cénevole." *Annales: économies, sociétés, civilisations* 39 (1984): 240–264.

Monluc, Blaise de. *Mémoires.* In *Nouvelle Collection des mémoires pour servir à l'histoire de France,* series 1, vol. 7, pp. 1–383. Edited by Joseph François Michaud and Jean Joseph François Poujoulat. Paris, 1838.

Montaigne, Michel de. *The Complete Essays of Montaigne.* Translated by Donald M. Frame. Stanford: Stanford University Press, 1958.

Montesquieu, Charles de Secondat. *De l'esprit des loix.* 3 vols. Geneva, 1750.

————. *The Spirit of the Laws.* Translated by Anne M. Cohler, Basia Carolyn Miller, and Harold Samuel Stone. Cambridge: Cambridge University Press, 1989.

Mousnier, Roland. *La vénalité des offices sous Henri IV et Louis XIII.* 2d ed. Paris: Presses Universitaires de France, 1971.

————, et al. *Le Conseil du roi de Louis XII à la Révolution.* Paris: Presses Universitaires de France, 1970.

Musée des Archives nationales. *Documents originaux de l'histoire de France exposés dans l'hôtel Soubise.* Paris, 1872.

Neely, Sylvia. "Michel de L'Hospital and the "Traité de la Réformation de la Justice: A Case of Misattribution." *French Historical Studies* 14 (1986): 339–66.

*Négociations, lettres et pièces diverses relatives au règne de François II, tirées du portefeuil de Sébastien de l'Aubespine, évêque de Limoge.* Edited by Antoine Louis Paris. Paris, 1841.

Nugent, Donald. *Ecumenism in the Age of the Reformation: The Colloquy of Poissy.* Cambridge, Mass.: Harvard University Press, 1974.

Olivier-Martin, François. *L'organisation corporative de la France d'Ancien Régime.* Paris: Sirey, 1938.

————. *Histoire du droit français des origines à la Révolution.* Paris: Domat Montchrestien, 1951.

*Ordonnances des rois de France de la troisième race.* Edited by Eusèbe de Laurière, Denis F. Secousse et al. 21 vols. Paris, 1723–1849.

Pagès, Georges. "La vénalité des offices dans l'ancienne France." *Revue historique* 169 (1932): 477–95.

Paschal, Pierre de. *Journal de ce qui s'est passé en France durant l'année 1562 principalement dans Paris et à la cour.* Edited by Michel François. Paris: Librairie Henri Didier, 1950.

Pasquier, Estienne. *Les Oeuvres d'Estienne Pasquier, contenant ses recherches de la France...* Amsterdam, 1723.

———. *Lettres historiques.* Edited by D. Thickett. Geneva: Librairie Droz, 1966.

———. "Lettre de Guillaume Poyet relative au mariage de Michel de l'Hospital." *Bulletin historique et scientifique de l'Auvergne* 12 (1882): 128–33.

P. D. L. *See* La Faye de L'Hôpital, Paul.

Pernot, Michel. *La guerre de religion en France, 1559–1598.* Paris: Sèdes, 1987.

———. "Le rôle du cardinal Charles de Lorraine dans la vie politique et religieuse de la France au troisième quart du XVIe siècle." *Les Cahiers Haut-Marnais* 188–189 (1992): 19–41.

Picot, Georges. *Histoire des Etats Généraux.* 2d ed. 5 vols. Paris, 1888.

Potter, David, L. "A Treason Trial in Sixteenth-century France." *English Historical Review* 105 (1990): 595–623.

Powis, Jonathan. "Gallican Liberties and the Politics of Later Sixteenth-Century France." *The Historical Journal* 26 (1983): 515–30.

———. "Order, Religion, and the Magistrates of a Provincial Parlement in Sixteenth-Century France." *Ardhiv für Reformationsgeschichte* 71 (1980): 180–97.

Rady, Martyn. *France: Renaissance, Religion and Recovery, 1494–1610.* London: Hodder & Stoughton, 1988.

*Registres des délibérations du bureau de la ville de Paris.* Edited by François Bonnardot et al. 19 vols. Paris, 1888–1892.

Regnault, Amable. *Histoire du Conseil d'Etat depuis son origine jusqu'à ce jour.* Paris, 1851.

Reynaud, H. *Jean de Monluc évêque de Valence.* Montpellier, 1893.

Reynolds, Beatrice. *Proponents of Limited Monarchy in Sixteenth Century France: François Hotman and Jean Bodin.* New York: Columbia University Press, 1931.

Ribier, Guillaume. *Lettres et mémoires d'estat, des roys, princes, ambassadeurs, et autres ministres, sous les règnes de François premier, Henry II & François II.* 2 vols. Paris, 1666.

Richelieu, Armand Jean du Plessis. *Testament politique.* Edited by Louis André. Paris: R. Laffont, 1947.

Richet, Denis. *La France moderne: l'esprit des institutions.* Paris: Flammarion, 1973.

———. "Aspects socio-culturels des conflits religieux à Paris dans la seconde moitié du XVIe siècle." *Annales* 32 (1977): 764–89.

Ritter, Raymond. "L'Hospital et Montaigne devant la guerre civile." *Bulletin de la société des amis de Montaigne* 30 (1964): 57–59.

Rocquain, Félix. *La France et Rome pendant les guerres de religion.* Paris: Champion, 1924.

Roelker, Nancy Lyman. *Queen of Navarre Jeanne d'Albret.* Cambridge, Mass.: Belknap Press, 1968.

Romier, Lucien. *Les Origines politiques des guerres de religion.* 2 vols. Paris, Perrin, 1913.

———. *La Conjuration d'Amboise: l'aurore sanglante de la liberté de conscience, le règne et la mort de François II.* Paris: Perrin, 1923.

———. *Catholiques et Huguenots à la cour de Charles IX.* Paris: Perrin, 1924.

———. *Le Royaume de Catherine de Médicis.* 2 vols. Paris: Perrin, 1925.

Rouse, Ruth, and Stephen Charles Neill. *A History of the Ecumenical Movement 1517–1948.* 2d ed. London: S.P.C.K., 1967.

Ruble, Alphonse de. *Antoine de Bourbon et Jeanne d'Albret.* 4 vols. Paris, 1881–1886.

———. "Le Colloque de Poissy." *Mémoires de la société de l'histoire de Paris et de l'Isle de France* 16 (1889): 1–56.

Sainte-Marthe, Scevole de. *Eloges des hommes illustres qui depuis un siècle ont fleury en France dans la profession de lettres.* Translated by G. Colletet. Paris, 1644.

Salmon, J. H. M. *Society in Crisis: France in the Sixteenth Century.* New York: St. Martin's Press, 1975.

Schneider, Mical H. "The French Magistracy 1560–1615." Ph.D. dissertation, University of North Carolina at Chapel Hill, 1973.

Seitte, Th. *Un apôtre de la tolérance au XVIe siècle, Michel de L'Hospital, chancelier de France.* Montauban, 1891.

Serbat, Louis. *Les assemblées du clergé de France, origines, organisation, développement 1561–1615.* Paris: Champion, 1906.

Seyssel, Claude de. *La monarchie de France et deux autres fragments politiques.* Edited by Jacques Poujol. Paris: Librairie d'Argences, 1961.

Shaw, A. E. *Michel de L'Hospital and His Policy.* London: Henry Frowde, 1905.

Shennan, J.H. *The Parlement of Paris.* Ithaca, N.Y.: Cornell University Press, 1968.

Skinner, Quentin. *The Foundations of Modern Political Thought.* 2 vols. Cambridge: Cambridge University Press, 1978.

Stapfer, Paul. *Montaigne.* Paris, 1895.

Stegmann, André. "Transformations administratives et opinion publique en France 1560–1580." In *Beihefte Der Francia, Histoire comparée de l'administration,* pp. 594–612. Munich: Artemis Verlag, 1980.

———, ed. *Edits des Guerres de Religion.* Paris: Librairie Philosophique J. Vrin, 1979.

Stocker, Christopher. "Office and Justice: Louis XI and the Parlement of Paris (1465–1476)." *Mediaeval Studies* 37 (1975): 360–86.

———. "The Parlement of Paris and Confessional Politics in the 1560s." *Proceedings of the Annual Meeting of the Western Society for French History* 15 (1988): 38–47.

Susta, Josef. *Die Romische curie und das Concil von Trient unter Pius IV: Aktenstücke zur geschichte des Concils von Trient.* 4 vols. Vienna: A. Holder, 1904-1914.

Sutherland, N. M. *The Huguenot Struggle for Recognition.* New Haven: Yale University Press, 1980.

———. "Calvinism and the Conspiracy of Amboise." *History* 47 (1962): 111–38.

———. *Catherine de Medici and the Ancien Régime.* London: Historical Association, 1966.

Taber, Linda. "Royal Policy and Religious Dissent within the Parlement of Paris, 1559–1563." Ph.D. dissertation, Stanford University, 1982.

Taillandier, A.H. *Nouvelles recherches historiques sur la vie et les ouvrages du chancelier de l'Hospital*. Paris, 1861.

Taillandier, Maurice. *Des Projets de réforme du chancelier de L'Hospital et de quelques réformes actuelles*. Arras: Imprimerie de la Société du Pas-de-Calais, 1903.

Tessereau, Abraham. *Histoire chronologique de la grande chancelerie de France contenant son origine, l'estat de ses officiers....* 2 vols. Paris, 1710.

Tessier, G. *Diplomatique royale française*. Paris: Picard, 1962.

———. "L'audience du sceau." *Bibliothèque de l'Ecole des Chartes* 109 (1951): 51–95.

———. "Parlement of Paris et style du 1er janvier." *Bibliothèque de l'Ecole des Chartes* 101 (1940): 233–36.

Testaud, Georges. *Des juridictions municipales en France, des origines jusqu'à l'ordonnance de Moulins*. Paris: Société du recueil général des lois et des arrêts, 1901.

Thireau, Jean-Louis. *Charles Du Moulin (1500–1566)*. Geneva: Librairie Droz, 1980.

Thompson, James Westfall. *The Wars of Religion in France, 1559–1576*. Chicago: The University of Chicago Press, 1909.

Thierry, Augustin. *Essai sur l'histoire de la formation et des progrès du tiers état*. Paris, 1868.

———. *Recueil des monuments inédits de l'histoire du tiers état*. 4 vols. Paris, 1850–1870.

Thou, Jacques-Auguste, de. *Histoire universelle depuis 1543 jusqu'en 1607*. 11 vols. Basel, 1742.

Tommaseo, M. N., ed. *Relations des ambassadeurs vénitiens sur les affaires de France au XVIe siècle*. 2 vols. Paris, 1838.

———. *Correspondance du Cardinal François de Tournon, 1521–1562*. Edited by Michel François. Paris: Champion, 1946.

Turchetti, Mario. *Concordia o tolleranza? François Bauduin (1520–1573) e i "Moyenneurs."* Geneva: Librairie Droz, 1984.

———. "Concorde ou tolérance? Les Moyenneurs à la veille des guerres de religion en France." *Revue de théologie et de philosophie* 118 (1986): 255–67.

———. "Religious Concord and Political Tolerance in Sixteenth- and Seventeenth-Century France." *The Sixteenth Century Journal* 22 (1991): 15–25.

———. "Une question mal posée: La qualification de 'perpétuel et irrévocable' appliquée à l'Edit de Nantes (1598)." *Bulletin de la société de l'histoire du protestantisme français* 139 (1993): 41–78.

Vaissière, Pierre de. *Charles de Marillac, ambassadeur et homme politique sous les règnes de François Ier, Henri II, François II*. Paris, 1896.

Valois, Nöel. *Inventaire des arrêts au conseil d'état (règne de Henri IV)*. Paris, 1886.

———. *Le Conseil du roi aux XIVe, XVe, XVIe siècles*. Paris, 1888.

———. "Projet d'enlèvement d'un enfant de France (le futur Henri III) en 1561." *Bibliothèque de l'Ecole des Chartes* 75 (1914): 5–48.

———. "Les Etats de Pontoise, août 1561." *Revue d'histoire de l'église de France* 29 (1943): 237–56.

———. "Les essais de conciliation religieuse au début du règne de Charles IX." *Revue d'histoire du l'église de France* 31 (1945): 237–76.

Van Dyke, Paul. *Catherine de Médicis*. 2 vols. New York: Charles Scribner's Sons, 1927.

————. "The Estates of Pontoise." *The English Historical Review* 28 (1913): 472–95.

Varillas, Antoine. *Histoire de l'hérésie de Viclef, Iean Hus, et Jérome de Prague.* Lyon, 1682.

Vic, Claude de, and Joseph Vaissètte. *Histoire générale de Languedoc.* 15 vols. Toulouse: E. Privat, 1889.

Vibraye, Henri de. *Histoire de la maison Hurault.* Blois: Imprimerie de J. de Grandpré, 1929.

Vieilleville, François de Scepeaux, sire de. *Mémoires.* In *Nouvelle collection des mémoires pour servir à l'histoire de France,* series 1, vol. 9, pp. 1–400. Edited by Joseph François Michaud and Jean Joseph François Poujoulat. Paris, 1838.

Villemain, Abel Framçoos. "Vie du Chancelierde L'Hospital." In *Etudes d'histoire moderne,* pp. 319–415. Paris, 1862.

Vindry, Fleury. *Les parlementaires français du XVIe siècle.* 2 vols. Paris: Champion, 1909–1912.

Viollet, Paul. *Histoire des institutions politiques et administrative de la France: le roi et ses ministres pendant les trois derniers siècles de la monarchie.* 4 vols. Paris, 1912; reprint ed., Aalen: Scientia Verlag, 1966.

Voltaire, [François Marie Arouet de]. *Voltaire's Correspondence.* Vol. 97. Edited by Theodore Besterman. Geneva: Institut et Musée Voltaire, 1964.

Vovelle, Michel. *Piété baroque et déchristianisation en Provence au XVIIIe siècle: les attitudes devant la mort d'après les clauses des testaments.* Paris: Librairie Plon, 1973.

Weber, Bernard C. "The Conference of Bayonne, 1565: An Episode in Franco-Spanish Diplomacy." *The Journal of Modern History* 11 (1939): 1–22.

————. "The Council of Fontainebleau (1560)." *Archiv für Reformationsgeschichte* 45 (1954): 43–62.

Weill, Georges. *Les théories sur le pouvoir royal en France pendant les guerres de religion.* Paris, 1892.

Wolfe, Martin. *The Fiscal System of Renaissance France.* New Haven: Yale University Press, 1972.

Wrangham, Francis. *An Epithalamium on the Marriage of Francis of Valois and Mary Stuart.* London, 1837.

Yardeni, Myriam. *La conscience nationale en France pendant les guerres de religion (1559–1598).* Paris: Béatrice-Nauwelaerts, 1971.

Zeller, Gaston. *Les institutions de la France au XVIe siècle.* 2d ed. Paris: Presses Universitaires de France, 1987.

# Index

ISBN 0-940474-38-7

9 780940 474383

54000>